To my great /. /. ?
6

MW01254223

GOVERNING TORONTO:

Bringing Back the CITY that WORKED

10/04/15

"The honourable member wants to de-amalgamate"

*– The Hon. Kelso Roberts responding to remarks of
Donald MacDonald MPP (York South) leader of the
New Democratic Party in the Ontario Legislature during
second reading debate on Bill 81 to amend
The Municipality of Metropolitan Toronto Act
(Ontario Hansard April 21, 1966).*

 **FriesenPress**

Suite 300 - 990 Fort St
Victoria, BC, Canada, V8V 3K2
www.friesenpress.com

Copyright © 2014 by Alan Redway
First Edition — 2014

All rights reserved.

No part of this publication may be reproduced in any form, or by any means, electronic
or mechanical, including photocopying, recording, or any information browsing,
storage, or retrieval system, without permission in writing from the publisher.

ISBN
978-1-4602-5199-7 (Hardcover)
978-1-4602-5200-0 (Paperback)
978-1-4602-5201-7 (eBook)

1. History, Canada, Post-Confederation (1867-)

Distributed to the trade by The Ingram Book Company

Inside...

INTRODUCTION

"Perhaps the sentiments contained in the following pages, are not YET sufficiently fashionable to procure them general favour; a long habit of not thinking a thing WRONG, gives it a superficial appearance of being RIGHT, and raises at first a formidable outcry in defense of custom. But the tumult soon subsides. Time makes more converts than reason."

The introduction to Thomas Paine's pamphlet *COMMON SENSE* February 14, 1776 Published on the eve of the American Revolution.

On January 1, 1998, in spite of strong opposition, the government of the province of Ontario totally amalgamated the Municipality of Metropolitan Toronto replacing it with the present Megacity of Toronto. Ever since then, a number of the megacity's closest observers have called it dysfunctional.

> *Why? Is it because the Province of Ontario downloaded extra costs on the city? That certainly didn't help. Or is it really because of amalgamation?* Amalgamation was intended to reduce the cost and increase the efficiency of running our city by eliminating our then existing Metro form of local government and reducing the number of municipal politicians. *Did it work or has it just resulted in a city government that costs no less and perhaps even more than the Municipality of Metropolitan Toronto it replaced?*

One thing is for certain, amalgamation has drastically centralized Toronto government. Accordingly it has diminished resident access to and participation in Toronto's decision making process. In many instances the role of residents has been replaced by lobbyists. Historically resident access to and participation in the municipal decision making process is what local government is all about. Today more city policies and the application of those policies originate with city officials and urban planners than with city residents. As a result of amalgamation, Toronto's residents have lost control of their neighbourhoods and communities.

1

I had the honour of serving three terms of two years each, six years in all as the Mayor of East York, a member of Metropolitan Toronto Council and Executive Committee from 1977 to 1982. During that time the Municipality of Metropolitan Toronto was made up of six area municipalities: Etobicoke, York, North York, East York, Scarborough and the old city of Toronto. The six Mayors and all of the Metro Councillors were initially elected by residents to their local Councils and then served on both their local and Metro Council. At that time Toronto not only worked but worked well. Some have called the Municipality of Metropolitan Toronto era, "the golden years of Toronto". The Metro form of local government was studied and admired around the western world.

When Metro Toronto was created it was anticipated that other local municipalities would be added to the Metro federation as the surrounding area became urbanized. Instead, the province of Ontario froze the Metro boundaries as they were originally established in 1954. By the 1990s it was clear to all that the surrounding regions of Halton, Peel, York and Durham were so interconnected with Metro Toronto that some form of regional co-ordination was necessary. But when the provincially appointed Anne Golden Task Force recommended a Greater Toronto Area (GTA) regional government, the Toronto and the GTA municipal politicians balked. They wanted change but not that kind of change.

The provincial government got the message. The result was something the old city of Toronto council and the Toronto's newspapers had been asking for since the end of World War II total amalgamation. At the same time the province of Ontario itself, assumed the role of the regional government for the GTA and beyond.

If amalgamation is the problem, how can we fix it? This book answers that question. It explains the evolution of Toronto's local government from the early annexations of nearby smaller municipalities to the decision to end of those annexations, which led directly to the creation and then to the subsequent development of the much admired Municipality of Metropolitan Toronto. It goes on, to detail the events leading to the creation of the present megacity and its financial consequences. Finally, it proposes a solution to the city's present dysfunctional structure, either through a return to a Metro federated form of government by way of de-amalgamation or at the very least a de-centralization of the city's present decision making process.

Is this possible? Yes it is. A comprehensive review of the present Toronto government is long over-due. Ten years after the Municipality of Metropolitan Toronto was established in 1954, it was reviewed by the Goldenberg Royal Commission. Ten years after that it was reviewed once again by the Robarts' Royal Commission. David Peterson's Ministers of Municipal Affairs publically reviewed the Metro government in 1986. Then in 1996 the Anne Golden Task Force established by the Bob Rae government completed further review, followed that same year by the Libby Burnham Task Force review on behalf of the Mike Harris government.

Well over ten years has passed since the Toronto megacity was created in 1997. To date it has never had a comprehensive public review by the provincial government. Prior to standing as a candidate for provincial office our present Premier Kathleen Wynne was a leader in the fight against amalgamation. She knows its problems and she knows that another review of Toronto city government is long overdue.

Nothing is impossible or insurmountable.

No means no

No more annexations

CHAPTER 1

"For the reasons reported, we urge with all the force of which we are capable, that further annexations to the city of Toronto be not made until such time as undoubted compensating advantages exist. This municipality is entering a period of prosperity unexampled in its history and we should be remiss in our duty if we did not combat with every effort any proposal which in our judgment would for several generations, cripple the municipality."[1]

The recommendation made of the thirteen Toronto civic department heads including the Chief of Police, which was adopted by Toronto city council in 1929.[2]

That was the city council's attitude in 1929, but that had not always been the case. The original city of Toronto, incorporated in 1834, consisted of an area bounded by the present Bathurst, Dundas, Parliament Streets and the waterfront. A surrounding territory known as the *Liberties* (which included the Toronto Islands, Ashbridge's Bay, the waters 500 feet from the *windmill line*, the land east of Dufferin Street, south of Bloor Street and west of the Don River as well as Queen Street as far east as Maclean Avenue), merged with the city in 1859.

These were the city boundaries until 1883. In the meantime, a number of towns and villages had grown up in the Township of York around the city. In 1929 the city council would adopt a policy of no more

---

1. City of Toronto Staff Report to Board of Control November 5, 1928
2. City of Toronto Council minutes 1929

annexations of nearby communities; however, that was certainly not their policy from 1883–1925. In 1883 Yorkville – at the request of its residents – was annexed by the city. Brockton (including High Park) and Riverdale were added in 1884. Between 1887 and 1889 the city annexed Rosedale, part of the Annex, Sunnyside and Parkdale. During those years Toronto residents went land crazy. City council caught the fever as well and annexed everything for miles around. Everyone was or expected soon to be a real estate millionaire. My father-in-law, Bob Harvey, who lived in Cobourg, Ontario told me that if he had bought land in Parkdale he would have made a fortune, but instead he bought land in western Canada and lost it all for property taxes in the Great Depression. But the real estate market crashed in 1890 bringing city annexations to a virtual halt for the next thirteen years.

By 1903, however, the annexation fever had returned. From that time until 1925 – with a pause during World War I – the city annexed Avenue Road, North Rosedale, Deer Park, the Baldwin Estate, East Toronto, Wychwood, Bracondale, West Toronto, Midway, Balmy Beach, Dovercourt, Earlscourt, the Helliwell property, Montclair District, North Toronto, Moore Park, the Glebe Estate, Mount Pleasant Cemetery, north of the Danforth east of Woodbine Avenue and fifteen acres of the Davies estate among others. A complete list of the city's annexations from 1883–1929 is shown on the accompanying map and table to the map.

There was little if any opposition to these mergers. Most if not all of the residents annexed to Toronto wanted in, for the improved services the city provided. For instance, West Toronto, an area known today as the Junction, was originally incorporated as a village in 1885. Later after merging with the villages of Carlton and Davenport, it became a town in 1892 and then later in 1908 as the city of West Toronto. The next year, deeply in debt, the city of West Toronto amalgamated with the city of Toronto.

North Toronto, incorporated as a town in 1890 was a different story. In a 1911 plebiscite, the residents wanting an adequate water supply, police protection and street car service voted overwhelmingly to join the city. But a city plebiscite held at the same time on the same issue rejected the proposed amalgamation. However, the very next year when North Toronto tried again for a merger, Toronto council following a heated debate turned down a proposal for another plebiscite and approved an application to the Ontario Railway and Municipal Board (now the Ontario Municipal Board) for annexation. This application was subsequently approved by the Board effective December 15, 1912. The following day Moore Park was united with the city as well after presenting the Board with a petition for merger signed by 128 out of the entire 196 Moore Park ratepayers.

By 1919, however, the bloom had faded from the rose as far as many of the North Toronto residents were concerned. Disillusioned that the city had done nothing to eliminate the double transit fares they were paying and what they considered to be an intolerable street car situation, the North Toronto residents organized a Secession Club aimed at forcing improvements. In 1920, despite a favourable North Toronto plebiscite, the city of Toronto Board of Control rejected the idea of secession so North Toronto remains a part of the city to this day.

Toronto daily papers have always been strong advocates of amalgamations. The Toronto World urged holus-bolus merger of everything east of the Humber River, west of Victoria Park Avenue and south of Wilson Avenue. It labelled those who opposed its proposal including then Toronto Mayor Geary as "Wee Yorkies". So did the Mail and Empire. The Globe advocated editorially for a metropolitan jurisdiction rather than total amalgamation but only as it pointed out for the sake of the poor Toronto taxpayers.

Meanwhile, by 1911, the city civic department heads were starting to voice their concerns about further mergers. That year they opposed a proposal to annex the more populated parts of the Township of York arguing that it was a land developer's plot that would push the limits of the city's services and drive up city property taxes.

One of those land developers, Mr. Home Smith (who acted for an English syndicate which owned land in the Humber Valley), offered the city 105 acres if Toronto would annex Swansea (then part of the township of York as well as some parts of the township of Etobicoke) and build a 100-foot wide parkway from the Lake to Lambton Mills. City council accepted this offer but took such a long time to search the title of the property that a year later Mr. Home Smith revoked the offer. Although the residents of what was then the Swansea district later to be incorporated as a village in 1925 were in favour of annexation at that time, the residents of Etobicoke Township were skeptical to say the least. Thus, despite the urgings of the Toronto newspapers, nothing was done.

In 1913, another land developer the York Land Company, the real estate arm of the Canadian Northern Railway, proposed to move its railway car repair shops from Winnipeg to Leaside (the repair shop building exists to this day as a Longo's super market) and to lay out a planned residential community, if Toronto would annex the entire Leaside area. Again the city civic department heads opposed the request saying that there was no benefit for the city but the York Land Company would make a fortune. A majority of the city Board of Control supported the idea, but when the vote was taken by city council as a whole on April 4, 1913, the proposal was defeated. The Toronto World called it a "jockeyed vote". One month later on May 9, 1913, the Ontario Legislature incorporated the town of Leaside.

That same year 1913 and again in 1914 the city turned down proposals to annex the Forest Hill area in the township of York. This time not only Toronto civic officials but the affected residents were opposed as well. In 1923 Forest Hill was incorporated as a village. One year later, the Hon. George S. Henry then a provincial cabinet minister with responsibilities for municipalities but soon to become the Conservative premier of Ontario, tabled a draft Bill in the legislature calling for the creation of a Toronto Metropolitan District with a governing body having powers similar to that of a county council. The Bill never became law, however, years later in 1935 when the idea surfaced again under a Liberal provincial government, Forest Hill Village council passed a resolution declaring that: "This council goes on record of being opposed to the Metropolitan Area idea in any shape or form." [3]

The original township of York had been created by the Baldwin Act in1850. In 1923 North York, formerly a part of the township of York, was

---

3.   Village of Forest Hill Council minutes, 1935

incorporated as a separate township. When that happened a portion of the urban area remaining in York Township north of St. Clair Avenue and west to Keele Street threatened to incorporate as York City. So as not to be left "holding the bag" lumped with the rural part of the township both of the other urban areas in the township, Mount Dennis and Humbervale (known by some as Humbercrest) also threatened incorporation. Immediately both the Toronto Star and the Globe advocated for a massive annexation arguing that since sooner or later it was inevitable, it should happen before new cities were created which would likely go bankrupt as the city of West Toronto had. But in spite of the urging of the newspapers, Toronto city council maintained a neutral position, while the residents who would have been affected voted by a wide margin to reject the idea of York City.

Then in 1926 the township of York asked for and received special provincial legislation to preclude annexation. Section 5, Chapter 108 of Statutes of Ontario 1926 reads:

> *(1) Notwithstanding the provisions of The Consolidated Municipal Act 1922 or any other Act, no part of the township of York shall be annexed to any adjoining municipality, nor be incorporated as a municipality separate and apart from the township of York, without the approval of the council of the corporation of the township of York to be expressed by by-law.*

> *(2) This section shall be and remain in force only until the first day of July 1931.*[4]

Never one to give up, the Toronto World clamoured for the annexation of Todmorden, a district east of the Don River north of the Danforth together with the plains of East York, arguing that it made no sense to let a municipality "sit across the fence and cash in on other

---

4.   Statutes, Ontario 1926, chapter 108 set

peoples' taxes". In 1914 the city council agreed to annex Todmorden, but the plan died when World War I broke out in August of that year.

The creation of North York as a separate township in 1923 had cut off East York from the rest of the township of York. So that same year – but effective in 1924 – the Ontario legislature incorporated the township of East York. Despite the fact that they were now in East York Township, the businessmen of Todmorden north of the Danforth asked the city to complete the annexation previously approved in 1914, however, the residents of Riverdale south of the Danforth opposed that idea so city council took no action. Just to be on the safe side, in 1926 following the lead of the township of York, East York, obtained identical special provincial legislation to preclude annexation or amalgamation.

The villages of Mimico, New Toronto and Long Branch were carved out of the township of Etobicoke's lakeshore district in 1911, 1913 and 1930 respectively. Mimico became a Town in 1917 and New Toronto in 1919. Although up to 1929 the city had been busily expanding its borders, it was not until after World War II that Toronto even considered annexing these lakeshore municipalities. Similarly, neither Weston incorporated as a village in 1881 nor then as a town in 1914; the township of Scarborough, created under the Baldwin Act in 1850, nor the township of North York was in the city's annexation sights at this time. With the exception of the Home Smith proposal no part of the township of Etobicoke, which was also created by the Baldwin Act in1850, was a target of the city prior to World War II.

With the onset of the "Great Depression", however, the circumstances of the villages, towns and townships around the city of Toronto changed drastically. Indeed, so much so that in 1931 the township of York obtained new provincial legislation allowing either it or the city of Toronto to apply to the Ontario Railway and Municipal Board for an order annexing the entire township to the city on terms and conditions agreed to by their respective councils. The township of York then joined by the township of East York commenced annexation negotiations with the city. T.S. Scott, Commissioner of Works for the township of York, Bill Heaton the long- time Comptroller of the township of East York and R.C. Harris, Commissioner of Works for the city of Toronto, were each appointed to represent their respective municipality in those negotiations.

R.C. Harris – the Toronto negotiator – was the same man for whom the R. C. Harris Filtration Plant on the shore of Lake Ontario is named. He modernized Toronto's water treatment system and also had the foresight to add the second deck to the Bloor Street Viaduct, thus enabling the Bloor Danforth subway line to be built years later.

Here, however, R.C. Harris reported on behalf of the three negotiators that they had agreed as follows:

"(a) Annexation of the townships would not confer any immediate financial benefits upon the city.

(b) Any compensation derived by the city for an indeterminate period (which cannot be estimated) will be wholly intangible.

(c) Annexation would at once confer marked benefits upon the townships but would result in reduced council representation.

(d) If annexation be favourably considered by the city the influencing factors must be broad grounds of public policy, the desire to assist lesser and weaker municipalities by absorption with the hope and expectation that in time material compensation will accrue therefrom.

Commissioner R.C. Harris went on to say that, "Having regard to the conclusions so expressed, the officers of the respective municipalities determined that they were not in a position to draft and report terms upon which annexation would be acceptable to all parties." In essence, this was the same recommendation as had been made by Toronto civic department heads including Works Commissioner R.C. Harris, which the city council had adopted two years earlier in 1929. So there the matter died.[5]

But the Depression continued to deepen and unemployment continued to rise so that by the mid-1930s, 36 Ontario municipalities were bankrupt including: Scarborough Township, Long Branch, Leaside, Mimico, Etobicoke Township, New Toronto, York Township, East York Township, North York Township and Weston. Each had defaulted on the payment of their debts and applied to the newly constituted Ontario Municipal Board to appoint a committee of supervisors to manage their

---

5.   City of Toronto Council Minutes Report of Toronto Works Commissioner R.C. Harris to the Toronto City Board of Control October 31, 1931

10

financial affairs. The city of Toronto, Forest Hill Village and the village of Swansea were the only Toronto area municipalities to escape bankruptcy at this time.

In 1935 for example, 47 per cent of the property owners in the township of East York were on relief (welfare), paid not by the federal or the provincial governments, but rather from the real estate property taxes of the municipality in which the unemployed worker resided. But of course the unemployed home owners could not pay their property taxes, so in the case of East York Township, 53 per cent of the homeowners were paying for 100 per cent of the municipal services including relief for the 47 per cent unemployed. No wonder they went bankrupt.[6]

Something had to be done but what? The newly elected Liberal provincial government of Premier Mitchell Hepburn established the Department of Municipal Affairs in part to remove the direct supervision of the 36 bankrupt municipalities from the work of the Ontario Municipal Board. The premier then appointed the Honourable David Croll (later a federal member of parliament, a Senator and author of influential Senate reports on poverty and aging) to be the first Minister of the new Department. Minister Croll then appointed Professor A.F.W. Plumtre of the Department of Political Science and Economics, University of Toronto, to investigate and report on the government of the metropolitan area of Toronto. The Professor published his typewriter written report just two months after he was appointed having visited and studied the governments of seven American cities: Chicago, Cincinnati, Cleveland, Pittsburg, Philadelphia, New York and Boston. Today such a report would take years to complete and cost millions of dollars.

Professor Plumtre's 1935 report dealt with the city of Toronto and the twelve adjacent municipalities of Leaside, Weston, Mimico, New Toronto, Forest Hill, Swansea, Long Branch, East York as well as the urban portions of Scarborough, North York, York and Etobicoke. In referring to the residents of the twelve adjacent municipalities in his report he stated: "They are often said to 'live in the suburbs'. But since they

---

6.   Golden Years of East York, page 82

largely work, meet their friends, engage in social activities and find their amusement in the city, they might better be said to live in the city and sleep in the suburbs. When asked by an outsider where they live they will (truthfully) mention the name of the city, not the suburb."

His report set out the following five possible courses of action:

1. Drift

2. The investing of greater powers in some larger geographical unit of government; in this case, the county of York.

3. Erection of a metropolitan board or a number of metropolitan boards with certain functions to exercise over the otherwise autonomous municipalities within the metropolitan area.

4. Unification of a few of the outlying sections with each other.

5. A general amalgamation of the municipalities of metropolitan Toronto [7]

Forest Hill Village council was responding to this report when in 1935 it resolved that: "This council goes on record of being opposed to the Metropolitan area idea in any shape or form." [3]

Minister David Croll chose option number 5 – a general amalgamation of the municipalities of Metropolitan Toronto and prepared a Bill to make the suburban municipalities into Toronto City electoral wards. However, the Toronto Star deviating from its usual editorial line, strongly opposed the Bill using virtually the same reasoning as the Toronto civic department heads had in 1929 saying:

> *"The city cannot be expected to shoulder a load of debt charges for which there is no adequate revenue obtainable in the territories where the debts were incurred."*

7. Report on the government of the Metropolitan Area of Toronto to the Hon. David Croll, Minister of Municipal Affairs in the Province of Ontario by A.F.W. Plumtre, Department of Political Science and Economics, University of Toronto, June 20, 1935

Then shades of the recent European debt crisis, the Star stated:

*"The first thing to do is to negotiate settlements between each
of the bankrupt municipalities and its bondholders: settlements
which will reduce the interest payable if not, in some cases, the
principal."*[8]

Thus the Liberal government of Premier Mitchell Hepburn, which
up to now had received nothing but good press from the Toronto Star,
backed off option number 5 and instead referred the matter to another
committee thereby adopting option number 1 – Drift, described by
Professor Plumtre in his report as "continuation of the present policy or
lack of policy". [7]

On October 4, 1937, city of Toronto Controller soon to become the
Mayor, Ralph Day, put forward a motion to Council: "That the province
appoint a Commission to study and report upon the feasibility of annexing
to the city of Toronto all or any part of the towns, villages and townships
adjacent to or in close proximity to the city of Toronto." Later in the same
meeting after one of his council colleagues had declared: "There is no
reason why Toronto should be penalized for being able to carry on its
own business and still maintain its credit," Controller Day withdrew his
motion.[9]

No still meant no.

8. Toronto Star, March 2, 1937
9. City of Toronto Council Minutes October 4, 1937

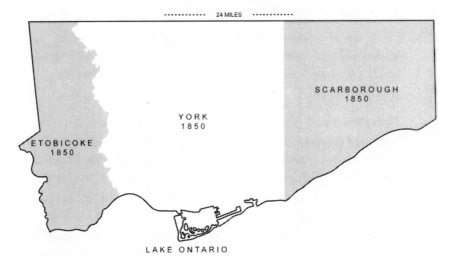

ORIGINAL TOWNSHIPS
SHOWING DATES OF INCORPORATION
AN AREA OF 240 SQ. MI

············ 24 MILES ············

SCARBOROUGH
1850

YORK
1850

ETOBICOKE
1850

LAKE ONTARIO

Map of the original Townships of Etobicoke *(created 1850)*, York *(created 1793)* and Scarborough *(created 1850)* *(Source: Valentine De Landro 2014)*

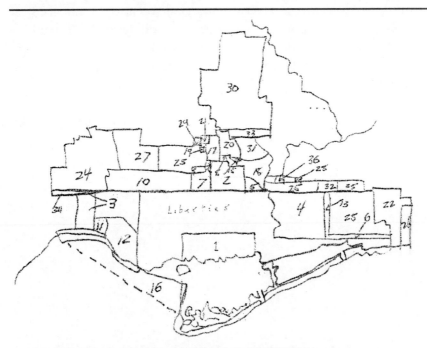

List of Annexations by the city of Toronto from 1883 to 1934
(Source: Archives of Ontario)

District	Acres of land	Date of Annexation
1. Original city	7,372.8	
2. Yorkville	556.8	Feb. 1, 1883
3. Brockton (including High Park)	975.9	Mar.25, 1884
4. Riverdale	1,236.6	Mar.25, 1884
5. Rosedale	98.5	Jan. 3, 1887
6. Strip North of Queen Street	57.7	Jan. 3, 1887
7. Annex	212.4	Jan. 3, 1887
8. Walker and Woodlawn Avenues	48.8	Jan. 2, 1888
9. Poplar Plains Road	16.1	Jan. 2, 1888
10. N. of Bloor and W. of Bathurst	1,082.4	Jan. 2, 1888
11. Sunnyside	115.2	Jan. 2, 1888
12. Parkdale	578.4	Mar.23, 1889
13. Greenwood Side Line	32.8	Jan. 6, 1890
14. Lakeshore Road	116.4	May 27, 1893
15. Summerhill Avenue	4.4	Oct. 2, 1903
16. Part of Humber Bay and Lake west of the Island		Oct.10, 1903
17. Avenue Road	126.4	Mar. 10,1905
18. North Rosedale	277.7	Jan. 1, 1906
19. Annex West of Avenue Road	29.3	Jan. 1, 1907
20. Deer Park	241.?	Dec.15, 1908
21. Baldwin Estate	51.4	Dec.15, 1908
22. East Toronto	602.7	Dec.15, 1908
23. Wychwood and Bracondale	582.2	Feb. 1, 1909
24. West Toronto	1,609.8	May 1, 1909
25. Midway	1,347.6	Dec.15, 1909
26. Balmy Beach	191.5	Dec.15, 1909
27. Dovercourt and Earlscourt	725.2	Jan.10, 1910
28. Helliwell Property	37.2	June 1, 1912
29. Montclair District	22.7	July 1, 1912
30. North Toronto	2,701.6	Dec.15, 1912
31. Moore Park	259.7	Dec.16, 1912
32. Glebe Estate	73.7	May 1, 1914
33. Mount Pleasant Cemetery	207.1	June27, 1914
34. South side Bloor Street (Swansea)	10.3	Jan. 2, 1920
35. North of Danforth Avenue and East to Woodbine Avenue	93.8	Sept.1, 1920
36. Davies Estate	15.1	Jan. 2, 1921
37. Annette Street, North Side	6.6	Jan. 4, 1922
38. Runnymede Road, West Side	6.4	Jan. 4, 1922
39. Rowntree Avenue, North Side	3.5	Jan. 4, 1923
40. Forest Hill	13.8	Jan. 4, 1924
41. Gunn's Road and Northland's Ave.	6.1	Jan. 4, 1924
42. Newmarket and Meagher Avenues	5.5	Jan. 4, 1925
43. Bayview Avenue (street only)	4.1	May 2, 1930
44. Lake Shore Bridge Approach	.4	April3, 1934
	21,759.8	

Map showing the city of Toronto annexations from 1833 until 1934
(Source: Archives of Ontario)

GROWTH OF THE CITY SHOWING LAST ANNEXATIONS

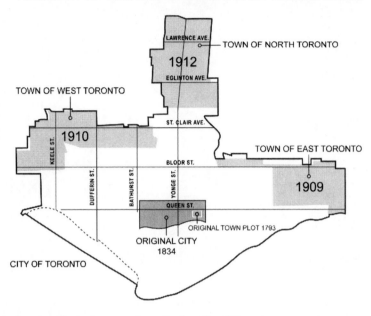

Map showing the last annexations by the city of Toronto
(Source: Valentine De Landro 2014)

Former Ontario Premier George S. Henry
(Source: City of Toronto Archives Fonds 1244 Item 8006)

Note ✓

TABLE VII

THE TEN DEFAULTING MUNICIPALITIES OF GREATER TORONTO.

Municipality	Date of Default	Debenture Debt as at December 31, 1934	Current Bank Loans as at December 31,1934
Scarborough Township	Dec.,1932	$ 4,240,000	$ 560,000
Long Branch	Dec.,1932	x	nil
Leaside	Jan.,1933	963,051	162,481
Mimico	Mar.,1933	1,907,000	100,368
Etobicoke Township	June,1933	3,490,000	95,479
New Toronto	Oct.,1933	1,601,000	85,000
York Township	Oct.,1933	18,000,000	1,116,684
East York Township	Oct.,1933	4,462,000	174,400
North York Township	Dec.,1933	3,244,000	562,500
Weston	Information not obtained.		

x Long Branch village, which separated from Etobicoke Township

in 1930, has no debenture debt of its own. Its contractual

obligations are chiefly to the township.

Indebtedness of the suburban Toronto municipalities in the 1930s
(Source: Archives of Ontario)

Former Ontario Premier Mitchell Hepburn
(Source: Archives of Ontario 1934-1942 F 10-2-3-8.1)

No becomes Yes

Good Times Return

CHAPTER 2

"One thing that is 100 per cent wrong is the establishment of a metropolitan area – this is poison." [1]

– Fred Gardiner, the Reeve of Forest Hill village in 1944,
(later the first Chairman of Metropolitan Toronto council in 1954).

"Amalgamation is as inevitable as the law of gravity" [2]
– Fred Gardiner, Chairman of the Toronto and York Planning Board in 1950.

Towards the end of and immediately following World War II, the Greater Toronto Area changed dramatically. Prosperity had returned. Population of the Toronto region fuelled by immigrants from Britain and Europe was growing rapidly. The sole exception, however, was the city of Toronto. It was completely built up with virtually no vacant land within its pre-war boundaries. In fact, the city population was actually declining somewhat. The increasing population of the region, however, created housing, transportation, water supply and sewage treatment problems for many of the municipalities surrounding the city. [3]

---

1.   Timothy Colton, Big Daddy: Frederick G. Gardiner the building of Metropolitan Toronto (University of Toronto Press) 60
2.   Timothy J. Colton, Big Daddy (University of Toronto Press) 64
3.   G.P. de T. Glazebrook, The Story of Toronto (University of Toronto Press, 1971)

The township of North York for instance had septic tanks. The water shortages in 1950 caused the Reeve of North York to write to the Mayor of Toronto requesting the city to supply it with water from Lake Ontario. "Otherwise," said Reeve Boylen, "all residential building must stop." The Reeve closed his letter by adding: "We repeat our situation is desperate."[4] That desperate situation wasn't solved until 1952 when Scarborough Township agreed to provide North York with the needed water.[5]

In 1944 the recently elected provincial Progressive Conservative minority government of Premier George Drew had created the Department of Planning and Development to encourage municipalities in Ontario to plan for future growth with consistent standards. Two years later the provincial legislature passed the first Planning Act, which was followed by the appointment of a nine-man Toronto and Suburban Planning Board, later re-designated as the Toronto and York Planning Board, to prepare an official land use plan for Toronto and its twelve closest suburbs.

Events leading to the reorganization of local government in the Greater Toronto area moved rapidly thereafter. On February 4, 1947, the town of Mimico applied to the Ontario Municipal Board for an order creating an interurban administration area composed of the thirteen municipalities in the Metropolitan Toronto area in order to provide region wide services for education, fire and police protection, the administration of justice, health and welfare, planning, sewage disposal, transportation and main highways.[6]

The city of Toronto reacted to this move by convening a meeting with the suburbs of York, North York, East York, Scarborough, Etobicoke, Forest Hill, Leaside, Weston, Swansea, New Toronto, Long Branch and Mimico during which it was agreed that the city of Toronto Civic Advisory Council would establish a committee to study and make recommendations for improving the organization of public services for the entire area.[7]

---

4. Archives of Ontario – Leslie Frost papers RG, B292271-2, 3 – 24 Box #35,36
5. Township of North York Council Minutes
6. Ontario Municipal Board, January 20, 1953 decision
7. G.P. de T. Glazebrook, The Story of Toronto (University of Toronto Press, 1991)

On December 1, 1949, the Toronto and York Planning Board chaired by Fred Gardiner released a report recommending that the seven municipalities between the Humber River and the Township of Scarborough (that is East York, Leaside, North York, Forest Hill, Swansea, Township of York and Weston), should be united with the city. Later the Board enlarged that recommendation to include all twelve of the suburbs. In doing so it rejected the obvious alternative stating:

"A metropolitan area of divided authorities between local municipalities and superimposed boards or commissions is less desirable and probably no answer. The creation of a borough system where you have a central financing authority is an arrangement designed for failure in that lack of cooperation and agreement will result. It would appear that nothing short of a unified municipality can command the support and provide the financial background for the successful development of what are the obvious requirements."[8]

Almost simultaneously the Civic Advisory Council's committee published its report. It is interesting to note that the Civic Advisory Council's report stated that the area to be reorganized should include the ten local municipalities located in the townships of Markham, Vaughan, Toronto Gore and Toronto township (the last two are now known as the city of Mississauga) in addition to the original thirteen municipalities that the committee had been mandated to study. It envisaged an urban government for an area as far east as the Rouge River as far north east as Stouffville and as far west as Port Credit. The report set out a number of alternative proposals for reorganizing the existing system of local governments but made no specific recommendation.[9] Dr. Albert Rose, a professor at the University of Toronto, and the research director for the committee was quoted as saying: "We don't know the appropriate system at this moment. We may decide for one system or compromise with various forms. There is a widespread belief that panaceas are available

---

8.   Archives of Ontario – Leslie Frost papers B292271-2, RG3-24 Box #35,36
9.   Archives of Ontario – Leslie Frost papers B292271-2, RG3-24 Box #35,36

to solve the problem. I don't believe that." He went on to say that, "The committee would make its decision as objectively as it can and it won't be stampeded by political considerations."[10]

However, in reality, the entire issue was wrapped up in political considerations. The new premier of Ontario Leslie Frost, who had been chosen by the provincial Progressive Conservative party to succeed premier George Drew when he resigned to become the leader of the federal Progressive Conservative party in Ottawa, had been watching the situation very carefully. He was consulting with his close Progressive Conservative party allies, Fred Gardiner and Robert Saunders, a former Mayor of Toronto who at that time was Chairman of the Hydro-Electric Power Commission of Ontario.[11] Frost was well aware of all of the political considerations and they required handling with kid gloves. In order to try to deal with the issue in a way which would sooth troubled waters rather than bring on a political tsunami, he invited the Mayors and Reeves of the city and the twelve suburbs to a meeting on January 16, 1950, in the Ontario government cabinet room at Queen's Park in Toronto to discuss and hopefully agree upon a municipal reorganization.[12]

Although the premier wanted to set a friendly and co-operative tone for the meeting, his Minister of Municipal Affairs, George Dunbar, inflamed the Mayors and Reeves two days before the meeting took place when he spoke to them at a civic luncheon saying: "We are going to let you decide what to do up to a point. If you are unable to reach that point then prepare for the consequences."

"If the provincial government would run its government as well as we do, they'd get along a lot better," responded William G. Jackson, the Mayor of New Toronto.

"Leaside always has been able to pay its own way," chimed in, Trace Manes, Mayor of Leaside. "We use some services from Toronto but we pay in full for all of them."

10. Archives of Ontario – Leslie Frost papers B292271-2, RG3-24 Box #35,36
11. Archives of Ontario – Leslie Frost papers B292271-2, RG3-24 Box #35,36
12. Archives of Ontario – Leslie Frost papers B292271-2, RG3-24 Box #35,36

Reeve Clive Sinclair of Etobicoke township, predicted that the township taxes would double under amalgamation.[13] "The inescapable fact," replied Toronto Mayor Hiram McCallum, "is that somebody has to make a decision – and soon. And it doesn't seem that any clear decision is going to come out of a general agreement of the municipalities concerned. If Toronto wanted to be selfish about the situation it is quite possible that we would be better off so far as the individual taxpayer is concerned if we remained just as we are and allowed the surrounding municipalities to stew in their own juice."[14]

For his meeting with the Mayors and Reeves, Fred Gardiner provided his friend Leslie Frost with draft speaking notes biased in favour of total amalgamation. After reviewing them the premier said to Gardiner, "That simply makes us a target for attack. I have wanted to leave the matter with them to see what they say, not that I am hopeful that they will come to any decision, but it helps to formulate public opinion."[15]

So at the Queen's Park meeting with the thirteen Mayors and Reeves, rather than throwing the fox into the chicken coup as Gardiner would have preferred, premier Frost opened by making use of his favourite adjective, "great", referring to "this great area", "undoubtedly one of the world's greatest cities and urban areas" and one with "a great future". Then after referring to the 23 municipalities mentioned in the Civic Advisory Council's report, outlining the municipal service problems and emphasizing that the situation in Greater Toronto is not static but will be constantly expanding, Frost added: "I am most anxious that this should be your meeting. I am sure that we have one thing in common – this is our desire to do the best job we can for all of our people. I should like to ask those present to express their views among others on the following matters:

"Firstly – as to the Toronto and York report. Does the recommendation for unification of eight centrally located

---

13. Globe & Mail, January 9, 1950
14. Toronto Telegram, January 10, 1950
15. Timothy J. Colton, Big Daddy (University of Toronto Press)

municipalities meet with your approval? (Note: The Board at a later date March 21, 1950, amended its recommendation to include the thirteen municipalities in their entirety.)

"Secondly – is there any consensus of opinion that amalgamation should include Scarborough on the east and Mimico, New Toronto, Long Beach and Etobicoke on the west?

"Thirdly – is there any consensus of opinion that the wider area recommended by the Civic Advisory Council including Scarborough, Toronto Gore, and the township of Toronto etc., 23 municipalities in all is a more appropriate area?

Fourthly — and perhaps, or is most important — what constructive suggestions do you have for solution of the problems common to the whole area? I place no restriction on the views you may care to express.

"Let us all remember," he told the Mayors and Reeves that the ultimate objective must be, "a municipal system which is going to meet the needs of our people. Human welfare and betterment is of paramount consideration."

After the premier finished speaking and following some inconclusive discussion the thirteen agreed at Frost's suggestion to form a continuing Toronto Area committee under the chairmanship of A.E.K. Bunnell of the Ministry of Municipal Affairs who unbeknownst to them was a strong advocate of total amalgamation.[16]

Almost simultaneously with this meeting at Queen's Park, the village of Long Branch Council applied to the Ontario Municipal Board for an order amalgamating the Lakeshore area consisting of Etobicoke, Mimico, New Toronto and Long Branch into one municipality.

Then a few days later on February 2, Toronto city council voted nineteen to two to endorse the recommendation of the Toronto and York Planning Board for unification and to apply to the Ontario Municipal

16. Roger Graham, Old Man Ontario, Leslie M. Frost (University of Toronto Press 1990)

Board for full amalgamation. One of the two votes against was cast by Alderman Nathan Phillips, a member of the premier's own political party and a future Toronto Mayor who would soon become an extremely strong amalgamation advocate. The other negative vote was cast by Alderman Norman Freed, a member of the Labour Progressive Party (Communist). According to Nate Phillips, after he had asked numerous questions during that council meeting concerning the finances of the suburbs, Mayor Hiram McCallum motioned him over and whispered in his ear that the recommendation was before council at the request of the Premier Leslie Frost. Phillips replied: "As far as I was concerned, I would not be a party to railroading such an important matter through council."[17]

It is interesting to note that Fred Gardiner appeared at that city council meeting as a witness urging council not only to vote for amalgamation but to do so without holding a public referendum on the subject because, in his words it was a "cinch to be rejected by the voters".[18] Did Fred Gardiner tell Mayor McCallum that the premier had requested this action? If so, did the premier actually ask him to do it? Or was this the same kind of tactic used on me as federal Minister of State (Housing) when a lobbyist friend of the prime minister told me that the prime minister wants this to happen. "If so," I replied, "have the prime minister call me." He never did. In this case we will never know.

Later in February the Warden of York county, Clive Sinclair, who was also the Reeve of Etobicoke circulated an another proposal envisaging a structure, similar to the one put forward in 1924 by Ontario Premier George S. Henry, designating a Metropolitan County comprising the county of York and the city of Toronto. The Warden pointed out that this was not a novel idea since the county governments of Los Angeles included 44 incorporated municipalities with populations ranging from 1000 to over one million, of Wayne County included the city of Detroit,

17. Nathan Phillips, Q.C., The Mayor of All the People
18. Timothy J. Colton, Big Daddy (University of Toronto Press)

of Cook County included Chicago, of Denver County included the city of Denver and of Erie County included Buffalo. His proposal met with a mixed reaction. [19]

The Toronto Area Committee of Mayors and Reeves chaired by Mr. Bunnell reported to the premier at the end of March that all four of his questions had been answered in the negative. Only the city and Mimico supported amalgamation while eleven suburbs including Fred Gardiner's Forest Hill Village were opposed.[20] Although the informal discussions dragged on until June, Frost realized that they were getting nowhere. So he gave the Ontario Municipal Board, which had been deliberately sitting on the Mimico application since 1947 and the Toronto application for almost six months, the go ahead to set a date for the formal hearings. [21]

The Ontario Municipal Board made up of a three-man panel was chaired by Lorne R. Cumming Q.C., from Windsor, Ontario, a man highly respected in the fields of municipal law and planning. The Board wasted no time in getting underway. But before the hearings began the OMB denied a request by the suburbs for an order requiring the city council's decision to apply for amalgamation to be put to a vote of its taxpayers. The hearings themselves lasted from June 19, 1950 to June 7, 1951. During that time the Board members listened to three million words of oral testimony from 85 witnesses while receiving 300 written documents. Although the hearings ended in mid-1951, the Board did not release its 92-page decision, which soon became known as the Cumming Report, until January 20, 1953.[22]

Witnesses for the city of Toronto at the hearings including Fred Gardiner on its behalf, all supported amalgamation emphasizing the efficiency and cost savings of one big government.[23] So did the three Toronto daily newspapers of course. On the other hand, the suburbs emphasized the errors, extravagance and inefficiencies of the city in handling its own problems claiming this would only increase with

---

19. Town of Leaside Council Minutes, February 10, 1950
20. Archives of Ontario – Leslie Frost papers B292-271-2, RG 3 – 24 Box #35,36
21. Archives of Ontario – Leslie Frost papers B292-271-2, RG 3 – 24 Box #35,36
22. Ontario Municipal Board, January 20, 1953 decision
23. Timothy J. Colton, Big Daddy (University of Toronto)

amalgamation and result in higher overall taxation without any improvement in services. Heavy emphasis was placed on public access to local government.[24] Mayor Howard Burrell of Leaside, for example, testified that the town's "community spirit" would disappear if it were merged with Toronto. Small scale governments like Leaside's were more accessible to the taxpayers and more familiar with their local problems, he maintained.[25] Former Swansea Reeve Elmer Brandon now a MPP (Member of the Provincial Parliament), put forward the idea that the city of Toronto should be split up into a number of smaller municipalities because larger cities get further away from the people.[26] York Township and the township of East York reflecting the views of their residents but also recalling how the city had said no to them during their time of need in 1931, were insistent on maintaining their own identities, their frugal administrations and their fiscal prudence.[27] Two other former suburban Reeves both now Progressive Conservative MPPs together with Scarborough, York and East York Townships, all insisted that their taxpayers be required to vote approval before any amalgamation or annexation was implemented. Etobicoke, Mimico, Long Branch and New Toronto all opposed amalgamation with the city but supported an amalgamation of their own.[28]

Despite the fact that there was nothing said publicly behind the scenes, Premier Leslie Frost was in constant communication with Chairman Lorne Cumming. From the opening of the OMB hearings until the release of its final report, the premier immersed himself in the problem for a very practical and a very political reason.[29] By 1953 all but one of the Toronto suburban members of the provincial Parliament (MPPs) were members of his government's caucus in the legislature. One of them had

24. Timothy J. Colton, Big Daddy (University of Toronto)
25. Timothy J. Colton, Big Daddy (University of Toronto)
26. Timothy J. Colton, Big Daddy (University of Toronto)
27. Timothy J. Colton, Big Daddy (University of Toronto)
28. Ontario Municipal Board, January 20, 1953 decision
29. Roger Graham, Old Man Ontario, Leslie M. Frost (University of Toronto Press 1990)

warned Frost of the bitter opposition to unification among suburban Progressive Conservative supporters. "Amalgamation will pile up such a cloud of grudge voting against us, we will be snowed under at the next election. Amalgamation is a hornet's nest; let us leave it alone."[30] At the same time four of his other MPPs had voted for amalgamation in 1950 as members of Toronto city council. Allan Grossman, then a Toronto Alderman and president of the St. Paul's Progressive Conservative Association, had previously written to the premier claiming to know that the vast majority of the people in the city and the suburbs favoured amalgamation as he did.[31] But another of his P.C. MPP's William Stewart, representing the Toronto riding of Parkdale and who had been Mayor of the city in 1931, still opposed amalgamation as he had then. It was indeed a real hornet's nest.[32]

As is the case with every political issue large or small, Premier Frost received a great deal of public input. All three Toronto newspapers, the Star, the Telegram and the Globe and Mail supported total amalgamation. At the same time he received letters pro and con from private citizens. One of those letters opposing amalgamation was written on behalf of North York Branch 66 of The Royal Canadian Legion. A.D. McKenzie MPP, the President of the Progressive Conservative Party of Ontario and the party's chief election organizer was a member of that Legion Branch. Scarborough's Reeve Oliver Crockford wrote to say: "Unification would be the first step in the formation of a dictatorship, which would exercise control over the Toronto area." Of course, Fred Gardiner kept sending him briefs in support of amalgamation. [33]

However, as well as reading his mail the premier – not only familiarizing himself with the political and the religious persuasions of the councils and boards of education members in each of the thirteen municipalities (see Appendix "A") – personally studied the financial impact of each option, including the breakdown between residential and

---

30. Peter Oliver, Unlikely Tory (Lester & Orpen Dennys)
31. Peter Oliver, Unlikely Tory (Lester & Orpen Dennys)
32. Archives of Ontario – Leslie Frost papers B292271-2 RG 3-24 Box #35,36
33. Archives of Ontario – Leslie Frost papers B292271-2 RG 3-24 Box #35,36

commercial assessments, the property tax rates, the actual expenditures and the provincial grants they received. Additionally, he reviewed the 163 inter municipal agreements which had been entered into among the thirteen municipalities since 1915 covering an assortment of municipal services all of which had financial implications, not only for the thirteen municipalities but for the remainder of York County as well (see Appendix "B"). The premier also immersed himself in reports describing, the forms of municipal governments and boards of education in other jurisdictions such as Los Angeles, California and Newark, New Jersey.[34] So, although Frost's concerns were very political, in order to determine what was doable and what was not, he did not overlook the financial implications for the Toronto area residents.

After Cumming had identified the main options, he met with Frost and other government officials at least ten times to discuss the content of the OMB report.[35] When it was finally made public in January 1953, the Cumming Report was a compromise acknowledging favourable points in each argument but ultimately finding that the objections to amalgamation were sufficient to outweigh its advantages.

"Amalgamation," Cumming wrote, "would result in increased taxes due to bringing all the suburban wages, salary scales and working conditions up to city levels. Costs would increase with the size of the municipality because of the larger number of employees per unit of population, and per capita costs in general tend to increase with the size of the municipality. A large city is able to pay more than a small one and to afford an almost endless list of desirable but unnecessary expenditures. It is unrealistic to expect any single council to give sufficient consideration to the many difficult problems in an area of more than 240 square miles and over one million people. The need for reform does not justify complete amalgamation. The loss of local autonomy would mean domination of the central city through their concentrated voting power.

---

34. Archives of Ontario – Leslie Frost papers B292271-2 RG 3-24 Box #35,36
35. Archives of Ontario – Leslie Frost papers B292271-2 RG 3-24 Box #35,36

An amalgamated city might be strong, efficient and well organized but it would not be local government. Local government, in a democracy, however, at least to the majority of Ontario people," he went on to say, "means a government which is very close to the local residents and is carried on by duly elected local leaders who offer their services from time to time in the interests of their local community and who learn at the same time something of the duties and responsibilities of public office."

Cumming also rejected the Mimico proposal for a joint administration area stating: "In the judgment of the Board these problems cannot be resolved by further reliance upon the process of voluntary inter municipal co-operation with its apparent inevitable delays. Apart from the interminable controversies involved in the method it would appear to be practically impossible to hope for unanimous approval of thirteen sets of local government when projects involving heavy capital expenditures, although located within some of the municipalities, must be financed by combining the resources of all."

In dismissing the applications of the city and of Mimico, Cumming also said: "The Board does not consider it necessary or desirable at this time to determine the proper limits of the future metropolitan area, provided the boundary recommended in the initial period is deemed a temporary boundary only and that there be no repetition of the errors of the past in neglecting to provide for growth. There seems to be no good reason why future additions to the area should not be permitted and even encouraged within reasonable limits. Such additions could be made either by an act of the legislature or by an order of this Board on application of Metropolitan council, any local council already within the area or any existing or future local council outside the proposed area."[36] If the Chairman was urging a future expansion of the metropolitan Toronto boundaries into Peel, Vaughan, Markham and Durham etc., as the urban area grew he would have been very disappointed with the recommendations of future reports, Royal Commissions and provincial government decisions.

---

36. Ontario Municipal Board, January 20, 1953 decision

Instead of amalgamation or the status quo, Cumming recommended a federation in the best tradition of the British North American Act that created Canada in 1867. A new Metropolitan Toronto council was to be created by the provincial legislature to be concerned with capital projects, property assessment, debenture borrowing, major trunk sanitary sewers, public transit, arterial roads and regional planning, while the thirteen municipalities continuing to exist within their present boundaries would provide for policing, fire protection, licensing, libraries, local planning and tax collection.

As soon as the report was released on January 20, 1953, the city of Toronto council wasted no time in convening a February 3 meeting to condemn the recommendations on a vote of 22 to 1. Speaking in the council debate that proceeded the vote then Alderman Allan Grossman, later a Progressive Conservative provincial MPP said: "This report seems to have been drafted by somebody with an anti-Hogtown psychosis."[37] Cumming came from Windsor, Ontario and Frost from Lindsay, Ontario. Grossman and others on the council were concerned that the central city would be reduced to a having no municipality and that its physical services would sadly deteriorate. The lone dissenting vote was cast by Mayor Allan Lamport, a former Liberal MPP who informed the council: "You haven't been given the full facts, because I had already arranged it with Frost that he was going to give us so much a head for every person in the area. And that was the teller because we were going to get an enormous boost for extra funds." That was the sweetener that Premier Frost had kept up his sleeve since the 1949 Dominion Provincial conference in Ottawa where he had managed to persuade the federal government to increase its transfer payments to Ontario.[38] When the city resolution denouncing the Cumming Report arrived in the premier's office on February 10 under the official city seal together with signatures of the City Clerk and the Mayor, it was accompanied in a small separate envelope containing a recipe card on the back of which was written:

37. Peter Oliver, Unlikely Tory (Lester & Orpen Dennys Publishers 1985)
38. Roger Graham, Old Man Ontario, Leslie M. Frost (University of Toronto Press 1990)

"Although my views are contrary to those expressed in this document, however, I am required to sign them according to Statute," signed Allan Lamport, Mayor (see Appendix "C"). [39]

The day after the city resolution, then Alderman Allan Grossman wrote to Premier Frost: "I am convinced that it would be a very grave mistake should the recommendations be adopted. Amalgamation was the best solution on practical grounds. I am also convinced that it would be – at least in the Toronto area – disastrous politically to implement the Board's recommendations. The Liberal members of city council are rubbing their hands gleefully in anticipation of becoming candidates in the next provincial election and conversely those of us who have been considering the possibility of standing as Conservative candidates, feel that under the same circumstances, it would be political suicide."

Frost replied: "I think you will agree that if the city of Toronto had done what was necessary, years ago in progressive annexations, then this situation would not exist and therefore the failure to take action on the part of many governments has further complicated the problem. Shortly after taking office in 1950 I initiated action, and I intend to do the very best I can and abide by the results." [40]

Despite advertisements placed by city council in the three daily newspapers praising the advantages of amalgamation, on February 25, 1953 Premier Frost personally moved first reading of Bill 80 in the Ontario legislature implementing the Cumming recommendations to establish The Municipality of Metropolitan Toronto. [41] The fact that the Bill containing more than 200 sections was prepared and introduced only one month after the Report was published demonstrates how closely the premier was involved in preparing the Report itself. In my personal experience federal legislative draftsmen take many months if not years to prepare a single simple Bill let alone a complex one with over 200 sections. That being so the draftsman likely worked on the Bill

39. Archives of Ontario – Leslie Frost papers B292271-2 RG 3-24 #35,36
40. Roger Graham, Old Man Ontario, Leslie M. Frost (University of Toronto Press 1990)
41. Roger Graham, Old Man Ontario, Leslie M. Frost (University of Toronto Press 1990)

continuously from the time the Board hearings ended in June 1951 until the report was released in January 1953.

Whether there were any objections to the Bill when it was discussed by the premier's Conservative caucus we do not know, but we do know that Frost was the most knowledgeable and dominant person in the legislature at that time. During Question Period at Queen's Park the premier would often motion one of his cabinet Ministers to whom a question had been directed by an Opposition member to sit down, while he stood and answered the question himself. He had the reputation of knowing every file of every provincial Department better than anyone else in the Legislative Assembly.[42]

Whether or not there were any objections in caucus the premier proceeded with Bill 80. The Bill closely followed the Report with the exception of the composition of Metropolitan Toronto council. The Board had recommended a council made up of nine members, four from the city, four from the suburbs, and a chairman appointed by the Lieutenant Governor in Council i.e. by the premier himself. One suburban member was to be appointed from each of four groupings of the twelve suburbs: the western division included Weston, Swansea, Mimico, New Toronto, Long Branch, and Etobicoke; the northwest division included York and Forest Hill; the northern division included Leaside and North York and the eastern division composed of Scarborough and East York. Those chosen were not to be delegates or representatives of any local council nor permitted to sit on two councils at the same time.[43] The makeup of the Metro Council and how its members were to be selected were among the most hotly debated issues following the release of the of the Cumming report.[44] The Bill 80 solution was a Frost compromise, imperfect perhaps, but saleable. It established Metropolitan Toronto council composed of the twelve Mayors or Reeves of the suburban councils plus the Mayor and two Controllers receiving the most votes in the city

42. Roger Graham, Old Man Ontario, Leslie M. Frost (University of Toronto Press 1990)
43. Ontario Municipal Board, January 20, 1953 decision
44. Timothy J. Colton, Big Daddy (University of Toronto Press)

together with the nine city Aldermen who led the poles in their Wards (see Appendix "D"). The Chairman of Metropolitan Toronto Council was to be appointed initially for a two-year term by the Lieutenant Governor in Council i.e. the Premier himself and thereafter to be elected by Metro council members. The Chairman was not required to be one of the elected members of Metro Council. It is interesting to note in the light of current remuneration that the Chairman's pay was not to exceed $15,000.00 per year; that the Metro council members pay was not to exceed $1,800.00 per year and that a Committee chair's pay was not to exceed $100.00.[45]

Bill 80 received a mixed reception but much better than that received by the Cumming Report itself. All the three Toronto daily newspapers had been opposed to the OMB report but they were split on the Bill. The Telegram supported it. The Globe, Mail and the Star were more critical. In the legislature there was little if any opposition likely because all of the MPPs from the affected areas were Progressive Conservatives with the exception of Joe Salsberg, a Communist who could find no one to second his motion to kill the Bill.[46] Although they didn't agree with every detail in Bill 80 the suburban councils supported it and in the words of Weston's Mayor Seagrave "would do everything to try to make it work". [47]

The burning question, however, was, who would the premier appoint to Chair Metro council? Various names including Lamport and Cumming were seriously considered but Frost had decided on Fred Gardiner with whom he had a long, close and friendly association. Although Gardiner had vigorously advocated in favour of amalgamation, he subsequently described the Cumming Report as "a thoroughly sensible and practical alternative". So Frost asked Gardiner to come to his office for a chat. When the position was offered Gardiner protested that he was too busy with his law practice but Frost replied: "You thought a hell of a lot about my law practice when you urged me to allow my name to stand

45. Ontario Legislative Assembly, Bill 80, 1953
46. Roger Graham, Old Man Ontario (University of Toronto Press 1990)
47. Archives of Ontario – Leslie Frost papers B292271-2 RG 3-24 #35,36

for leader." Gardiner gave in and in doing so gave up an income of $50,000.00 a year practicing law for the job of the Chairman of Metro paying only $15,000.00 a year, but he agreed to serve for two years only.[48] Frost could not have made a better choice. Gardiner who stayed on much longer than two years became known as the "Big Daddy of Metro".

A year after his appointment, Gardiner wrote to Frost: "While I supported amalgamation you convinced me that the metropolitan form of government is a more appropriate answer to the problems involved and I am now satisfied you were right."[49]

48. Roger Graham, Old Man Ontario (University of Toronto Press 1990)
49. Timothy J. Colton, Big Daddy (University of Toronto Press)

Municipality	Name	Politics	Active Yes-No	Religion
Toronto	Lamport, Allan A.	Liberal	Yes	Baptist
	Saunders, Leslie H.	Conservative	Yes	Salvation Army
	Shannon, Louis, J.	Liberal	Yes	United Church
	Allen, Wm. A.	Liberal	Yes	Roman Catholic
	Dennison, Wm.	C.C.F.	Very	Unitarian
	MacVicar, J. A.	Liberal	Yes	Roman Catholic
	Grossman, A.	Conservative	Yes	Hebrew
	Gould, J. M.	Liberal	Yes	Hebrew
	Robinson, Mrs. M.	Conservative	Yes	United Church
	Davidson, W. C.	Conservative	Yes	United Church
	Lipsett, R.	Conservative	Yes	Anglican
	Belyea, R. E.	Conservative	Yes	United Church
York	Hall, Fred W.	Conservative	Yes	Baptist
	Gell, Mrs. Florence	Conservative	Quite	Anglican
North York	McMahon, Frederick	Liberal	Yes	?
	Douglas, F. A.			
East York	Simpson, Harry G.	Conservative	Yes	Anglican
	Webster, George	Liberal	No	?
Scarborough	Crockford, Oliver	Conservative	Yes	Baptist
	Cook, Norman	Conservative	No	Protestant
Etobicoke	Lewis, Beverley	Conservative	Yes	?
	Parker, J. D.			
Forest Hill	Bick, Charles O.	Conservative	Yes	Protestant
	Long, J. A.	Conservative	No	Baptist
Leaside	Burrell, Howard T.			
	Rogers, W. M.			

Appendix A *(Source: Archives of Ontario)*

Mimico	Norris, A. D.	Liberal	No	Anglican
New Toronto	Grant, E. W.	Conservative	No	United Church
	Morrison, Angus H.	nil	No	Protestant
Long Branch	Curtis, Mrs. Marie	C.C.F.	Very	United Church
Weston	Seagrave, R. C.	nil	-	Presbyterian
Swansea	Hague, Mrs. Dorothy	Liberal	No	?
	Bonham, J. T.	Liberal	No	?

February 10, 1953

Please add to list :

North York	McMahon, Frederick	Liberal	Yes	Roman Catholic
	Douglas, F. A.	nil	-	Anglican
Leaside	Burrell, Howard T.	Conservative	No	Baptist
	Rogers, W. M.	Conservative	No	United Church

Appendix A - cont'd *(Source: Archives of Ontario)*

What if we complied
all into one school
area?

Would it not merely raise
all cents to Toronto Level

Appendix B *(Source Archives of Ontario)*

There are only 2 or 3 of these municipalities
in trouble - North York - Mimico -
East York - due entirely to
over centralization of houses & lack of
industry -

(a) give them to Toronto

(b) empty all schools

Appendix B - cont'd *(Source: Archives of Ontario)*

Feb. 10, 1953.

Although my views are contrary to
those expressed in this document,
however I am required to sign them
according to Statute.

Mayor.

Appendix C *(Source: Archives of Ontario)*

Former Ontario Premier Leslie M. Frost QC (on the left) with former OMB Chairman Lorne Cumming QC (on the right)
(Source: The Globe and Mail, February 26, 1953)

Former Ontario Premier Leslie M. Frost QC (on the left) with former old city of Toronto Mayor Allan Lamport (on the right)
(Source: "Harold Barkley/ GetStock.com")

There are difficulties in all schemes no use to escape difficulties in one scheme to run blindly into another and accept in turn all the difficulties there — Better to alleviate where possible all difficulties

THE ONTARIO MUNICIPAL BOARD

IN THE MATTER OF SECTIONS 20 AND 22 OF "THE MUNICIPAL ACT,"
(R. S. O. 1950, CHAPTER 243

THE CORPORATIONS OF THE CITY OF TORONTO and THE TOWN OF MIMICO,

APPLICANTS

- and -

THE CORPORATIONS OF THE COUNTY OF YORK, THE TOWNS OF LEASIDE, NEW TORONTO and WESTON, THE VILLAGES OF FOREST HILL, LONG BRANCH and SWANSEA, and THE TOWNSHIPS OF ETOBICOKE, YORK, NORTH YORK and SCARBOROUGH,

RESPONDENTS

D E C I S I O N O F T H E B O A R D

Dated January 20, 1953

Press Release

Toronto Papers and Radio	Thursday, January 22 at 3 p. m.
Outside Papers	Thursday, January 22 at 1.30 p. m.

Govt 1 each suburb
1/2 Toronto
Chairman

Committee
Water Chairman
Sewers Information committee

Appendix D: Cover page of the 1953 OMB decision with notes inscribed by Leslie Frost *(Source: Archives of Ontario)*

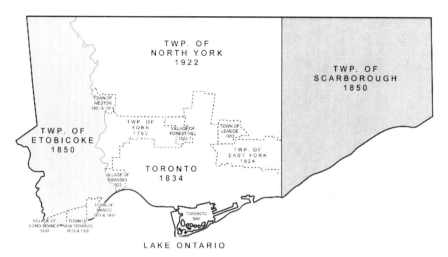

Map showing the original 13 local municipalities of The Municipality of
Metropolitan Toronto *(Source: Valentine De Landro 2014)*

Former Metropolitan Toronto Chairman Frederick Gardiner QC (on the left) with former Ontario Premier Leslie M Frost QC (on the right) *(Source: "Leo Harrison/ GetStock.com")*

Leaving a Trail

CHAPTER 3

"Do not go where the path may lead;
go instead where there is no path and leave a trail"

Ralph Waldo Emerson

Frederick Goldwin Gardiner, Q.C. had been the Reeve of Forest Hill Village, Chairman of its Hydro Commissions, a member of the Toronto and York Planning Board and Warden of York County. He was also a principal fund raiser for the Ontario Progressive Conservative Party and had nominated Leslie Frost as party leader meaning he had actually nominated Frost as the premier of the Province of Ontario. Gardiner had municipal politics in his blood and could not resist the challenge of blazing a new trail with the newly created Municipality of Metropolitan Toronto.

It was the first Metropolitan Municipality of its kind in North America. According to the Globe & Mail: "Cities throughout the western world are looking towards Metropolitan Toronto in hope that the new municipal government is also the answer to their problem." Within the first year of its existence the Globe & Mail reported: "Information dealing with Metropolitan Toronto has been requested from the United States, Japan, England, New Zealand, Australia and Ireland." The new trail required a real leader to blaze the trail and that leader was Fred Gardiner.

Premier Frost had indeed chosen the right person for the job of Metropolitan Toronto council's first Chairman. "If I was going to get anywhere," Gardiner said later, "I had to know more about any given subject than any individual councillor and more about metropolitan business than all the members of council combined."[1] In that respect he mirrored the way in which his friend Leslie Frost dealt with his cabinet, his party caucus and the entire Ontario legislature.

Gardiner was not only knowledgeable but he was a dynamo as well. During Metro's first years under his leadership, in a flurry of action the Chairman established a competent municipal bureaucracy and drove through a vast program of public works including carefully planned extensions of water and sewers to Etobicoke, North York and Scarborough. The septic tanks and contaminated water disappeared while the cost of financing projects was reduced because there was now one rather than thirteen separate borrowers.

Many, including East York Reeve True Davidson called Gardiner a bulldozer. "When I call him a bulldozer," she explained, "I am not being critical. A bulldozer knocks things about a bit, but not wantonly. There is a purpose and usually the purpose is to prepare for construction." He had to clear away obstacles in order to build the region.[2]

Shortly after he took the job Fred Gardiner went to New York City for a few days to discuss capital projects and spending with that city's famous but controversial chief of construction Robert Moses, a man whom Gardiner admired and to whom Gardiner has frequently been compared.

"The thing that impressed me about Moses was that the first question he asked me was, 'What the hell are you going to do with that mess up there now that you're in charge of it?' I had to think fast, but I knew what to say. I said I was going to be like Stalin. I'd have a five-or-ten-year plan and I'd lay out exactly what I had and how I was going to spend it and I'd know exactly where the money was going. His only comment was, 'Never mind those high-minded advisers. Keep your staff small. Don't let them boss you around. Hire them when you want and

1. Timothy J. Colton, Big Daddy (University of Toronto Press)
2. True Davidson, The Golden Strings (Griffin House 1973)

fire them when you want. Make them work for you and not the other way around.' He didn't have to convince me. This was how I intended to proceed. I was going to run my own show. That's why they called me a bulldozer."[3]

But while Fred Gardiner held Robert Moses in high regard, Jane Jacobs, the well- known and highly respected author of The Death and Life of Great American Cities, did not. During his long career working with the numerous Mayors of the city of New York, the various Governors of the State of New York and with Franklin D. Roosevelt the President of the United States, Moses played a dominant role in the creation or the reshaping of roads, bridges, tunnels, parks, playgrounds, housing projects and other physical projects, not only in the New York metropolitan area but in the State of New York and in other US cities. He was the moving force behind the construction of the Lincoln Centre and the locating of the United Nations headquarters building in New York rather than Philadelphia. He is credited with the creation of the New York State Parks System and the concept of limited access highways or parkways, a concept now employed internationally. He had a reputation for getting things done at a time when there was no such thing as an environmental assessment. That is what attracted Fred Gardiner. The Robert Moses Parkway along the American side of the Niagara River, the Robert Moses Power Dam on the St. Lawrence Seaway and the Robert Moses State Park are just a few of the many sites that bear his name today.[4]

But in 1962, eight years after his meetings with Gardiner, Robert Moses crossed swords with Jane Jacobs over the proposed construction of the Lower Manhattan Expressway. Jane Jacobs, then a resident of New York City, became the chairperson of the "Joint Committee to stop the Lower Manhattan Expressway". Moses had already bulldozed through numerous huge urban renewal projects as well as thirteen other expressways right across the heart of New York City, but in the process he had destroyed more than twenty established local New York City neighbourhoods. The preservation of neighbourhoods was Jane Jacobs'

---

3.   Timothy J. Colton, Big Daddy (University of Toronto Press)
4.   Robert A. Caro, The Power Broker (Alfred A. Knopf 1974)

issue. To do so the expressway had to be stopped and so it was. Jacobs was instrumental in killing Moses' plan for the Lower Manhattan Expressway just as she was in stopping the Spadina Expressway after she moved to Toronto in 1968.[5]

Like Robert Moses when they met in 1954, Fred Gardiner got things done. Toronto Mayor Nathan Phillips, who continued to press for total amalgamation because he strongly believed that "Metro was milking the Toronto taxpayers to the advantage of the suburbs" found Gardiner "as being deeply knowledgeable about every aspect of civic administration and as time went on I saw that it was his genius that made Metro tick."[6]

But since the Mayor of Toronto, his city council and the three Toronto daily newspapers, the Star, the Telegram and the Globe & Mail were continuing to press for total amalgamation tension on Metro council between the city and the suburban members was inevitable. In spite of that, however, there were very few direct clashes along city-suburban lines. In the first six years of Metro's existence, the Chairman was required to cast a deciding vote on only one occasion when all twelve city members and all twelve suburban members were on opposing sides of a question. On one other occasion, city Controller and Metro council member Jean Newman, broke ranks and voted with the suburbs against the otherwise unanimous city opposition to a uniform wholesale water rate for all thirteen municipalities. Mayor Nathan Phillips never forgave her for that and used it against Mrs. Newman when she ran against him for Mayor in the next election.[7]

Although Lorne Cumming is called the father of Metro, the real author or at the very least co-author of the Cumming Report, Premier Leslie Frost, continued to keep a very close eye on the Metro scene. In a letter to Frost dated November 26, 1956, Dorothy Hague, the Reeve of Swansea wrote: "Personally, I can see very little wrong with the

5. Anthony Flint, Wrestling with Moses (Randon House 2011)
6. Nathan Phillips, Q.C., The Mayor of All the People (University of Toronto Press)
7. True Davidson, The Golden Strings (Griffin House 1973)

metropolitan form of government."[8] In spite of the Reeve's vote of approval, however, the premier together with his economic advisor George Gathercole continued to monitor the population, assessment, property tax and provincial subsidies gains and losses for the thirteen municipalities. He was also still receiving numerous letters from Chairman Gardiner but now concerning Metro finances and provincial grants. [9]

As the population of the suburbs grew so did their concerns about their representation on Metropolitan Council versus the city and versus each other. Swansea a small municipality may have been happy to have only one member on Metro Council but the larger municipalities of North York, Scarborough and Etobicoke were not. The original 1953 Act provided for twelve city members on the Metro Council with the twelve suburbs having one member each. Not only that hot potato but also policing, licensing and the never ending calls by the city for total amalgamation soon blossomed into issues for Metro Council.

When the Municipality of Metropolitan Toronto was established, the Ontario government had agreed to review its experience within five years. But only three years later the province moved to address two of the Metro concerns by passing amending legislation to merge the thirteen individual police departments into one and the thirteen individual licensing bodies into one licensing commission both reporting to Metro Council. Later in 1957, Premier Frost who was known to many as the "Silver Fox" and to others as "Old Man Ontario", appointed a Metropolitan Toronto Commission of Inquiry to examine not only the issue of council representation but also the extent to which the 1953 Act was meeting the need for a better local government.

The Commission of Inquiry was composed of Chairman Lorne Cumming Q.C. as well as four Progressive Conservative members of the provincial Legislature: Allan Grossman, a former Toronto City Alderman; William J. Stewart, a former Mayor of Toronto; Bev Lewis, a former Reeve of Etobicoke and Tom Graham, a former Deputy Reeve of York

---

8.   Archives of Ontario – Leslie Frost papers B292271-2 RG 3-24 Box #35,36
9.   Archives of Ontario – Leslie Frost papers B292271-2 RG 3-24 Box #35,36

Township. The Commission held 32 public hearings, received 46 written briefs and 32 volumes of exhibits totalling in all 900,000 words of evidence. [10]

One of those briefs was presented by the "Mayor of all the People" as Toronto Mayor Nathan Phillips called himself. He argued that Metro was headed for amalgamation; that it was only a question of "when" and that "the amalgamation of those municipalities that were ready for it should not be delayed until the entire thirteen were ready; municipalities should be considered ready if amalgamation would not place a burden of taxation on the taxpayers of the amalgamated municipalities" and that "upon partial amalgamation Metro should be dissolved and a commission set up to deal with those remaining services which affect the entire Metro area".[11]

No final Report was ever made but in its 1958 Interim Report the Commission found:

>*"It is quite evident that, notwithstanding previous differences and doubts, the experience of the past four years has shown beyond question that the application of the principle of federation was a sound and practical approach to an acceptable and workable solution of the complex problem of providing adequate municipal services in the Toronto Metropolitan Area ....*

>*"It has shown beyond question that with the development of a wider understanding of the basic principles of the legislation on the part of the citizens, together with the able and constructive leadership of the Metropolitan Chairman and persistent and sincere efforts of the elected representatives, great progress has been made in removing the serious obstacles to the economic growth and development of the area, which seemed insurmountable under the former outdated system of rigidly divided jurisdictional areas and in equally rigid and unbalanced distribution of taxable resources."*

10. Peter Oliver, Unlikely Tory (Lester & Orpen Denny Publishers 1985)
11. Nathan Phillips, The Mayor of All the People (University of Toronto Press)

According to that Report there was "a surprising amount of satisfaction with the present type of council and school board and an unwillingness to make any drastic change in the existing organization at the present time or in the immediate future".

Although a great many of the submissions dealt with the city-suburban split the Commission pointed out that: "Only once has an exact division occurred on only one issue of the many hundreds that have been decided in the history and proceedings of the council."

On the question of the method of selecting the Chairman of Metropolitan Toronto Council, the Commission had this to say:

> "The Commission is of the opinion that this important provision must be retained in its present form so long as the legislation continues to provide for an equal division of political power between the city and the outer area municipalities, and that unless and until the existing legislation is amended to provide for the direct election by an overall Metropolitan vote of a substantial number of the members of the Metropolitan council, there is no advantage to be gained by requiring candidates for this vitally important position to undergo the expense and uncertainty of a political campaign extending over the 240 square miles of the metropolitan Area."

> The Report went on further, to argue that advocates of direct election of the Metro Council Chairman "misconceive the true nature of the office". In the view of the Commission, the Chairman should be far more an impartial presiding officer with a vote to cast in the event of an equal division of the council: "He should be the Chief Executive Officer responsible for continuous and detailed supervision and correlation of the work and activities of all the administrative departments in accordance with the policies adopted by the elected body .... His duties and responsibilities should correspond closely with those of the General Manager of a large corporation."[12]

---

12. Albert Rose, Governing Metropolitan Toronto 1953-1071 (University of California Press 1972)

Although the Commission did recommend some minor changes to the governing legislation, its finding can really be described as being stand pat. This was not really surprising bearing in mind the close relationship between the Commission Chairman Mr. Cumming known as the father of Metro and the premier.

However, the city of Toronto council and its bureaucrats had not given up their belief in one big city. On the other hand the suburban municipalities were even more opposed to the idea of amalgamation than they had been in 1950. Since Metro had been created not only had their population increased but they had also developed a local pride in each of the respective suburban municipalities. So by 1960, although absolutely committed to the metropolitan concept, the inequality of representation on Metro Council had become a very lively issue for the suburbs. A Toronto Progressive Conservative member of the Ontario legislature, the former city Alderman, Allan Grossman, urged the province to get involved, arguing that differences between the city and the suburbs were hardening.[13] A number of proposals for change were advanced by council members themselves and of course by the newspapers but none appealed to the provincial government since the city still had roughly 50 per cent of the total population and property assessment value for the entire metropolitan area.

Then in January 1961, Fred Gardiner who had been Chairman of Metro Council since its inception announced that he would be stepping down at the end of the year. But before doing so, acknowledging the need for changes in the metro system, he stated: "It is my view that there is no body better calculated, to have the knowledge and experience to determine the best form of government for this area than this council constituted as it is, with representation from all of the constituent municipalities. There is a reservoir of knowledge and experience in this council with respect to what should be the best form of government for this area, which cannot be matched by any other governmental institution

13. Peter Oliver, Unlikely Tory (Lester & Orpen Denny Publishers 1985)

or by any consultants who might be engaged to investigate the subject and make a report upon what should be done. My recommendation is that this council should constitute itself into a special committee of the whole council under the chairmanship of the Chairman of the council to give consideration to what would be the form of governmental institution best calculated to provide the best municipal government for this area in the most efficient and economical manner."

He also pointed out, however:

> *"There is one thing that all should remember and that is that there is financial amalgamation already in existence. On January 1, 1954, Metro assumed all the debenture debt of all the constituent municipalities with the exception of $70,585,000.00. That un-assumed debt has now been reduced to $35,150,000.00 and will disappear entirely at a relatively early date.*

> *"All of the assumed debt and all new debt created since January 1, 1954, now amounts to a total of $628,176,000.00 as January 1, 1961 and that debt is the joint and several liability of the Metropolitan Corporation and each of the thirteen municipalities.*

> *"Whether any individual municipality likes it or not, what it can now finance can be no longer determined by, itself. That decision must be determined by the Metropolitan council .... The members of this council should be calculated to know in an objective, practical, and realistic way the extent to which there is or is not duplication of administrative services and duplication of costs."[14]*

So, Metropolitan Council created a Special Committee on Metropolitan Affairs comprised of all the members of council. It requested two reports to help the Committee make recommendations for the changes that Gardiner felt were needed.

First a committee of Metro department heads was asked to report on their functions and the extent to which Metro services overlapped with

---

14. Albert Rose, Governing Metropolitan Toronto 1953-1971 (University of California Press 1972)

those of the thirteen area municipalities. Then Premier Leslie Frost volunteered the provincial Department of Economics and Municipal Affairs directed by the premier's close advisor George Gathercole, the Deputy Minister of Economics to prepare a further report for the Special Committee. Metro Council members welcomed this offer in the hope that a report coming from a source so close to Frost would result in recommendations that the provincial legislature would actually implement.[15]

The report of the committee of department heads provided a snap shot of the total administrative and government structure in the entire metropolitan area, but understandably it concluded that the real decisions rested with council and not the bureaucracy.[16]

The Gathercole Report, as the Provincial study came to be named, made no recommendations either. But a number of possibilities were examined. The Report put forward three alternative detailed solutions: total amalgamation, a five city (borough) system and a four city (borough) system of Metro government. It was mainly concerned with the "disparities in representation and economic balance". In dealing with the consolidation of the thirteen area municipalities under a four city (borough) plan, the Report described the needed changes as follows:

1.   *The borough of Toronto would consist of the city of Toronto and five additional municipalities described as an "inner group of six municipalities", which in 1960 would have included 58 per cent of the total population of Metro and 60.3 per cent of its total assessed valuation.*

2.   *The borough of North York would consist of North York and one additional small municipality, which in 1960 would have included 16.8 per cent of the total population and 16.5 per cent of the total assessed valuation.*

15. Albert Rose, Governing Metropolitan Toronto 1953-1971 (University of California Press 1972)
16. Albert Rose, Governing Metropolitan Toronto 1953-1971 (University of California Press 1972)

3.   *The borough of Scarborough, composed only of the township of Scarborough, in 1960 would have had 13 per cent of the total population and 10 per cent of the total assessed valuation.*

4.   *The borough of Etobicoke, composed of the township of Etobicoke and three additional small area municipalities, in 1960, would have had 12.2 per cent of the total population and 13.2 per cent of the total assessed valuation.*

"It will be noted that under this suggested consolidation of area municipalities, representation by population could be made fairly consistent with representation by financial interest. The borough of Toronto's proportion of total population and assessment would exceed the combined population and assessment of the other three boroughs but would steadily decline, reaching parity with them in 1970."

The Gathercole Report assumed that the membership of Metro Council would expand from 24 to 26, but that the city (borough) of Toronto would still have one half of the total while the other half would be divided among the three new boroughs in proportion to their population with five, four and four members respectively, excluding the Chairman.[17]

The retiring Metro Chairman initiated a full scale council debate following receipt of the two reports, in which he personally recommended the five city (borough) proposal versus total amalgamation which was still insisted upon by Toronto city members and the daily newspapers. The debate which started in the early afternoon raged until the wee hours of the next morning. In the result, council divided twelve to twelve on a motion to apply to the Province for a reorganization of the Municipality of Metropolitan Toronto. Chairman Gardiner cast the deciding vote to defeat the motion on the grounds that when the vote was so evenly split

---

17. Albert Rose, Governing Metropolitan Toronto 1953-1971 (University of California Press 1972)

it was not appropriate for him to come down on the side of drastic reform. Instead he felt that the new Metro Chairman should initiate a further council debate but, even more importantly, should feel out the Ontario government's position before proceeding. A subsequent motion by Toronto Mayor Nathan Phillips for total amalgamation was defeated on a vote of eighteen to five.[18]

As the Frederick Goldwin Gardiner era at Metro drew to a close, Big Daddy as he was known or Metro Goldwin Mayor as he often called himself, could look back and see that most of the large trunk sewers and water-mains were now in place; that the Gardiner Expressway and the Don Valley Parkway had been built and that on the very last day before he retired council had agreed to build the Spadina Expressway. Without it he had told the members, the provincial government would not construct an interchange at Yorkdale and Highway 401, now known as the basket weave.[19]

Paul Godfrey, later a Metro Chairman himself, told me that on one occasion, he personally observed Fred Gardiner in action at a Metro Council meeting, having an angry exchange with Toronto Alderman and Metro Councillor George Ben. Ben was opposing a proposal put forward by Gardiner. Gardiner stood up waving a thick report in his hand telling Ben in anything but a soft voice that if he had read this report he would be very embarrassed since it refuted everything Ben had said. After the vote which Gardiner won almost unanimously, Godfrey asked his friend and Metro Councillor and North York Reeve Norman Goodhead what was in that report? Goodhead said he didn't know but took Godfrey to meet Gardiner privately. When asked about the contents of the report, Gardiner replied, that there was no "report" just a sheaf of papers he had picked up from his desk, but since no one else on council had read the "report" either they all voted for Gardiner's proposal. As Godfrey told me Fred Gardiner ruled with a heavy hand.[20]

---

18. Albert Rose, Governing Metropolitan Toronto 1953-1971 (University of California Press 1972)
19. Timothy J. Colton, Big Daddy (University of Toronto Press)
20. Interview with Paul Godfrey December 20, 2012

During his time as Metropolitan Toronto Chairman, Gardiner's staff consisted only of two stenographers, a receptionist and a messenger. He deliberately retained no advisors or consultants whom he felt would inhibit his work by measuring his proposals against some theoretical standards as to how a city should be built or governed. The letters PHD he said "stands for pile it high and deep".[21] He was as Nate Phillips described him "the genius that made Metro tick". He did indeed blaze a new trial.

---

21. Timothy J. Colton, Big Daddy (University of Toronto Press)

The first council of Metropolitan Toronto in 1954 *(Source: City of Toronto Archives)*

Jane Jacobs
(Source: "Patti Gower/ GetStock.com")

Former old city of Toronto Mayor Nathan Phillips QC (on the left) with former
Metro Chairman Frederick Gardiner QC (on the right)
(Source: City of Toronto Archives Fonds 220,Series 65, File 155, Item 16B)

"What way ought I to go from here?"

CHAPTER 4

That Depends a good deal on where you want to go

Lewis Carroll – Alice in Wonderland

As the year 1962 opened there was a new premier at Queens Park and a new Chairman of Metropolitan Toronto Council. The previous October John Robarts Q.C. had succeeded Leslie M. Frost Q.C. as leader of the Ontario Progressive Conservative Party and as Premier of Ontario. In January 1962, William Allen Q.C. a lawyer, a former Toronto Alderman, a member of Toronto city's Board of Control and a member of Metropolitan Toronto Council, was elected by Metro Council members to succeed Fred Gardiner Q.C. as Chairman by a vote of fourteen to ten over his opponent North York Reeve Norman Goodhead.

The election of a new Chairman did not solve the issue of Metro reorganization. It had been assumed that Allen would be more sympathetic to the city's position on amalgamation than either Gardiner or Goodhead. However, Chairman Allen interpreted his position to be that of an appointed administrator or a city manager. This was on all fours with the description Lorne Cumming had given the job in his 1958 interim Report on behalf of the Metropolitan Toronto Commission of Inquiry when he said the Chairman should be far more than an impartial presiding officer with a vote to cast in the event of an equal division of the council. "He should be the Chief Executive Officer responsible for continuous and detailed supervision and correlation of the work and activities of all the administrative departments in accordance with the policies adopted by the elected body …. His duties and responsibilities should correspond closely with those of the General Manager of a large corporation."[1] Paul Godfrey, a former Metro Chairman himself and a keen observer of every one of his predecessors and his successors, describes Bill Allen as using a velvet glove as opposed to Fred Gardiner's iron fist. Allen had a smoother more planned approach, according to Godfrey.[2]

Nathan Phillips nominated Bill Allen for Metro Chairman "because of his municipal experience in both city and Metro council" and also because he "possessed a rare combination of political astuteness and shrewd administrative ability". Phillips later wrote: "I rate Allen as the top administrator in Canada today." [3]

In his book Front Row Centre, Tony O'Donohue, a long-time Toronto Councillor, said: "Allen was known as 'Wiley Willie'. Allen could be very sharp and cutting without raising his voice. He used very few words to get his message across ... he was a very capable and dedicated chairman."[4]

Under William Allen's guidance the subway system was extended to include the Bloor-Danforth and the University lines. But while he continued to emphasize the building of hard services, he also brought to Metro a new emphasis on social services advocating an expanded regional public housing program: establishing an independent Metropolitan Housing Authority; building Metro homes for the aged and initiating a Metropolitan Department of Welfare. Allen was once quoted as saying: "It is simpler to send a man into space than to solve the human problems of providing decent housing to the lowest third of the population in our western urbanized societies." During his term the existing Metropolitan housing administration was transferred to a new provincial housing authority where it belonged. Unfortunately, however, the province refused

1. Albert Rose, Governing Metropolitan Toronto 1953-1971 (University of California Press 1972)
2. Interview with Paul Godfrey – December 20, 2012
3. Nathan Phliips, Q.C., The Mayor of all the People (University of Toronto Press)
4. Tony O'Donohue, Front Row Centre (Abbeyfield Publishers, Toronto)

to assume the total cost of welfare payments.[5] The provincial government with its income, sales, liquor and gasoline tax revenues, not Metro with only its real estate property tax revenue, had the necessary resources to finance these very essential social services. The financing of social services as well as primary and secondary education from property taxes remains a major issue plaguing the city of Toronto to this day.

When he died, the then Metro Chairman, Paul Godfrey said that William Allen had given Metro its "human touch".[6] But the main event during Allen's time as Chairman was the radical reorganization of the Municipality of Metropolitan Toronto by the province of Ontario.

In January 1962, a meeting of Metro Progressive Conservative MPPs chaired by Fred Cass then the Minister of Municipal Affair, held to consider the Gathercole Report, concluded that "the basic system should remain unchanged" pending a study to correct possible inequities. The Liberal opposition argued that the government should make welfare, education and justice Metro responsibilities. But John Robarts facing his first general election as premier knew he needed to elect as many PC MPPs members as possible in the Metro ridings. So he took a leaf from Leslie Frost's book by setting up a cabinet committee to consider the Municipality of Metropolitan Toronto government. The committee chaired by Allan Grossman included all the cabinet ministers representing Metro constituencies, the new Minister of Municipal Affairs, Wilf Spooner and his Deputy Minister the father of Metro Toronto, Lorne Cumming. They discussed going to a borough system as described in the Gathercole Report but again decided more study was needed because a borough system "would stir up too much opposition to the government which would not be desirable at this time". Most thought there should be a general review by an independent commission but Deputy Minister Cumming felt it would be impossible to find commissioners who could understand this complex system.[7]

---

5. Albert Rose, Governing Metropolitan Toronto 1953-1971 (University of California Press 1972)
6. Toronto Star – October 1, 1985
7. Peter Oliver, Unlikely Tory (Lester & Orpen Denny Limited Publishers 1985)

Then on April 19 the premier announced that he was establishing a Royal Commission on Metropolitan Toronto naming H. Carl Goldenberg OBE Q.C. LLD a Montreal labour lawyer as the Commissioner. It seemed to be a strange choice but Goldenberg, who had just finished chairing a provincial royal commission on the Ontario construction industry arbitrating a labour dispute at Ontario Hydro and mediating a CPR hotel dispute, was highly regarded by the premier.[8] Inevitably, because he was not an Ontarian, Goldenberg's appointment was strongly criticized in the Toronto newspapers.[9]

Before the Commission's public hearings got underway, the city of Toronto Council, likely realizing that the combined population of the suburbs would soon outstrip that of the city, renewed its application to the Ontario Municipal Board for total amalgamation. The Ontario government responded quickly, however, suspending the powers of the OMB to hear the city's application prior to receiving Mr. Goldenberg's study and recommendations.[10]

The Commission began its public hearings on April 21, 1964. They lasted for two months while receiving approximately 75 submissions from MPP's municipal councils, boards, commissions, ratepayer associations and individuals.[11]

This time Toronto had a new Mayor, Donald Summerville. Not unexpectedly, he was in favour of total amalgamation because as he put it: "Amalgamation could hang another eighteen mills at least $100.00 per house around the necks of 'the suburban taxpayers' while 'Toronto taxes will go down'." In his submission to the Commissioner, however, he, like most others, recognized that the Town of Leaside would be a special problem because over 50 per cent of its total property assessment was industrial giving it the lowest property tax rate in Metro.

---

8.   A.K. McDougall, Robarts: His Life and Government (University of Toronto Press 1986)

9.   Albert Rose, Governing Metropolitan Toronto 1953-1971 (University of California Press 1972)

10. Albert Rose, Governing Metropolitan Toronto 1953-1971 (University of California Press 1972)

11. Report of the Royal Commission on Metropolitan Toronto, H Carl Goldenberg OBE, Q.C., LLD, Commissioner dated June 10, 1965

Former city Mayor now city Controller, Allan Lamport, said he had always believed that the Municipality of Metropolitan Toronto was only a stepping stone to total amalgamation and now believes that he had been "double crossed".[12]

Norman Goodhead, the Reeve of North York who had once been the main spokesman for the suburbs at Metro Council, now spoke in favour of "One Big City". It was no wonder then that he had been replaced as the suburban advocate by Albert Campbell, the Reeve of Scarborough.[13]

In his brief to the Commission supporting either four, five or six boroughs, Reeve Campbell made his feelings clear that, "If representation and financing problems are corrected and the subsidiary functions more closely attuned to the principle of the two-tier system, the Municipality of Metropolitan Toronto will develop properly. What started out as an experiment will become an example of responsible government." He also quoted from the United Kingdom's Royal Commission on Local Government for Greater London: "It is essential therefore that the system of government should be one that promotes efficiency and economy in the use of both human and financial resources.

> *"Local Government is not just a machine or a piece of organization. Local Government is to us an instance of democracy at work and no amount of potential administrative efficiency could make up for the loss of active participation in the work by capable, public spirited people elected by, responsible to, and in touch with those who elect them."*

John MacBeth, the Reeve of Etobicoke, felt the Metro form of government was sound and his township's brief made that clear: "We believe it is a fallacy to equate equalization of educational opportunity with centralization.

---

12. Toronto Telegram – September 12, 1963
13. Albert Rose, Governing Metropolitan Toronto 1953-1971 (University of California Press 1972)

"This is the age of megalopolis, the development of great co-urbanization in which men are alienated by distance from the political and other institutions which govern their lives." [14]

Reeve Jack Mould of York Township supported a six city plan quoting the Cumming Report that municipal government involved "direct and personal contact between electors and elected representatives".[15]

The York Township six borough plan had Swansea merging with Toronto, Mimico, New Toronto and Long Branch merging with Etobicoke, Forest Hill and Weston joining York Township. Scarborough as is; the part of North York south of Highway 401 and east of Yonge Street merging with East York and Leaside and parts of Markham and Vaughan south of Highway 407 merging with the remainder of North York.[16]

"East York," its Reeve True Davidson told the Commission, "has within it a rare vitality – its people wish to survive as a group. This is not because of any favourable financial position, for the township enjoys none. East York is small enough to know what services and amenities its people want and need, and large enough to supply them. More than 700 people are engaged in some sort of voluntary work with or for the township and there is a remarkable sense of fellowship. There is a tremendous community pride, which gives residents a sense of security and of significance."

True also cited the writing of Jane Jacobs, who at that time was at doing battle with Robert Moses in New York, saying that a municipality needed to remain small so that "a district 'could be' big and powerful enough to fight City Hall".

According to the East York Township Clerk Doris Tucker, True Davidson bullied Carl Goldenberg into a Saturday morning meeting during which she paraded in all the senior East York staff to talk about what they did so that he would know what a good viable municipality

14. Archives of Ontario – John Robarts papers (RG 7-1-0-1026 Box 40)
15. Archives of Ontario – John Robarts papers (RG 7-1-0-1026 Box 40)
16. Archives of Ontario – John Robarts papers (RG 7-1-0-1026 Box 40)

East York really was. "One hundred thousand population isn't to be sneezed at," True told the Commissioner. "That's a better type of population than a great big one and if they put us in with some others it wouldn't be nearly as well run." [17]

Leaside's brief, presented by its Mayor Beth Nealson echoed True's comments: "Metropolitan Toronto's greatest asset, its provision for flexible self-determination would preserve desirable local autonomy and avoid increased burdens of costs, red tape and as well the inevitable inefficiency that goes with excessive centralization."[18]

Metro Chairman Bill Allen as well as the Mayors of Weston, Mimico and New Toronto and the Reeves of Long Branch, Forest Hill and Swansea, all spoke in favour of the metropolitan system and opposed total amalgamation with the city.[19]

As one can imagine, there was a fight on Metropolitan Toronto council. Its official position was debated on and off from September 10, 1963 to March 11, 1964, when after defeating motions in favour of total amalgamation, the holding of a plebiscite and a modified system of metropolitan government, it finally adopted a motion by city of Toronto Alderman Mary Temple, seconded by Mayor Donald Russell of New Toronto, to approve the continuation of a metropolitan system of government.[20]

In June 1965, Commissioner Goldenberg submitted his report to the Ontario government recommending: "That the thirteen diverse municipalities – one city, four towns, three villages and five townships – should be consolidated into four cities as follows:

"Reorganization of Metropolitan Toronto.

(i) "The system of metropolitan government should be maintained, with a consolidation of the thirteen area municipalities into four cities, as follows:

17. Eleanor Darke, Call Me True (Natural Heritage/Natural History Inc. 1997)
18. Archives of Ontario – John Robarts papers (RG 7-1-0-1026 Box 40)
19. Albert Rose, Governing metropolitan Toronto 1953-171 (University of California Press 1972)
20. Metropolitan Toronto Council minutes – March 11, 1964

"The city of Toronto, consolidating the city of Toronto, the township of York, the village of Forest Hill, the town of Leaside, the township of East York, and the village of Swansea.

"The city of North York, consolidating the townships of North York, York and the town of Weston.

"The city of Scarborough.

"The city of Etobicoke, consolidating the township of Etobicoke, the village of Long Branch, the town of New Toronto, and the town of Mimico."

In his Report, Goldenberg also dealt with the outer boundaries of Metro or what he called "the fringe municipalities", pointing out that they were part of the Metropolitan Toronto Planning Area. He identified these as consisting on the north of the township of Vaughan, the village of Woodbridge, the town of Richmond Hill, the township of Markham, the village of Stouffville, the village of Markham and the township of Toronto Gore. On the east of township of Pickering, the village of Pickering and the town of Ajax and on the west of the township of Toronto, the town of Streetsville and the town of Port Credit, all together having a total population in 1963 of 178,382. Goldenberg compared this with the total population of 310,743 for the twelve suburban Toronto municipalities when the metropolitan system was created in 1950. At that time York Township with 95,659 people had the largest population of the twelve suburban Toronto municipalities followed by North York with 62,646, East York with 60,155, Scarborough with 48,146 and Etobicoke with 44,137. In 1963 the five largest "fringe municipalities" by population were the township of Toronto with 70,859, the township of Pickering with 21,891, the town of Richmond Hill with 18,606, the township of Vaughan with 17,493, and the township of Markham with 14,800. Goldenberg noted that large portions of the "fringe municipalities" were still rural but failed to mention that large portions of Scarborough, North York and Etobicoke were still rural as well.

65

His report went on to say: "The brief from the city of Toronto has raised the question of the location of our outer boundaries. It is my submission that in those cases where it becomes necessary to alter the outer boundaries of Metropolitan Toronto, it can be done more easily through a district system than through a totally amalgamated system. The essential point of our system of government in this area is that we must retain a high degree of flexibility for the future. The rigidity of total amalgamation would place restrictions on the future growth and development of our area and make it difficult, if not impossible, to develop regional government for the urbanized area that exists between Oshawa and Niagara Falls."

On the subject of Metro's boundaries and the "fringe areas", Goldenberg recommended:

"Before considering extension of Metro's boundaries, the province should give consideration to the position and function of the counties and to municipal reorganization in the fringe areas, including the possible creation of a smaller 'Metro' on the western fringe.

i. *"Failing satisfactory arrangements by Metro and the Ontario Water Resources Commission to provide the required water and sewage facilities on the northern fringe, the appropriate built-up area north of Steeles Avenue in Vaughan and Markham Townships should be annexed to North York without undue delay, with compensation for loss of assessment to the townships and the County of York.*

ii. *"The Provincial Government should formally recognize the special situation of dormitory municipalities adjacent to Metro by appropriate adjustments in grants for municipal and school purposes."*[21]

21. Report of the Royal Commission on Metropolitan Toronto, H. Carl Goldenberg OBE, Q.C., LLD, Commissioner dated June 10, 1965

Soon after the Goldenberg Report was released Allan Grossman – now a cabinet minister in the Robarts' government – wrote to his colleague the Minister of Municipal Affairs Wilf Spooner with a copy to the premier pointing out that the four-city concept would essentially eliminate the essence of the two tier system without bringing about the so-called advantages of total amalgamation. Leaside, Forest Hill, East York, Swansea and Weston communities with "the greatest degree of local pride" would be merged with four big cities.

He went on:

> "I am also deeply concerned about the proposed political structure. Here the Commissioner seems to have been impressed with the necessity of retaining an even balance of votes between the city proper and the other municipalities, and then to have constructed the municipal and electoral boundaries to accomplish such a purpose without regard to the practicability and implications of same .... The lack of political electoral experience of the Commissioner may be in evidence here.

> "The political structure and electoral systems he recommended were the things that made me bite my nails. How could he make such recommendations? To me it was evidence of the fact that we were dealing with a person who knew nothing about politics or the political implications of his recommendations. And in fact they weren't carried out. There was no educational council, no educational districts, no change as suggested in the electoral system, no four-city federation."

Grossman who had intimate experience with the Toronto municipal scene as a city Alderman, as a Metro Councillor, as a member of the 1957 Commission of Inquiry and as chairman of the Cabinet committee on Metro, was surprised and disappointed that Goldenberg never took him up on his offer to provide the Commissioner with informal advice.[22]

---

22. Peter Oliver, Unlikely Tory (Lester & Orpen Denny Publishers 1985)

Grossman was not the only critical voice in the Robarts' cabinet; on this subject, a number of other ministers shared Grossman's views including the Minister of Economics and Development, Stanley Randall MPP. Representing a portion of East York, Randall had discussed the Goldenberg report with then East York Councillor later the Mayor of East York, Willis Blair even before it was publically released.[23] Unlike Premier Leslie Frost who ran a virtual one-man government, his successor Premier John Robarts allowed his cabinet to carry much of the burden of government. His style was closer to that of Chairman of the Board so he would have taken the criticisms of Grossman and other cabinet and caucus colleagues very seriously. A provincial election was imminent. In 1962, the federal Progressive Conservative government of John Diefenbaker had suffered a disastrous defeat, particularly in metropolitan Toronto ridings. None of this escaped the premier as he considered the government's response to the Goldenberg Report. [24]

Robarts also had to reflect on the York Township Council submission to the Commissioner endorsing a six borough city as well as letters on the subject, such as those from two East York Councillors, Norman Maughan and Jim McConaghy, urging the survival of their municipality.[25] In addition, one from his own Minister of Labour, Leslie Rowntree, making it quite clear that the suburbs wanted the Metro Chairman to continue to be elected by council itself and not elected at large by a Metro wide public vote, when he wrote: "Re: Bill #81 – Metro, the Reeve of Etobicoke and I have had a detailed conversation about the position of Chairman and he points out that Etobicoke and other suburbs do not want to see an election, as such would give the three Toronto newspapers a stranglehold on the outcome. In the meantime the three Toronto newspapers give no publicity or news reporting on the views of the suburbs on this matter."[26]

Of course the Goldenberg Report satisfied none of the thirteen municipalities. While it was clear that the final decision would be up to

23. Interview with Willis Blair - January 9, 2012
24. A.K. McDougall, Robarts (University of Toronto Press 1986)
25. Archives of Ontario – John Robarts papers (RG-7-1-0-1026 Box 40)
26. Archives of Ontario – John Robarts papers (RG-7-1-0-1026 Box 40)

the provincial government, that didn't stop the suburban municipalities from continuing their efforts to try to influence that decision.

Long Branch council recommended a five-city government with the fifth city to be composed of York and East York Townships, Leaside, Forest Hill and the part of Toronto north of St. Clair.[27] In August the town of New Toronto, opposing both total amalgamation and Goldenberg's four cities asked the province to amalgamate it with Mimico, Long Branch, parts of Etobicoke and Swansea to be known as Lakeshore City, thus creating a seven-borough metropolitan system.[28] Both Mimico and Long Branch later agreed with that concept[29] but of course, the province did not.

When the Progressive Conservative Metro MPPs either asked to meet with suburban councils or were invited to do so in order to discuss the Goldenberg Report, the suburban councils considered this as their opportunity to give the local MPP marching orders to oppose the Goldenberg recommendations. For example, in September at a packed public meeting held in Leaside High School Hollis Beckett, Q.C. MPP for York East told 500 residents that he opposed total amalgamation as well as the Goldenberg four-city plan but he recommended a six-borough plan in which Leaside would merge with the township of East York to create an East Toronto Borough. He pointed out that under the Goldenberg plan, Leaside would become part of the city of Toronto and thus have no direct representation on Metro Council. The rowdy meeting sent Mr. Beckett on his way after unanimously passing the following resolution:

> *"That Mr. Hollis Beckett Q.C. MPP York East be requested to oppose amalgamation of any form when the Report of the Royal Commission is considered in committee and when presented in the legislature."* [30]

27. Long Branch Council minutes – September 7, 1965
28. New Toronto Council minutes – August 16, 1965
29. Mimico Council Minutes – November 23, 1965 & Long Branch Council Minutes – December 8, 1965
30. Leaside Council Minutes – September 9, 1965

Mr. Beckett replied to Leaside Council, in a letter dated November 15, 1965, advising that he would do everything in his power to carry out the resolution passed at the public meeting opposing any kind of amalgamation.[31]

Former Leaside Councillor Keith Stainton told me that while Leaside Council clearly preferred the status quo, his personal fallback position was a merger with East York rather than the city of Toronto, because as a former member of the Leaside board of education, he considered the Leaside education system was more closely aligned to that of East York than to that of the city of Toronto.[32]

Meanwhile at Metro Council East York, Reeve True Davidson was taking a position most unexpectedly in favour of total amalgamation, but with the addition of local district councils somewhat similar to the present community councils. On September 21, 1965, she moved the following motion:

> "Whereas the Report of the Royal Commission on Metropolitan Toronto, commonly called the Goldenberg Report, satisfies no one; whereas it doesn't help tax inequities; whereas total amalgamation would solve all the above problems; therefore be it resolved that the Ontario government be asked to consider the possibility of establishing immediately an amalgamated city of Toronto divided into districts ... with district councils and committees for local affairs and representatives to the amalgamated city council, school boards, etc., in proportion of about one for every 67,000 or major part thereof."

That Motion finally came to a vote on October 19, 1965, when it was defeated with only True Davidson voting in favour. But the following amendment moved by Toronto City Alderman David Rotenberg and seconded by True Davidson was adopted:

31. Leaside Council Minutes – November 5, 1965
32. Interview with Keith Stainton – October 5, 2012

"Therefore it be resolved that the Government of the Province of Ontario be asked to consider amalgamation of the thirteen area municipalities into one city of Toronto, and then divide such city into a number of districts with limited legislative and taxation powers such districts to have their own councils, school boards and such districts to have populations of about between 200,000 and 300,000 people." [33]

The amendment differed from the original motion not only by the enlarging the population of each district but unlike the present community councils the district councils were to have taxing powers as well.

The Globe & Mail chimed in with: "Government Out of Touch.

"We believe that the people of Metro Toronto care little for municipal boundary lines which run invisibly down the middle of some streets, in spite of the bugle call ballyhoo of their elected representatives. They are aware, rather, of belonging to Greater Toronto; sleeping in one part and working in another, perhaps but living in the whole of it."[34]

In the months that followed the release of the Goldenberg Report, the Metro Area Progressive Conservative MPPs and Cabinet Ministers reviewed and debated every detail in the Report. Finally, just before Christmas 1965, the Minister of Municipal Affairs Wilf Spooner presented the PC caucus recommendations to the premier. These were fundamentally different from the Goldenberg recommendations in that Metro would have a six-borough city not four; East York and York would continue to exist; the city of Toronto would have twelve Metro Council Members and the other boroughs would have a total of twenty. The city and the boroughs would each have an equal number of Metro Executive Committee members.[35] According to a former provincial Intergovernmental Affairs Deputy Minister, Don Stevenson, "The PC

---

33. Metropolitan Toronto Council Minutes – October 19, 1965
34. Globe & Mail – November 15, 1965
35. Peter Oliver, Unlikely Tory (Lester & Orpen Denny Publishers 1985)

government was not ready to agree to anything that would promote the opposition."[36]

The premier then wasted no time in making the Ontario government's position clear. On January 10, 1966, he delivered a policy statement in the legislature, the forerunner of the new Municipality of Metropolitan Toronto Act, Bill 81. During its introduction in the Assembly the premier said: "The Bill cannot be expected to please all of the people of Metro Toronto, but is in the best interests of all." Rather than total amalgamation the metropolitan system of government, which had been endorsed by Commissioner Goldenberg, was to continue as a two-level federated system but consolidated into a smaller number of local municipalities.

The city of Toronto would be made up of the existing city together with Forest Hill and Swansea. The borough of Etobicoke would consist of the former township of Etobicoke plus Long Branch, New Toronto and Mimico. The borough of York would be made up of the former township of York plus Weston. The borough of East York would consist of the former township of East York together with Leaside, while the townships of North York and Scarborough would each remain as is but become boroughs. The new Metro council was to have 32 members of elected local councils plus a Chairman to be elected by the members of Metro Council. The Metro Council membership was to be made up as follows:

City of Toronto	12
Borough of North York	6
Borough of Scarborough	5
Borough of Etobicoke	4
Borough of York	3
Borough of East York	2
Chairman	1
	33

36. Albert Rose, Governing Metropolitan Toronto 1953-1971 (University of California Press 1972)

The new system retained the principle of choosing the members of the Metropolitan Council indirectly, through their election to the local councils. Also it retained the principle of Metro Council members rather than Metro citizens electing the Chairman. Each of the six local area Mayors and each of the members of a Board of Control (if the local municipality had a Board of Control), were to be ex-officio members of the Metropolitan Council.

The additional members allocated to a municipality were to be appointed by the municipal council following each election prior to the inaugural meeting of that council. In the case of the city of Toronto, this meant that its twelve members would be composed of the Mayor, four members of the board of control, and seven aldermen. Since the city was subdivided into nine wards, the formula was an immediate cause of concern. The previous system of representation had included one councillor from each city ward. Ultimately the province agreed to reduce the representation from the city of Toronto Board of Control to two members, retaining the previous system of representation as far as the city was concerned.[37]

Conventional wisdom in East York credits True Davidson with convincing Goldenberg to recommend six rather than four boroughs.[38] However, as we have seen, Goldenberg recommended four boroughs and not six.[39] The same day that Premier Robarts announced the plan for a six-borough Metro, the provincial Liberal Leader Andrew Thompson accused Hollis Beckett, the PC MPP for York East, of exercising undue influence on the premier when he said, "The creation of East York owes more to the opportunism and the persuasive voice of Mr. Beckett than it does to the careful considerations of Dr. Goldenberg. The local municipalities make absolutely no sense. By no stretch of the imagination – except perhaps in the mind of Hollis Beckett – is East York and Leaside a community in any sense of the word."[40] After the Goldenberg report

37. Eleanor Darke, Call Me True (Natural Heritage/Natural History Inc. 1997)
38. Report of the Royal Commission on Metropolitan Toronto, H Carl Goldenberg OBE, Q.C., LLD, Commissioner dated June 10, 1965
39. Toronto Star – January 11, 1966

was released. Beckett had proposed a six-borough Metro. At the time he claimed his plan was favoured by a majority of the 26 MPPs on a special committee made up of seventeen PCs, four Liberals and five NDPs appointed to rule on the future form of government for Metro. "They don't care much for Goldenberg's proposals," Beckett said at the time.[41] Former Toronto Mayor David Crombie, who teaches a course on the history of Toronto believes it was York East MPP Hollis Beckett notwithstanding his letter to Leaside Council of November 15, 1965, was the key to saving East York through its merger with Leaside. Then, Crombie says, in order not to show a preference for East York the PC caucus committee recommended six rather than five boroughs by merging Weston with York Township.[42] Darcy McKeough, a former Ontario Minister of Municipal Affairs, wrote to me to say that: "It was really the Tory caucus MPPs who were in favour of doing nothing. They were a large group (not many opposition MPPs). They got along well with the borough mayors and councils who vociferously did not want to be amalgamated with the big spending, erratic, city of Toronto council. Robarts didn't feel strongly about amalgamations and didn't feel strongly enough to take on Toronto caucus."[43] While the Beckett plan and the Robarts' plan had many similarities, they differed with respect to the borough boundaries. The Beckett plan carved up the city of Toronto and the township of North York arbitrarily to increase the population of York and East York[44] while the Robarts' plan respected the existing local boundaries as had the original Frost plan for Metropolitan Toronto.

The Robarts' plan highlighted two other issues that divided his PC caucus, and both of which would come back to haunt Metro later: the direct election of Metro Councillors and a Metro wide direct election for the Metro Chairman. Some but not always the same PC MPPs opposed

40. Toronto Star – August 28, 1965
41. Interview with David Crombie – January 9, 2013
42. Letter from Darcy McKeough dated November 26, 2012
43. Letter from Major-General Richard Rohmer DFC QC dated January 28, 2012
44. Ontario Hansard – April 26, 1966, page 2599

one or the other or both. Once again, however, the premier opted for the tried and true approach successfully tested by the original Frost plan. Members of Metro Council would to be chosen indirectly through election to their local councils and the Metro councillors, not the general public, would elect the Chairman.[45]

When Premier Robarts said: "The Bill cannot be expected to please all of the people of Metro Toronto," he knew what he was talking about. Less than two weeks after the premier's statement in the legislature, the Toronto Star declared: "Local Councils have no place in new Metro.

> *"The Star acknowledges a certain merit in local government – but only so long as it performs a useful function. And in the case of the boroughs proposed by Premier Robarts, we mention that they do not serve a useful purpose and are in fact, costly window dressing for a principle that no longer has any validity in Metro Toronto.*

> *"If the responsibilities of borough councils were assumed by departments of central Metro government, taxpayers would have the same opportunity to meet with responsible civic officials as they have now.*

> *"It appears more logical to assume that Premier Robarts has bowed to pressure from local politicians anxious to retain their jobs, even with meagre authority, at the expense of logical, cohesive and effective government over the entire Metro community."*[46]

Shades of the megacity to come.

However, according to section 92(8) of the British North Act 1867 now the Canadian Constitution Act 1982, municipalities are the creatures of the provinces and like it or not the Province of Ontario had spoken. Premier Robarts had decided "on where he wanted" Metro "to go".

---

45. Toronto Star – April 26, 1966
46. Toronto Star – January 22, 1966

Former Metro Chairman William Allen QC
(Source: City of Toronto Archives Fonds 1257, Series 1057, Item 5011)

Former Ontario Premier John Robarts QC (on the left) with Carl Goldenberg QC , Royal Commissioner (on the right) *(Source: John Gillies/ The Globe and Mail June 15, 1965)*

Former old city of Toronto Mayor Allan Lamport
(Source: Toronto Reference Library election for Alderman 1969 brochure)

Former East York Reeve and later Mayor True Davidson
(Source: "Boris Spermo/ GetStock.com")

Here's Goldenberg's Master Plan for a new Metro

Here's Goldenberg's Master Plan for a new Metro *(Source: Toronto Star June 17,1965)*

79

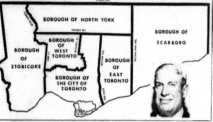

Hollis Beckett QC, MPP's proposed restructuring of Metro
(Source: Toronto Star, August 28, 1965)

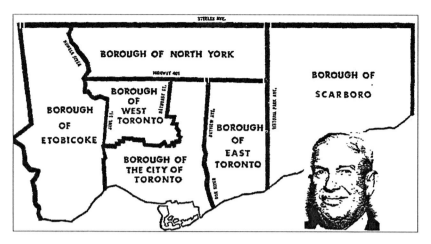

Hollis Beckett QC, MPP's proposed restructuring of Metro *(Source: "Walter Arthur Bett/ Toronto Star Pages of the Past, August 28, 1965")*

Hollis Beckett QC MPP for York East (immediately to the right of the memorial plaque for former Ontario Premier George S. Henry a previous MPP for York East) with former Ontario Premier Leslie M. Frost QC (at the far left)
(Source: "Walter Arthur Bett/ Toronto Star Pages of the Past, August 28, 1965")

81

The 1965 Metropolitan Toronto Council the last 13 local municipality council
(Source: City of Toronto Archives)

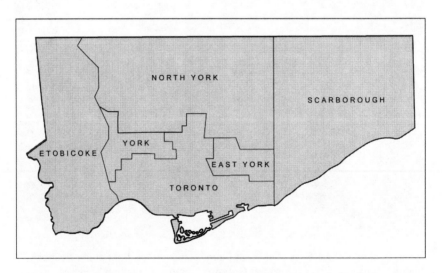

Map of the Municipality of Metropolitan Toronto after it was reduced from 13 to 6 local municipalities *(Source: Valentine De Landro 2014)*

"Now We Are Six"

A. A. Milne

CHAPTER 5

Two of the many submissions made to the Goldenberg Commission called for the direct election of Metro Councillors and for the election at large of the Metro chairman. The Commissioner adopted the first but rejected the second.[1] Premier Robarts rejected both of them.[2] Each would return to play an important role in the future of Toronto government.

On the Metropolitan Toronto boundary issue, Goldenberg recommended that the province should consider a smaller "Metro" on its western fringe because the municipalities to the west of Metro bordering on Lake Ontario were in a position to supply their own water and sewage services. Then after pointing out that the six dormitory municipalities on Metro's northern border only access to Lake Ontario is through Metropolitan Toronto, he recommended that the appropriate built-up area north of Steeles Avenue in Vaughan and Markham townships should be annexed to North York without delay unless satisfactory arrangements were made to provide them with water and sewage facilities.[3] Nothing

---

1.   Report of the Royal Commission on Metropolitan Toronto, H. Carl Goldenberg OBE, Q.C., LLD, Commissioner dated June 10, 1965

2.   Albert Rose, Governing Metropolitan Toronto 1953-1971 (University of California Press 1972)

3.   Report of the Royal Commission on Metropolitan Toronto, H. Carl Goldenberg OBE, Q.C., LLD, Commissioner dated June 10, 1965

was said about these recommendations in either the premier's statement of January 10, 1966, nor in Bill 81, which followed.

But, the government did not ignore the Metro boundary question. In April 1966, the premier announced a policy called "Design for Development", which envisioned a series of fourteen regional governments to the west, north and east of the Metro boundaries.[4] This reopened both the question of the Municipality of Metropolitan Toronto's external boundaries and the question of total amalgamation within Metro. The Mayor of Toronto immediately called for amalgamation to be followed by expanding Toronto city boundaries into "one big city". Chairman Allen and other Metro Councillors argued that if Metro was to grow and prosper it was essential for the boundaries to be expanded to the north and east. But there was no need for total amalgamation, they said, since Metro was doing just fine, thank you very much.[5] At the same time, the province commissioned a report on municipal restructuring west of Metro, which recommended the total amalgamation of the southern portions of Peel and Halton counties.[6] Needless to say this was soundly rejected by the residents and subsequently by the Provincial Minister of Municipal Affairs, Darcy McKeough, when he was quoted as saying: "Commissioner Thomas J. Plunkett of Queen's University isn't Moses leading the Israelites and he isn't God."[7]

In early 1969, several municipalities east of Toronto held meetings with Metro officials in the hope of being annexed by Metro before they were incorporated into another regional government extending as far east as Oshawa. Metro welcomed these initiatives and at the same time applied pressure to the provincial government to permit a formal annexation. That year both Pickering and Woodbridge residents voted to be annexed by Metro.[8]

4. Albert Rose, Governing Metropolitan Toronto 1953-1971 (University of California Press 1972)
5. Albert Rose, Governing Metropolitan Toronto 1953-1971 (University of California Press 1972)
6. Tom Urbaniak, Hazel McCallion and the Development of Mississauga (University of Toronto Press 2009)
7. Tom Urbaniak, Hazel McCallion and the Development of Mississauga (University of Toronto
8. Albert Rose, Governing Metropolitan Toronto 1953-1971 (University of California Press 1972)

Later the same year former Metro Chairman Fred Gardiner weighed in on the subject with an article in the Toronto Star entitled: "Metro Must Expand or Be Strangled" followed by a second article entitled: "An Iron Curtain Must Not Stifle Metro" in which he wrote:

> *"If Ontario's Minister of Municipal Affairs, Darcy McKeough, persists in freezing the boundaries of Metropolitan Toronto, he will be making a tragic mistake.*
>
> *"Right now, Metro has an unlimited potential for future development into one of the important cities on the continent. If Metro is surrounded by an iron curtain of municipalities preventing its natural growth, the development of the whole area would be thwarted ….*
>
> *"While Metropolitan Toronto is not a regional government in the accepted use of the term, it is in many respects, similar to one. It should be allowed to expand naturally without artificial boundaries ….*
>
> *"The main difficulty at the moment is that practically all of the land in Metropolitan Toronto is developed and future development must either be on land, which is far beyond an economical cost, or the development must be a vertical one, with multi-storey buildings for residential purposes and, in the case of industry, it will go where single storey buildings can be built at an economical cost."* [9]

Gardiner also wrote to his good friend the former Premier Leslie Frost to say in part: "Actually I am much concerned about our good Conservative Party. When McKeough was made Minister of Municipal Affairs I spent a couple of hours with him and of course there is quite a generation gap between your and my generation, and his, and I think there is a reluctance in the younger generation to listen to what is intended to be humble advice from some of us who have been through the mill." [10]

---

9. Toronto Star - October 11,1969
10. Darcy McKeough, unpublished autobiography

The next year the Metro Planning Board recommended that the Metro boundaries be expanded to include Vaughan, Markham and Pickering townships.[11] The Toronto Star then chimed in an editorial entitled: "Metro's Invisible Walls" in which it opined: "Toronto land won't be fit to live in unless we get the go-ahead to expand."[12]

In May of that year the Ontario government published "Design for Development: Toronto Centered Region", which if implemented, would have expanded Metro's planning area from its original 240 square miles to 8,600 square miles, representing at the time 50 per cent of the population of Ontario. This gave Metro hope that at the very least its boundaries would be enlarged northerly into York county up to the route of a new major east–west highway, the exact position of which had yet to be established (now Highway 407).[13] According to Darcy McKeough: "York county was complicated by the fact that Metro Toronto Council, vigorously supported by all three newspapers, thought that Metro should be allowed to grow west, north and east. (They never to my knowledge wanted to annex Lake Ontario to the south.) This gorilla approach did not have the strong support of the Tory MPPs in Metro – although a future MPP & Minister Margaret Scrivener was very vocal. The Metro MPPs were also aware of the strong opposition from the surrounding counties, York, Peel and Ontario, both their councils and their MPPs – nearly all Tories."[14] Because both Vaughan and Markham had made strong representations directly to Premier Robarts opposing the expansion of Metro into their territory, the province incorporated the regional municipality of York immediately to the north of Metro with its southern boundary on Steeles Avenue, which was the northern boundary of Metro itself.[15] Even then Metro still had high hopes of expanding east into Pickering township. But in Darcy McKeough's words: "Pickering was

---

11. Albert Rose, Governing Metropolitan Toronto 1953-1971 (University of California Press 1972)
12. Toronto Star – February 7, 1970
13. Albert Rose, Governing Metropolitan Toronto 1953-1971 (University of California Press 1972)
14. Darcy McKeough, unpublished autobiography
15. Albert Rose, Governing Metropolitan Toronto 1953-1971 (University of California Press 1972)

part of Ontario County. To put it mildly Metro 'lusted' to expand and include Pickering. At some point, we said Pickering Township, Ajax and Pickering Village would remain part of Ontario County (later renamed Durham). Metro was not happy but plans for restructuring in this area moved ahead."[16] In fact, the hopes for Metro expansion to the east were really dashed when the provincial and federal governments announced plans to build the Pickering Airport together with a new city (Century City) in north Pickering.[17] Neither of which has ever materialized.

Soon after that the province completed the "Iron Curtain" by creating the regional municipality of Peel in 1974.[18] There was never any real hope of Metro expansion to the west especially after Bill Davis replaced John Robarts as the Progressive Conservative Premier of Ontario in April 1971. Davis, who was raised and has lived all his life in Brampton, was elected as the MPP for Peel County in 1959 making no bones about his intentions to protect his home base.[19] According to Darcy McKeough: "Mr. Gardiner wanted Metro to expand to include Vaughan, Markham and Pickering on the premise that the province would not be prepared to see expansion to the west."[20] Apparently, Gardiner knew Bill Davis very well.

Unlike the Berlin Wall, the wall around Toronto has never come down. The Metro boundaries established in 1953 remain the boundaries of the megacity of Toronto today. "I have no recollection of a decision being made that the 'present Metro was it' but it happened," says Darcy McKeough.[21] However, the retired provincial Deputy Minister of Intergovernmental Affairs Don Stevenson told me: "There is an anti-Toronto sense in Queen's Park that poisons decisions."[22] Was it a mistake for the Ontario government to surround Toronto with an 'Iron Curtain'? Fred Gardiner believed that industry would "go where single storey

16. Darcy McKeough, unpublished autobiography
17. Albert Rose, Governing Metropolitan Toronto 1953-1971 (University of California Press 1972)
18. Albert Rose, Governing Metropolitan Toronto 1953-1971 (University of California Press 1972)
19. Claire Hoy, Bill Davis (Methuen Publications Toronto 1985)
20. Darcy McKeough, unpublished autobiography
21. Darcy McKeough, unpublished autobiography
22. Interview with Don Stevenson, November 20, 2012

buildings can be built at an economical cost". If Mississauga, Brampton and Markham had been part of Metro Toronto rather than part of the regions of Peel and York, then would the vast number of industries that have left Toronto have relocated within the expanded boundaries of Metropolitan Toronto? Would the property tax revenues that Toronto has lost have helped to improve social services and the quality of life in an expanded Metro Toronto? Fred Gardiner said: "Future development in Metro Toronto must either be on land, which is far beyond an economical cost, or development must be a vertical one with multi-storey buildings for residential purposes." Has the proliferation of high rise residential developments in Toronto as foreseen by Fred Gardiner created the same local community involvement and concern for one's neighbours as found in detached, semi-detached and townhouse neighbourhoods? Has the iron curtain stopped urban sprawl or is it still taking place on the 'fringes' of Toronto? Finally, would premier Mike Harris' government ever have amalgamated Metropolitan Toronto if it had included Mississauga, Brampton, Markham, Richmond Hill, Pickering, Ajax and Whitby, thus creating a municipal, government larger than that of the Province of Ontario itself?

While the province was reducing the Municipality of Metropolitan Toronto from thirteen to six area municipalities, another event was taking place that would also significantly shape the future of the metropolitan area – namely, the Spadina Expressway. The plan, which not only called for the Spadina but also the Crosstown and Christie Expressways, raised the major concerns that the Spadina was just the first step in a road building program threatening a huge number of neighbourhoods in the city with expropriation followed by the wholesale demolition of the residents' homes. Construction began in 1963 on the North York Township portion, running south from what we now know as the basket weave interchange on Highway 401. However, by the time it reached Forest Hill Village and York Township, strong citizen opposition had emerged in the form of the "Stop Spadina, Save Our City" Co-ordinating Committee. One of the key members of that committee was Jane Jacobs, who had moved to Toronto in 1968 after playing a major role in stopping the construction of Robert Moses' planned Lower Manhattan Expressway in New York City.[23] In 1971 the Spadina Expressway was scrapped completely. Once again the future shape of the city was determined by a personal decision of the premier of Ontario who was soon to face a provincial election, in this case by Progressive Conservative Premier Bill Davis, who said:

> *"In the final analysis, in determining how best to serve the future needs of Metropolitan Toronto, we must make a decision as to whether we are trying to build a transportation system to serve the automobile or one which will best serve the people.*

> *"If we are building a transportation system to serve the automobile, the Spadina Expressway would be a good place to start.*

> *"But if we are building a transportation system to serve people, the Spadina Expressway is a good place to stop."*[24]

In the provincial election, which followed a few months after this decision, Premier Davis and his party were swept back into office.

But the Province of Ontario had not finished tinkering with the Municipality of Metropolitan Toronto. On September 10, 1974, Premier Davis appointed his predecessor John Robarts as a Royal Commissioner to report on a "Framework for the Future of Metropolitan Toronto". The Commissioner issued his report in June 1977.[25]

As Premier of Ontario from 1961 to 1971, John Robarts had appointed the Goldenberg Commission, but it was Robarts' own decision to reduce the thirteen area municipalities to six. In that regard the Robarts' Royal Commission Report was in the words of Yogi Berra: "Déjà vu all over again." He agreed with the work done by his predecessors, Lorne Cumming in 1953 and Carl Goldenberg in 1966, as well as his own previous decisions.

---

23. Anthony Flint, Wrestling with Moses (Random House Trade Paperbacks, New York 2009)

24. Albert Rose, Governing Metropolitan Toronto 1953-1971 (University of California Press 1972)

25. Report of the Royal Commission on Metropolitan Toronto, John Robarts, Q.C. dated June 1977

His report gave Metro a glowing endorsement:

"The Metropolitan system of local government has served the Toronto area well and its achievements are many.

"During the past twenty years the population of Metropolitan Toronto has more than doubled. A major factor contributing to this increase has been immigration: Metropolitan Toronto has consistently attracted more than 25 per cent of all immigrants to Canada. In addition, many people from other parts of Ontario and indeed of Canada have been attracted to Metro by the variety of its employment, and by its social and recreational opportunities.

"To accommodate rapid growth was a challenge the metropolitan system was able to meet without undue stress. Throughout this period Metro residents have enjoyed a high level of employment, expanding educational opportunities, housing that is the envy of many cities of the world, and an environment that has been safe yet stimulating. By any comparison, Metro residents have also enjoyed modest property taxes during this period.

"Several features in its governmental structure have contributed to making Metro the lively, prosperous, progressive place it is. In particular, the Metro system was and is a single system of local government. Competition between Metro and the area municipalities has been kept to a minimum, partly because Metro Council is made up of local representatives. For the most part, the system has resulted in a healthy balancing of local interests and area-wide concerns. As a result, Metro has been able to establish sound planning, servicing, and development policies and to build a first-class transportation system to help implement them.

"Municipal planning and development policies have certainly contributed to Metro's healthy central core, which combines both residential and working environments. Since the Metro system was introduced, the population of the central city has remained relatively

stable. Unlike many large American cities, rapid growth in the suburbs has not brought about a deterioration of the central core. Growth in Metro has been accompanied by a growth in employment opportunities in its outer municipalities, but no commercial centre has emerged to offer strong competition to the core. Development policies during the past quarter-century have favoured the concentration of office development in the downtown area and Metro's investment in transit and roads serving the area has supported them. During the same period many downtown industries have relocated in outlying areas on less expensive land, making the central city more desirable as a residential area today than it was some years ago. In turn, the stable residential areas in downtown Toronto have been credited with keeping it livable and relatively free of crime.

"The existence of Metro government has made it possible to use the wealth of the entire area, and particularly that of the City of Toronto, to finance services needed in the outer municipalities to accommodate growth. The financial role assigned to Metro Council has served to equalize the availability and quality of services throughout the Metropolitan area.

"The years of Metro's development have happily coincided with an extended period of almost unprecedented prosperity. With buoyant revenues from a rapidly increasing tax base and from ever-increasing provincial grants, local services have been quickly expanded and substantially enriched. Special purpose bodies within the Metro system have been in a position to take fullest advantage of the opportunities presented, unfettered by concerns about determining priorities among competing demands. Without the discipline of having to make allocations between such services as libraries, education, conservation, and transit, the special purpose bodies have individually devoted themselves to improving one single aspect of civic service (their own) almost regardless of cost. It is doubtful whether such service enrichments could have been

accomplished with so little political difficulty had the financial circumstances not been so auspicious.

"A system alone does not make for good government or for a successful community. A community is its people and their traditions. Early Toronto was known for its thrift, its cleanliness, its high regard for work and sober living, and the integrity it demanded from those in public life. These characteristics have had a major influence on present-day Metropolitan Toronto and the institutes that serve it."

Robarts also made it clear that Metropolitan Toronto's 1953 boundaries would not change:

"It is assumed that the present external boundary of Metropolitan Toronto will remain the same.

"The consideration of major alterations in the external boundary of Metropolitan Toronto was not explicitly included in the Commissions' terms of reference, and it is clear from the views expressed by many during the Commission's work that there is widespread opposition to any expansion of Metro's jurisdiction. It is also the policy of the provincial government that the present Metro boundary remain unchanged.

"There are valid reasons for this view. It has been argued that the regional municipalities of Peel, York, and Durham have been created only recently and should be allowed to develop and consolidate before any boundary changes are considered. In addition, evidence given to the Commission showed that much of the taxable assessment and population of these surrounding regions and their constituent municipalities is located in the area immediately adjacent to the Metro boundary. Severe disruption in the finances and services of those municipalities would result from any loss of territory to Metro.

"Stopping the expansion of Metro's land area will have a significant implication for the provincial government. There is a

conventional wisdom in local government that major metropolitan areas must have room to breathe, so that their own governments can provide new physical services, transportation, housing, recreation, and other facilities in a planned manner. The provincial government has assumed a number of these responsibilities (for example, trunk sewers) in the central Ontario region. The Commission believes that the acceptance of the present Metro boundaries must result in the provincial government playing an even stronger role in the development of this region. This role can be harmonized with that of local government in the area by the establishment of the regional co-ordination machinery suggested in this report.

"For the system of government within it, the impact of accepting the current Metro boundary is enormous. With the major physical facilities in place and little further growth to service, the local government system will become increasingly concerned with redevelopment, conservation, and the preservation and improvement of the quality of life in this large, stable city. Growth in tax revenues resulting from new development will decline substantially, while the need for such costly services as assisted housing, income support, and transit will continue to rise.

"The assumption that the Metro boundary is fixed is therefore extremely important for the Commission's report."

Obviously the representations made by Fred Gardiner and others about "Metro's Invisible Walls" had made no impression on Mr. Robarts. But after all, the Commission's terms of reference had been approved by the Premier Brampton Bill Davis, who no doubt was looking over Mr. Robarts' shoulder when he wrote his Report. However, just to make sure the Commission did not consider expanding Metro to the west on January 1, 1974 prior to appointing the Robarts' Commission, Mr. Davis' government had created the regional municipality of Peel.

Without specifically naming it Robarts did make reference to the "Stop Spadina, Save Toronto" movement:

93

"It is assumed that the demands of citizens for participation in municipal government in Metropolitan Toronto will continue and grow.

"The increased involvement of private citizens in local government in metropolitan Toronto is one of the most important changes that has taken place since the system was last reviewed in 1963–65. While there have been fluctuations in public interest during the intervening period as various issues arose and were resolved, citizens are now much more aware of and involved in their local government's decisions. In part this awareness is rising because local governments are now making clearly political choices among priorities in areas that directly affect the daily lives of people. The people themselves are better educated than ever before and have more leisure time, which gives them the means to participate. The Commission assumes that, as specific issues are brought to the fore, the trend to greater citizen involvement will continue in the future."

The Robarts' Report endorsed the status quo for the existing metropolitan system recommending:

4.1 The two-tier form of local government in Metropolitan Toronto be continued.

4.2 Metropolitan Toronto continue to be made up of six area municipalities, subject to revisions in boundaries proposed in this report.

4.3 The constituent municipalities of Metropolitan Toronto be called, the city of Toronto and the boroughs of North York, Scarborough, Etobicoke, York, and East York.

4.4 All distinctions between the powers and eligibility for grants of the city of Toronto and the boroughs be removed from provincial statutes and regulations.

4.5 A general review of the Metropolitan system be instituted in not less than five nor more than ten years.

But The Report also recommended major and significant internal boundary changes for the area municipalities: Chapter 9: Boundaries.

9.1   The boundaries of the city of Toronto be the Humber River from lake Ontario to St. Clair Avenue; St. Clair Avenue from the Humber River to Bathurst Street; Bathurst Street from St. Clair Avenue to Highway 401; Highway 401, Wilson Avenue, and York Mills Road from Bathurst Street to Bayview Avenue; Bayview and the Bayview Avenue Extension from York Mills Road to Danforth Avenue; Danforth Avenue from the Bayview Avenue Extension to Warden Avenue, and Warden Avenue from Danforth Avenue to Lake Ontario.

9.2   The boundaries of the borough of North York be the Humber River from St. Clair Avenue to Steeles Avenue; Steeles Avenue from the Humber River to Warden Avenue; Warden Avenue from Steeles Avenue to Ellesmere Road; and Ellesmere Road; Parkwoods Village Drive, York Mills Road, Wilson Avenue, and Highway 401 from Warden Avenue to the Humber River.

9.3   The boundaries of the borough of Scarborough be Warden Avenue from Lake Ontario to Steeles Avenue; Steeles Avenue from Warden Avenue to the western boundary of the Regional Municipality of Durham, and the western boundary of the Regional Municipality of Durham from Steeles Avenue to Lake Ontario.

9.4   The boundaries of the borough of Etobicoke be the eastern boundary of the Regional Municipality of Peel from Lake Ontario to Steeles Avenue; Steeles Avenue from the eastern boundary of the Regional Municipality of Peel to the Humber River, and the Humber River from Steeles Avenue to Lake Ontario.

9.5   The boundaries of the borough of York be the Humber River from St. Clair Avenue to Highway 401; Highway 401 from the Humber River to Bathurst Street; Bathurst Street from Highway 401 to St. Clair Avenue; and St. Clair Avenue from Bathurst Street to the Humber River.

9.6   The boundaries of the borough of East York be the Bayview Avenue Extension and Bayview Avenue from Danforth Avenue to York Mills Road; York Mills Road, Parkwoods Village Drive and Ellesmere Road from Bayview Avenue to Warden Avenue; Warden Avenue from Ellesmere Road to Danforth Avenue, and Danforth Avenue from Warden Avenue to the Bayview Avenue Extension.

9.7   The transfers of population resulting from the proposed boundary changes be accompanied by a corresponding transfer of municipal employees, whose bargaining rights, salaries, and benefits should be protected as far as possible.[26]

This was like throwing a fox into the hen house. A primary principle of the Municipality of Metropolitan Toronto as created by Premier Leslie Frost and admired around the world was that of maintaining the existing historic municipal boundaries for each of the original thirteen. It was based on an understanding of local pride for one's own municipality not only on the part of local council members but also on the part of the local municipal residents themselves. Although the number of area municipalities had been reduced from thirteen to six that principle had not been violated existing boundaries had been maintained when Weston was merged with York; Leaside merged with East York; Mimico, New Toronto and Long Branch merged with Etobicoke and Swansea and Forest Hill merged with the city of Toronto.

The recommendation for internal boundary changes was, as can be imagined, strongly opposed by those losing and supported by those gaining territory. In my capacity as the Mayor of East York, at that time, I publicly debated with Mayor Mel Lastman of North York in Flemingdon Park territory, which Robarts' recommended should be removed from North York and transferred to East York. I had a similar public debate with then Toronto Alderman and later Mayor John Sewell concerning the portion of his ward

26. Report of the Royal Commission on Metropolitan Toronto, John Robarts, Q.C. dated June 1977

recommended to be transferred to East York. In his yet to be published book Darcy McKeough writes that as Minister of Treasury, Economics and Intergovernmental Affairs (TEIGA) at the time that: "I rejected rather quickly any boundary changes. Cabinet balked and on June 20, 1978, I said in a speech that we would not be proceeding at this session of the legislature with the proposals for Metro."[27] Clearly Darcy had his way because in the end Premier Davis and his provincial government rejected Robarts' recommendations and made no changes at all in the internal Metro boundaries.

Other Commission recommendations dealt with the election of the Metro Councillors and the Chairman:

> *5.16 Members of Metropolitan Council (other than local mayors) be elected directly from districts made up of groupings of three adjacent local wards.*

> *5.17 Directly elected Metro Councillors be full members of the councils of the area municipalities from which they are elected, except that they be precluded from membership on any executive or other local committee.*

> *5.18 The Metropolitan Chairman be chosen from among the directly elected members of Metropolitan Council at the first meeting of the municipal term, and hold his positions on his local council and Metro Council and the Chairmanship for the duration of that term."[28]*

The Province rejected the direct election of the Chairman and took no immediate action on the direct election of Metro Councillors. But this issue would return later to help put a nail in Metro's coffin.

Realizing some of the problems created in 1966 by his "Iron Curtain" approach to the external boundaries of Metro Toronto, Robarts recommended: Chapter 8: Intergovernmental Relations.

> *8.1 A Toronto Region Coordinating Agency be created by provincial legislation, with responsibility for facilitating the planning*

---

27. Darcy McKeough, unpublished autobiography
28. Report of the Royal Commission on Metropolitan Toronto, John Robarts, Q.C. dated June 1977

and development of the Toronto region and for providing such services and advice to the regional municipalities and the province as may be delegated to it by its participating governments.

8.2   Membership in the Toronto Region Coordinating Agency consist of representatives chosen by the councils of the regional municipalities in the Toronto region and Metropolitan Toronto ... and the provincial minister designated with responsibility for the Toronto region.

8.3   The Toronto Region Coordinating Agency be empowered to examine and comment on the budgets and plans of the existing operating bodies of a regional nature, the Toronto Area Transit Operating Authority and the conservation authorities.[29]

Back in 1947, Mimico had applied to the Ontario Municipal Board for an order creating an interurban administration area for all of the thirteen municipalities. Both OMB Chairman Lorne Cumming and Premier Leslie Frost realizing the problems with this approach rejected it in favour of the metropolitan concept. By not tearing down the wall surrounding Metro the "Greater Toronto Area" now faces a similar problem to that faced by the former metropolitan Toronto area in 1947.

Nothing really changed as a result of the Robarts' 1977 Report. Responding to the Report in a 1978 White Paper, the Ontario government said it would adopt the principle of direct election for Metro councillors while allowing them to remain as members of their local councils.[30] But that was not implemented so Metropolitan Toronto government continued to function, as constituted by the province in 1966 under the direction of successive Metro Chairmen namely: Bill Allen, Albert Campbell, Paul Godfrey and Dennis Flynn and Alan Tonks.

---

29. Report of the Royal Commission on Metropolitan Toronto, John Robarts, Q.C. dated June 1977
30. White Paper, Government Statement on the Review of Local Government in the Municipality of Metropolitan Toronto dated May 4, 1978

In 1969, shortly after Metro had been reduced from thirteen to six area municipalities, Scarborough Mayor Albert (Ab) Campbell followed Bill Allen as Metro Chairman. According to former Toronto Councillor Tony O'Donohue: "Campbell did not have the drive or vision of his two predecessors and was very cautious in his approach to anything new. He looked on Metro as an extension of Scarborough. If it was good enough for Scarborough it was good enough for Metro," was his philosophy.[31] Willis Blair, the Mayor of East York at the time, says he got along well with Campbell but described him as a "plodder".[32] Paul Godfrey told me that Campbell's approach was "that of a referee leaving it to Council to make the decisions".[33] In fairness, however, for much of his time in the office Ab Campbell was not a well man. He passed away from cancer in 1973 after less than five years as Chairman.

North York Controller Paul Godfrey, chosen by Metro council members to succeed Ab Campbell as Chairman, told me that he had always wanted to be the Metro Chairman. His mother who was deeply involved in behind the scenes politics had been urged to run for office herself but with only a grade 8 education was reluctant to do so. It was, however, her great ambition that her son Paul should run for public office. So from a very early age, encouraged by his mother Paul Godfrey started to attend Metro Council meetings as a spectator.

Godfrey is probably best known for bringing Major League Baseball to the city a move that not only provided a boost to local pride but also enhanced Metro's reputation as a world class city. Metro's international reputation was further enhanced after Godfrey's wife Gina read an article in the Toronto Star about a seven-month-old New York City boy Herbie Quinones, who needed an operation that could only be performed at Toronto's Sick Kids' Hospital. She told her husband that he should "do something about it". Paul Godfrey says he replied: "That health care was not in my job description," at which Gina shot back that:

---

31. Tony O'Donohue, Front Row Centre (Abbeyfield Publishers, Toronto)
32. Interview with Willis Blair, February 10, 2013
33. Interview with Paul Godfrey, January 13, 2013

"Bringing the Blue Jays to Metro was not in your job description either." At that moment the "Herbie Fund" was born, which headed by Gina Godfrey, has with private donations to date helped 675 kids from around the world.

During Godfrey's time as Chairman from 1973 to 1984, the Toronto Transit Commission under Metro was known as one of the best transit systems in North America; women and visible minorities were recruited for the Metro police force after height and weight restrictions were changed; more assisted seniors' housing was built and the subsidized day care system was instituted. Paul Godfrey attracted a first class personal staff and senior bureaucracy that could hold its own with provincial and federal civil servants. Although he ran a nonpartisan government, Paul Godfrey who was a Progressive Conservative, had an excellent relationship with PC Premier Bill Davis. Godfrey could be tough with the Davis behind closed doors but was always careful never to blind side or embarrass the premier in public.[34]

In his book, Front Row Centre, Tony O'Donohue wrote: "Godfrey was a great Chairman. Not only intelligent but hard working, he knew how to handle people." "Godfrey had another quality also, which is rare in people who sit at the top. If he gave you his word, you could count on it." "Godfrey was also a master at nailing down the vote when it was needed. I cannot ever remember him losing when the crunch came. He could always call the vote on any major issue." "He knew how everyone would vote before the debate ended – an art he had perfected."[35]

As Mayor of East York I served on Metro Council for six years from 1977 to 1982. Paul Godfrey was Chairman for all of those years. I had my disagreements with him. He could not always count on my vote but Metro worked exceedingly well when he was Chairman. Godfrey was

34. Interviews with Paul Godfrey, December 19, 2012 and January 13, 2013
35. Tony O'Donohue, Front Row Centre (Abbeyfield Publishers, Toronto)

neither the iron fist, nor the velvet glove nor merely the chairman of the board. I have great respect for him. He was a true leader.

When Paul Godfrey stepped down in 1984, Etobicoke Mayor Dennis Flynn was elected by Metro council members to replace him as Chairman. Flynn served only one three-year term, losing the job to York Mayor Alan Tonks in 1987. As Tony O'Donohue described it: "Dennis Flynn molded the office of Chairman into a much more co-ordinating role." [36]

Alan Tonks told me: "I had a huge respect for Flynn, who was not given the credit he deserved. He had a short fuse but was good leading council and balancing local concerns with Metro concerns." [37]

"Flynn was a consensus Chairman," said Paul Godfrey. But Dennis Flynn may never have really wanted to be Chairman. After two or three years in the job, he confided to Godfrey that he should have stayed on as Mayor of Etobicoke, which he felt was his real calling because he was not enjoying the job of Chairman. [38]

1985 was an eventful year for the Province of Ontario. Premier Bill Davis resigned. Frank Miller was chosen by the Progressive Conservative Party to succeed Davis. An election followed resulting in a Miller minority government. It didn't last long. Frank Miller's government was defeated that same year by the combined forces of the Liberal and New Democratic opposition parties in a vote of confidence in the Ontario Legislative Assembly. The 42 year reign of the Progressive Conservative Party as the government of Ontario had come to an end. Liberal Leader David Peterson replaced Miller as Premier.

With a Liberal provincial government now at Queen's Park, there was a feeling among many Metro Councillors that a Chairman who was a member of the Liberal party such as Alan Tonks, would be better suited to make progress for Metro with Liberal Premier David Peterson than a Progressive Conservative like Dennis Flynn. Like Paul Godfrey Alan Tonks too had always harboured the ambition to be Metro Chairman. Municipal politics was part of his DNA, his father Chris Tonks' municipal

36. Tony O'Donohue, Front Row Centre (Abbeyfield Publishers, Toronto)
37. Interview with Alan Tonks, December 28, 2012
38. Interviews with Paul Godfrey, December 19, 2012 and January 13, 2013

political career went back to the days of the York county council. Immediately following his election as Mayor of the city of York, in 1982, he challenged Paul Godfrey for the position of Metro Chairman. Not discouraged by his defeat he ran again unsuccessfully against Dennis Flynn. But persistence finally paid off when he defeated Flynn in 1987. Tonks told me that he ran against Godfrey and Flynn not because he felt that they had done a bad job but because he felt the position needed someone younger with more energy, someone who would make Metro work for the smaller area municipalities.[39]

Paul Godfrey says that, "It's easy to govern when times are good, not so when times are bad."[40] Unfortunately for Alan Tonks, times were bad during most of his term as Metro Chairman. In 1994 just after a Liberal government had come to power in Ottawa the feds announced a $410 million infrastructure program for Metro. Tonks had a long wish list of infrastructure projects waiting to take advantage of that money. But the very next year 1995, federal Finance Minister Paul Martin in his much praised budget, drastically cut federal programs and downloaded others to the already debt and deficit plagued provincial governments. As a result Metro was forced to raise taxes just to maintain its existing services. The Metro infrastructure program was a dead duck. Apparently the tax situation so upset the Metro business community that the Toronto police fearing violence recommended Tonks wear a bullet proof vest. Alan Tonks told me that he still has the vest but he isn't wearing it anymore.[41]

Although, Metro Councillor Howard Moscoe has been quoted as saying: "Many of us like Tonks because he is weak,"[42] but David Lewis Stein of the Toronto Star has written: "In his own way, Tonks was a leader and a damned good one. He allowed Metro politicians to work their way toward tough decisions. He stepped in only to broker a deal when council got bogged down."[43] East York Mayor Michael Prue has called him "a

---

39. Interview with Alan Tonks, December 28, 2012
40. Interview with Paul Godfrey December 19, 2012
41. Interview with Alan Tonks, December 28, 2012
42. Toronto Star – October 29, 1994
43. Toronto Star – April 4, 1997

man of vision".[44] "Tonks is a good guy," according to North York Mayor Mel Lastman.[45] "Alan Tonks was a smoother version of Dennis Flynn," says Paul Godfrey, "always smiling, never angry – a consensus builder finding the middle ground – never complained."[46]

In 1986, Premier Peterson's Minister of Municipal Affairs Bernard Grandmaître established a Task Force made up of staff representatives from Metro and its six area municipalities to assist the province in examining the Metro Toronto issues of representation, accountability and responsiveness.[47]

Responding to the staff Task Force Report, a Metropolitan Toronto Council Review Committee made up of the Chairman Dennis Flynn and Metro Council members, Ron Kanter and June Rowland both city of Toronto Council Members as well, North York Mayor Mel Lastman, Etobicoke Councillor Lois Griffin, Scarborough Councillor Maureen Prinsloo, York Mayor Alan Tonks and East York Mayor Dave Johnson, recommended direct election of Metro Councillors to sit only on Metro Council but not on their local councils.[48]

Former Toronto Mayor John Sewell says that Toronto Councillor Richard Gilbert had been pushing the idea of direct election of Metro Councillors before the Review Committee made its recommendation.[49] Toronto Councillors Ron Kanter, Michael Gee, and David Reville had also been actively advocating for this. After the 1985 provincial election, Ron Kanter, a Liberal himself, told me he had several very persuasive discussions on the subject with his friend the new Liberal Deputy Premier Robert Nixon.[50] However, according to a most emphatic Sean Gadon, who was then an Executive Assistant to a provincial cabinet minister, it was Health Minister Elinor Caplan who actually convinced Premier David Peterson that Metro Councillors should be directly elected. Caplan a

44. Toronto Star – December 8, 1994
45. Toronto Star – December 8, 1994
46. Interview with Paul Godfrey, January 13, 2013
47. Analysis and Options for the Government of Metropolitan Toronto prepared by the Task Force on Representation, and Accountability in Metropolitan Toronto dated November 1986
48. The Response of Metropolitan Toronto review Committee dated April 1987
49. Interview with John Sewell, January 14, 2013
50. Interviews with Enid Slack & Ron Kanter, August 7, 2012

former North York Councillor had dearly wanted to sit on Metro Council herself, but had never been chosen by Mayor Mel Lastman and her local council colleagues. Gadon says that Eleanor wanted to make sure this could never happen again to anyone else.[51] On the other hand former Premier David Peterson told me that for him "it was a no brainer. It just evolved."[52] Thus, in 1988 the Provincial Legislature finally implemented the part of the 1978 White Paper calling for the direct election of Metro councillors. However, rather than retaining their membership on both local and Metro councils as set out in the White Paper, the legislation provided that Metro Councillors except for the Mayors would not be members of their local council.[53] It was of course a "no brainer". It was the democratic thing to do; elect the people who represent you at every level of government. Implementing the same theory each and every cabinet minister should be directly elected to their cabinet portfolio rather than merely being appointed by the premier or the prime minister. Years ago in Canada we used to do that. Once the prime minister appointed a cabinet minister that minister had to resign their seat and stand for office again in a by-election. We don't do that in Canada any more even if it is a "no brainer". This Metro Council "no brainer" of course violated one of the key principles of the Municipality of Metropolitan Toronto as created by Premier Leslie Frost and admired around the world, that Metro Councillors should also be members of their local councils in order to ensure that the area municipalities would have an effective voice at Metro Council and that the co-ordination between the two levels of government would be facilitated. John Sewell told me he feels that Toronto megacity's second Mayor David Miller lacked an understanding of local issues because he had previously served on Metro council but had never served on a local council.[54]

The rationale for this 1988 "no brainer", which Metro and local councillors alike supported almost unanimously and was based on the

---

51. Interview with Sean Gadon formerly Sean Goetz-Gadon, December 10, 2012
52. Interview with David Peterson, January 15, 2013
53. Bill 29, An Act to Amend the Municipality of Metropolitan Toronto Act, 1988
54. Interview with John Sewell, January 14, 2013

theory that it was the democratic thing to do to, let the voters – not the local councillors they had elected – choose who should serve on Metro Council. Metro Councillors except for the Mayors would now, so the theory goes, devote full time and be accountable to the voters for Metro issues only. According to this line of thought, taxpayers would welcome the opportunity to hear Metro issued debated exclusively during the election process. There is little or no evidence that metropolitan residents were demanding the direct election of their Metro councillors. Public involvement on the issue appears to have come only after the province, Metro and the six local councils raised it themselves. Public reaction after the fact was quite modest and certainly not unanimous. For instance, in a letter dated January 20, 1987, Orville Leigh a past President of the Leaside Property Owners Association told East York council it should leave a system that was working well alone and not make any changes.[55]

The "no brainer" created what some have described as dysfunctional municipal government. Now that no local councillors sat on Metro Council they were free to blame Metro Council for everything. The inevitable result was increasing friction between the Metro and the local Councils, especially the former city of Toronto council, which began to see the newly independent Metro Councillors as competitors and rivals.[56] In 1992 this was exacerbated when Metro Council moved from the Queen Street City Hall where it had shared accommodation with the Toronto City Council since 1964 to the newly built Metro Hall on John Street. Previously, the Mayor of Toronto and the Metro Chairman's offices were side by side in City Hall separated only by a wall and furnished exactly the same in Burma teak furniture. Thus before the move to Metro Hall the Mayor and the Chairman had been in and out of each other's offices on a daily basis discussing the issues.[57] After the move there was a natural and growing estrangement. By 1994 Toronto Councillor Michael

55. Borough of East York Council minutes – March 4, 1987
56. Interviews with Sean Gadon, December 10, 2012 and Barbara Hall, January 21, 2013
57. Interview with Alan Tonks, December 28, 2012

Walker had convinced Toronto Council to hold a plebiscite[58]asking the question: "Are you in favour of eliminating the Metro level of government?" That year 73,510 residents of the former city of Toronto voted in favour while only 53,055 voted no, however, the total votes cast were less than the 163,159 cast for Mayor.[59]

Was this "no brainer" for Metro government significant in any other way? Former Toronto Mayor David Crombie, known as the defender of neighbourhoods, says it was the key factor that turned him into a supporter of total amalgamation. In 1996, prior to amalgamation, Crombie was appointed by the Ontario Premier Mike Harris as Chair of the "Who Does What" panel. Crombie told me that once Metro Councillors were directly elected with no local responsibilities there was no real difference between that and direct election to a "one big city council".[60] Without really understanding all of the implications, the Peterson government, as well as Metro Chairman Alan Tonks who told me that direct election seemed to him "so natural" because "it was democratic"[61], together with the councillors and the residents who supported direct election had, unintentionally, I presume, helped to drive a nail into the coffin of the Municipality of Metropolitan Toronto. The form of municipal government admired around the world.

58. Tony O'Donohue, Front Row Centre (Abbeyfield Publishers, Toronto 2001)
59. Toronto City Council minutes, December 6, 1994
60. Interview with David Crombie, January 9, 2013
61. Interview with Alan Tonks, December 28, 2012

The 1967 Metropolitan Toronto Council the first 6 local municipality council
(Source: City of Toronto Archives)

Former Ontario Minister of Municipal Affairs and Housing later Minister of Treasury, Economics and Intergovernmental Affairs (TEGA) Darcy McKeough *(Source: "John McNeill"/The Globe and Mail)*

Former Metro Chairman Fred Gardiner QC *(Source: City of Toronto Archives Fonds 1653, Series 975, File 2262, Item 32745-6)*

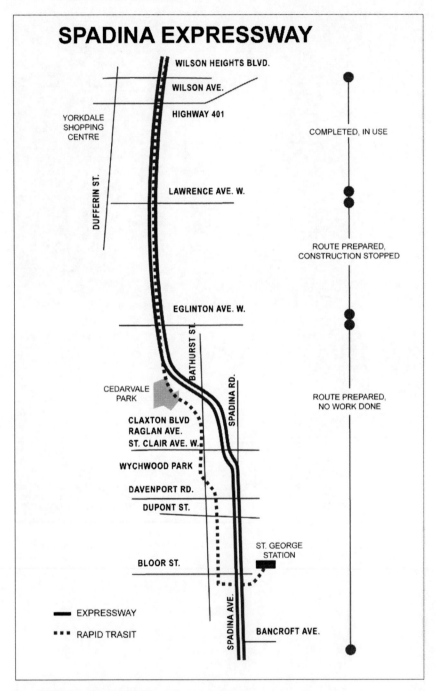

SPADINA EXPRESSWAY

WILSON HEIGHTS BLVD.

WILSON AVE.

HIGHWAY 401

YORKDALE SHOPPING CENTRE

DUFFERIN ST.

LAWRENCE AVE. W.

EGLINTON AVE. W.

BATHURST ST.

SPADINA RD.

CEDARVALE PARK

CLAXTON BLVD
RAGLAN AVE.
ST. CLAIR AVE. W.

WYCHWOOD PARK

DAVENPORT RD.

DUPONT ST.

ST. GEORGE STATION

BLOOR ST.

SPADINA AVE.

BANCROFT AVE.

COMPLETED, IN USE

ROUTE PREPARED, CONSTRUCTION STOPPED

ROUTE PREPARED, NO WORK DONE

━━ EXPRESSWAY

▪▪▪ RAPID TRASIT

Map of the proposed Spadina Expressway *(Source: Valentine De Landro 2014))*

Former Ontario Premier William G. Davis QC *(Source: "Steve Russell/ GetStock.com")*

Royal Commissioner and former Premier of Ontario John Robarts *(Source: F 15-7-1-16 ca. 1960 Photographic Illustrators ca from the files of the Archives of Ontario)*

The Toronto Star

ROLAND B. BENDRICK, *President and Publisher*

KENNETH B. TROLL, *Vice-President, Director*
HARRY A. HINDMARSH, *Secretary, Director*
WILLIAM J. CAMPBELL, *Director*
J. D. ARMSTRONG HINDMARSH, *Director*
STEWART S. WOODS, *Director*
WILFRID L. GIBBON, *Director*
BORDEN SPEARS, *Editorial Page Editor*
GEORGE R. RIMMER, *Director*

MONDAY, JUNE 18, 1973

"...it's not fair... our age group has been overlooked altogether as far as summer opportunities are concerned... what can WE do all summer...?"

Omens for the summit look good

Terminal 2: Confusion, delays, ugliness

Intolerable strikes can be avoided

Professional protection for the public

Naval flute-players?

The race for the biggest municipal job in the country

Secretariat's position

Uniquely successful

Odds are long

Sound administrator

METRO CHAIRMAN AB CAMPBELL
Illness forced him to resign the job

Former Metro Chairman Albert (Ab) Campbell *(Source: Toronto Star June 18, 1973)*

Godfrey at 34 youngest ever to head Metro- Gina and Paul Godfrey
(Source: Toronto Star July 3, 1973)

Former Metro Chairman Paul Godfrey who brought major league baseball to Toronto, later President of the Toronto Blue Jays Baseball Organization at the Sky Dome later the Roger's Centre *(Source: "Toronto Star/ GetStock.com")*

Former Metro Chairman Dennis
Flynn *(Source: 1980 Etobicoke mayoralty
election brochure Toronto Reference Library*

Former Metro Chairman Dennis Flynn *(Source: "Toronto Star/
GetStock.com")*

Former Metro Chairman Alan Tonks *(Source: "Toronto Star/ GetStock.com")*

Former Metro Councillor Ron Kanter *(Source: 1985 municipal election brochure Toronto Reference Library)*

Former North York Alderman,
later both an Ontario provincial
and a federal cabinet Minister
Elinor Caplan
*(Source: 1980 election campaign brochure
Toronto Reference Library)*

Former Ontario Premier
David Peterson
*(Source: Erik Christensen/ The Globe and Mail
April 19, 1989*

The Road To Ruin

CHAPTER 6

"Provincial policy in Ontario implies that the provincial government knows best how to organize local government and assign functions to different local government units as evidenced by provincially imposed reorganizations, including amalgamations. This parallels a classical central planning perspective where one assumes that local knowledge is easy to obtain and some optimal organization can be identified by central authorities.

"Provincial policy in Alberta and British Columbia is much different. In both these provinces their municipal acts set out procedural rules whereby citizens may incorporate, dissolve or amalgamate local government with the initiative coming from citizens or local governments themselves. Both provide for the creation of regional governments but do not impose them. The approach is one where structure itself is left to the local people with the expectation that they will pursue their own interests and evolve appropriate structures of local government over time. It is assumed that local people know best. This would appear to be a far superior system to one where problems build up until the provincial government comes in and imposes massive reorganization of local government activities including amalgamation, which reduce democratic control, eliminates comparison and competition with nearby municipalities, and may result in large bureaucracies where

diseconomies of scale result for a majority of local government activities if it tries to produce most services in-house."

Robert L. Bish
Professor Emeritus and Co-Director of Local Government Institute
University of Victoria, British Columbia
Canadian Journal of Regional Science – Spring 2000

Bob Rae became the first NDP Premier of Ontario following the election defeat of the David Peterson's Liberal government in 1990. It did not take the new premier long to realize the consequences of the "iron curtain", which his predecessors Premiers Robarts and Davis had constructed around Metropolitan Toronto. So in April 1995, spurred on by Metro Toronto's request for a review of Greater Toronto Area government as well as complaints that local municipalities both inside and outside the boundaries of Metro Toronto were not paying their fair share for the services they were receiving,[1] Premier Rae established the Greater Toronto Task Force chaired by Anne Golden. Its mandate was to recommend potential restructuring of responsibilities and practices of municipal and provincial governments in order to provide direction for the quality of life, the future governance and competitiveness of the Greater Toronto Area (the GTA). In the letter of transmittal to the Task Force the province described the GTA as a highly interdependent region greater than the sum of its parts.

The GTA was identified as the Municipality of Metropolitan Toronto and the regional municipalities of Peel, Halton, York and Durham comprising 72,000 square kilometres with 30 local municipalities. In its report the Golden Task Force report described the GTA as "no longer merely a geographic area but a powerful, single economy, an independent planning unit and an emergent political jurisdiction".

Among its many recommendations were the following very significant ones: **Governing the City-Region**

---

1.   Metropolitan Toronto Council minutes – April 6, 1994

The Province should implement the following changes in the governance of Greater Toronto: replace the five existing regional governments with a single Greater Toronto regional government with a more limited number of functions; strengthen local municipalities with added powers and the responsibility for delivering a wider range of local services.

"Revision of the external boundaries of the Greater Toronto region, consistent with the criteria of commuter shed, cohesiveness, and anticipated development, should be referred to the Greater Toronto Implementation Commission and considered in conjunction with the municipal restructuring process."[2]

It should be noted that Golden merely recommended the establishment of a Greater Toronto Implementation Commission. None existed at that time nor has one ever been established since.

By the time the Golden Report was released in January 1996 the Bob Rae government had been defeated in the provincial election of June 1995 ushering in a new Ontario Progressive Conservative government led by Premier Mike Harris. Harris had campaigned on the theme of "the Common Sense Revolution"[3] and subsequently made it quite clear that he intended to reform local government before the next municipal election due in November 1997. [4]

Mississauga Mayor Hazel McCallion didn't like Anne Golden's idea of a single Greater Toronto regional government. In fact she really didn't like the idea of regional governments at all. Certainly not the regional municipality of Peel in which Mississauga is located.[5] In August 1995, Mississauga issued a report entitled: Running the GTA "Like A Business" Mississauga's Recommendations for GTA Reform. One of those recommendations was:

2.   Report of the GTA Task Force, January 1996
3.   Ontario PC, The Common Sense Revolution
4.   Bill 26, the Savings and Restructuring Act, November 1995
5.   Tom Urbaniak, Her Worship, Hazel McCallion and the Development of Mississauga, page 209 (University of Toronto Press 2009)

"Legislation to abolish the five regional governments, establish ten to fifteen cities and create the Greater Toronto Area Services Commission by December 1, 1997."[6]

The same month as the Golden report was released four of the GTA Mayors Hazel McCallion of Mississauga, Mel Lastman of North York, Nancy Diamond of Oshawa and Barbara Hall of the city of Toronto issued their own report entitled "Moving Forward Together". Although appearing to be a response to the Golden Report, the four Mayors chaired by Hazel McCallion had been meeting together since the fall of 1995 with a view to reaching the following consensus on the question of GTA reform:[7]

"We believe that the existing system of regional government no longer meets the needs of our present situation and is not capable of effecting real changes needed for the future. When founded in 1954, Metropolitan Toronto spanned the urbanized GTA. Today about half of the population and some 43 per cent of the jobs are located beyond Metro's boundaries. In the early 1970s, this two-tiered structure was replicated, leaving us with five regional governments: Metropolitan Toronto, Halton, Peel, York and Durham.

"Today, Metro is too small to solve the problems that affect the GTA and too large to provide cost-effective or flexible neighbourhood services. Direct election to Metro Council, initiated in 1988, has been a disappointment, resulting in turf wars, not responsive government. Outside of Metro, regional governments have been ineffective in promoting a coherent growth management strategy and too often the focus has been on rivalry or competition for limited funding.

---

6.   Running the GTA "Like A Business" Mississauga Recommendations for GTA Reform, August 1995
7.   Moving Forward Together, A Discussion Paper, January 1996 and Interview with Barbara Hall, January 21, 2013

"Our proposal calls for the elimination of the regional level of government across the GTA in favour of a system of strong local government. Local government in the urbanized areas of the GTA has matured over the past twenty years and many municipalities are recognized among the best managed in North America.

"Time and again, local government has demonstrated the ability to provide high quality service at low cost. On the basis of this proven experience, local municipalities should be strengthened by broadening the range of services they provide.

"We believe that local government preserves local community identity for residents and businesses and promotes the efficient use of resources. These are the key building blocks and foundation of a reformed government structure in the GTA.

"Where coordination of limited 'utility' services is required across the urban municipalities of the GTA, we believe an Intermunicipal Services Board, representing a partnership of municipalities, should be established to provide such coordination.

"We see this type of partnership as a superior means of cross-boundary service delivery than the creation of a super-GTA level of government. That model is premised on the notion that bigger government is more efficient, which we don't believe has been demonstrated. A single government would be too large to be cost-effective and too far removed from communities and businesses to be responsive or even accessible.

"Strong local government, with a co-ordination mechanism designed to ensure that area services are provided at the lowest possible cost, is certainly a more workable structure. Urban municipalities, in most instances, are large enough to take advantage of economies of scale, but not so large as to be remote from their citizens.

"We are disappointed that the Task Force did not make specific recommendations relating to new GTA boundaries. Although the report clearly recognizes the need to contain growth so that future infrastructure will be affordable, it leaves boundary adjustments to

a 'Greater-Toronto Implementation Commission'. We believe strongly that this decision is crucial to any changes, in tax reform or governance, and should be made by the government as the first step in the reform exercise.

"The Task Force's recommendation for the creation of a 'Greater Toronto Council' calls for a government with taxing powers – a recreation of the old Metro on a larger scale. We feel this fails to achieve the goals of reducing the layers of government and of eliminating confusion for the taxpaying public.

"We believe that this regional level of government is not necessary and the co-ordination and delivery of cross-boundary services can better be accomplished through a management board representing member municipalities. It would provide services to municipalities, not to taxpayers, thereby allowing citizens to receive all local government services from their local city hall."

The four Mayors' "Moving Forward Together" Report then made the following recommendations among others:

Strong Cities – Strong Province
- Retain only two levels of government-strong local municipalities and a strong province.
- Empower local municipalities to deliver substantially all municipal services.

1. A Healthy, Redefined GTA
- Define the existing nineteen urban municipalities as the urban GTA.
- Restructure the remaining eleven rural municipalities into two counties.

2. Co-ordinated Intermunicipal Services
- Establish an Intermunicipal Services Board to coordinate a limited number of cross-border services, such as water/sewer supply and treatment, waste disposal, coordinated economic development and tourism, and transit coordination.

- Municipalities pay for what they consume.
- Appoint Mayors to the Board.
- Establish a system of voting based on one vote per 100,000 population.
- Coordination of transit services across the GTA to achieve "seamless" service, fare integration, cross-boundary service, and coordination for transit capital planning; but still allowing service to be delivered locally, through intermunicipal partnerships or existing service providers, such as the TTC.
- Police services to be more accountable to local councils and the establishment of true community-based policing with a phase-in over several years.
- Fire services to be delivered locally, combined with emergency ambulance service to improve overall response time and achieve administrative and operational efficiencies." [8]

The rationale for this report, at least as far as the two Metro Mayors Hall and Lastman were concerned, was as stated that, the "no brainer" decision initiated in 1988 for the direct election to Metro Council "has been a disappointment, resulting in turf wars, not responsive government". Ultimately when the megacity was created it could be argued that the provincial government had actually adopted the "Strong Cities – Strong Province" recommendations of the four GTA Mayors, at least where Metro was concerned, for only two levels of government (the city of Toronto and the Province of Ontario with the amalgamated city of Toronto delivering substantially all municipal services). But this, of course, wasn't what the Mayors had in mind.

In February 1996, faced with Golden and the four GTA Mayors diametrically opposing sets of recommendations, the Minister of Municipal Affairs Al Leach decided to establish a review panel to see what the public thought. It was chaired by Libby Burnham QC, a

---

8.   Moving Forward Together, A Discussion Paper, January 1996 and Interview with Barbara Hall, January 21, 2013

Progressive Conservative party activist and corporate lawyer well known in the field of women's healthcare. The Burnham panel held eighteen public meetings, listened to over 284 delegations and received 86 written briefs over a one-month period.[9] In the course of preparing its report the Golden Task Force had met with 165 organizations and individuals besides receiving more than 300 written submissions. Golden did not hold public hearings, however, because the newly elected Harris government, anxious to get on with changes to municipal government had reduced the time for her to issue her report.[10]

Why did the government reduce Golden's reporting time thereby, making it impossible for her Task Force to hold public hearings and then turn around and create the Burnham Panel in order to hold public hearings? According to John Ibbitson in his book Promised Land inside the Mike Harris Revolution, Al Leach praised the recommendations in the Golden Report when it was released and promised swift implementation.[11] But a short time later, faced with the opposing recommendations of Golden and the four GTA Mayors, it became obvious that more sober thought was needed. Thus, the Burnham Review panel was born.

The Burnham Review Panel arrived at very different conclusions from those of Golden. Its findings released on April 17, 1996, mirrored closely those of the four GTA Mayors in "Moving Forward Together". Burnham's findings can be summarized as follows:

"GOVERNANCE
- Reject the creation of a Greater Toronto Council (GTC) and a Greater Toronto region.
- Concern over the potential power of the council, as the governing structure.

---

9.   Review Panel on the Greater Toronto Area Task Force Report, April 17, 1996
10. Report of the GTA Task Force, January 1996
11. John Ibbitson, *Promised Land inside the Mike Harris Revolution* (Prentice Hall Canada Inc. 1997)

• Concern over type of representation on the proposed GTC, control by urban areas.
• Rural sectors want representation by area factored with population.

Need of a co-ordinating function or body for inter-regional and inter-urban issues across the GTA.

Call for the province to take a stronger role in co-ordinating inter-regional issues and to play a role in economic development for the broader GTA (a Minister for the GTA or a Co-ordinating Committee).

• Maintain regional government especially in Durham, Halton, Peel.
• In York, support is mixed.
• In Metro, stronger support for local government only.

Disentangle responsibilities and service delivery. Clearly identify responsibilities of province/regions/local municipalities.

Deal with governance issues province-wide not just GTA.[12]

In May 1996, the provincial government locked into the Burnham Review panel's call for disentangling provincial-municipal responsibilities when it appointed the "Who Does What" Panel chaired by former Toronto Mayor and former Progressive Conservative federal cabinet Minister David Crombie.[13] For many years Metro Toronto and other municipalities across Ontario, supported by a number of studies and reports had been advocating for a redistribution of municipal-provincial responsibilities and funding. In 1991 the Rae government had established a committee to examine the issue based on the principle of disentanglement with fiscal neutrality. One of the Metro staff members participating in this effort was none other than Al Leach, then the General Manager of the Toronto Transit Commission (the TTC) now the Minister who appointed the David Crombie "Who Does What" panel. The Rae

12. Review Panel on the Greater Toronto Area Task Force Report, April 17, 1996
13. Who Does What Panel Chair letter to The Honourable Al Leach dated December 23, 1996

committee had arrived at a draft agreement involving the transfer of responsibilities and funding for police, welfare, roads, property assessment and provincial grants but nothing was finalized prior to the Rae government's defeat by the Mike Harris PCs. [14]

In October 1996, the six Metro Mayors, Scarborough's Frank Faubert, Etobicoke's Doug Holyday, York's Frances Nunziata, Toronto's Barbara Hall, North York's Mel Lastman and East York's Michael Prue met with the Minister of Municipal Affairs Al Leach who told them that total amalgamation was in the works for Metro. The Mayors then asked for and were given 30 days to come up with their own plan. [15]

Anticipating that the Metro Mayors' plan would recommend the elimination of Metropolitan Toronto Council, Alan Tonks, soon to be the last Chairman of Metropolitan Toronto, although having previously together with Metro council opposed amalgamation reversed his field and pre-empted the Mayors when on November 28, 1996 he wrote to Minister Al Leach endorsing amalgamation: "We have done some more thinking about creating one unified municipality that I want to share with you.

"A united city of Toronto model is quite consistent with the principles that I have adhered to throughout the Metro and GTA reform debate. In fact, it is a logical step towards taking Metro and the GTA governance into the next millennium.

"In August of 1995, Metro Council adopted 'There's No Turning Back: A Proposal For Change'. This plan was Metro's input to the GTA Task Force. It called for the creation of a strong accountable, effective regional government for the urban GTA. It was premised on the logic of strong two-tier government (i.e. effective and accountable at both levels). It was conditional upon any new government structure having at least as much capacity for region-wide co-ordination and tax pooling as Metro and the existing regions have now. A unified city will preserve the existing benefits of Metro-wide co-ordination, scale economies, tax pooling and equalization of resources. All of this adds up to opportunities and cost

---

14. Metropolitan Toronto Council minutes, April 14, 1993
15. Changes For The Better, December 12, 1996

savings. I expect that this letter will arrive in your hands at about the same time as Metro's six Mayors' 'eliminate-Metro-and-save-money' document."[16]

Chairman Tonks knew what he was talking about. The six Mayors' document which they called: "Change For The Better" was delivered to the province on December 12, 1996. It advocated a GTA reorganization resembling in many ways the Four GTA Mayors' Report "Moving Forward Together". That should not be surprising since two of the same Mayors signed both documents. In this one they said:

> *"We believe in strong local governments, and so do our citizens. Local councils are the cornerstone of government in our country. Local government allows our citizens to deal directly with their elected representatives and to shape the attitudes, the image and even the future of the neighbourhoods where they live.*

> *"Our local government understands the people it serves. We know the neighbourhoods, the local business community and the arts and cultural groups. We are in the best position to deliver vital services. We are in the best position to promote local business development, to provide recreational programs and to respond quickly to community needs. We are in the best position to ensure safe and liveable local communities.*

> *"We do not believe that a city of 2.3 million people is a local government.*

> *"Our citizen's want stronger, more effective, less confusing local government, they expect us to work together to manage services like transit, police, sewers, water and garbage disposal. They expect us to take the lead in finding solutions to problems which span not only Metropolitan Toronto but also the Greater Toronto area.*

> *"They also want to be consulted on any changes to their local government and to have their voices heard. We agree.*

---

16. Letter from Metro Chairman Alan Tonks to the Honourable Al Leach, November 28, 1996

"The Government of Ontario is considering various ways to reform local government, including the amalgamation of our municipalities. We oppose this amalgamation. Our view is shared by the experts on this subject. Recent studies of the governance of the Greater Toronto Area have not recommended large scale amalgamation. Studies of the amalgamation of larger municipalities in other areas of Canada and from around the world show that amalgamation increases rather than reduces costs. Rather than solving financial and policy problems, amalgamation would create more problems by eliminating the healthy benefits of strong local municipalities competing to provide their citizens with services which they need and value"

And then they went on to propose among others:

"That locally-elected officials in each city be responsible for the delivery of all municipal services to their citizens, that the current upper tier of local government in Metropolitan Toronto be eliminated. Services which require co-ordination across Metropolitan Toronto, such as police, transit and sewer, water and waste management, will be overseen by a Local Municipal Co-ordinating Board with elected representatives from each city."

"That by the year 2000, a Greater Toronto Area Co-ordinating Board, which would be composed of locally-elected officials from each of the municipalities in the region, be established to replace the Local Municipal Coordinating Board. This will provide effective planning and co-ordination of Greater Toronto area-wide services, including transit, sewer, water and waste management."

"That by the year 2000, a Greater Toronto Area Coordinating Board, which would be composed of locally-elected officials from each of the municipalities in the region, be established to replace the Local Municipal Coordinating Board. This will provide effective planning and coordination of Greater Toronto area-wide services, including transit, sewer, water and waste management."

131

"That a public consultation process begin immediately in our local municipalities. It is essential that our citizens be involved in the decision-making process."

"In the coming days and weeks, we will be holding public meetings on our municipalities to hear from our communities."

"We urge the Government of Ontario to join us in allowing citizens to vote for their future in a binding referendum."[17]

Chairman Tonks and the six Mayors had forgotten the warning given to the American colonists on the eve of the American Revolution: "If we don't hang together we will hang separately."[18]

By rejecting both the continued existence of Metropolitan Toronto Council and the Golden Reports' recommendation to replace the five existing regional governments Metro Toronto, Peel, Halton, York and Durham with a single Greater Toronto Council, the six Metro Mayors, the four GTA Mayors and the Burnham panel were rejecting the form of metropolitan government created by Premier Leslie Frost and OMB Chairman Lorne Cumming, which despite its challenges, had produced a quality of urban life consistently ranked among the highest in the world. "A city" that the late actor Peter Ustinov described as one "that works".[19] Why did they do it? The seeds were sown when the "no brainer" decision was made that directly elected Metro Councillors would no longer sit on their local council. That "no brainer" resulted in increased friction between Metro and local councils. It led directly to some people concluding that Metro should be eliminated while others concluded that total amalgamation was the answer. If Peter Ustinov was right, both of these conclusions were wrong.

In addition to its mandate on disentanglement, the government of Ontario had also asked the Crombie Panel to advise it on the governance

---

17. Changes For The Better, December 12, 1996
18. Benjamin Franklin, signing of the Declaration of Independence July 4, 1776
19. Report of the GTA Task Force, January 1996, page 30

of the GTA. Although the "Who Does What" Panel's final report on governance was not delivered to Al Leach until December 6, 1996, after the Minister had made known to the Metro Mayors the decision for total amalgamation, Crombie's personal opinion had already been conveyed to the government in a private meeting.[20] On that subject of GTA governance, the Panel's final report like the reports of the four GTA Mayors, the Burnham panel and the six Metro Mayors recommended a Greater Toronto Services Board but in sharp contrast to the other reports it recommended "consolidation" of Metro or in plain English, total amalgamation. Specifically the final "Who Does What" Panel Report said:

> 1. *The Panel recommends that the Province implement a GTA governance structure based on three fundamental and interrelated imperatives:*
>
> * *Creation of a Greater Toronto Services Board (GTSB) eliminating the five upper-tier municipalities*
>
> * *Consolidations of member municipalities into strong cities;*
>
> * *Consolidations in Metro that create a strong urban core for the GTA.*
>
> *The Panel agreed that a Greater Toronto Services Board is of overwhelming importance. The Panel was unanimous in endorsing the importance of a strong urban core, with views on strengthening the core ranging from one city to four. All were agreed that consolidations should significantly enhance the political strength of the core city within the Greater Toronto Area.*

David Crombie told me that the panel did not reach a consensus on the question of governance until shortly before its final report was issued;

20. Interview with David Crombie, January 9, 2013

however, he personally became a supporter of total Toronto amalgamation after Premier David Peterson's government instituted the direct election of Metro Councillors. After seeing Metro Councillors directly elected he could then no longer see an argument against total amalgamation. Before the direct election of Metro Councillors, Crombie as the Mayor of Toronto was often asked to speak in American cities about how Metro worked and when he was asked by Mississauga officials how to solve the GTA problems he told them "Look at Metro".[21]

But in David Crombie's mind the amalgamation of Toronto had to go hand in hand with the creation of a Greater Toronto Services Board to solve those GTA problems the Mississauga officials had asked him about:

The Panel recommends the Greater Toronto Services Board should have the following characteristics:

- *Represent a geographic area for the planned provision of services for the next 25 years.*
- *Representation from municipalities based on population.*
- *No direct taxing authority. Member municipalities and their residents pay on the basis of user charges, assessment or population. For different functions, different revenue sources will be utilized.*
- *An important function of the GTSB would be to act as a forum for discussion, co-ordination and innovation.*

The GTSB should focus on ensuring the coordination of:
- *Regional roads and expressways.*
- *Waste management.*
- *Sewer and water – distribution and treatment.*
- *Hydroelectric distribution.*
- *Public transit integration and co-ordination.*
- *Police board coordination.*
- *Regional and infrastructure planning.*
- *Social planning and co-ordination.*
- *Watershed management.*

---

21. Interview with David Crombie, June 8, 2011

It is the Panel's view that the GTSB should have a limited central administration. Most functions would be provided by member municipalities or private and partnership arrangements.

The GTSB external boundaries would be porous, allowing participation by contiguous neighbouring municipalities through purchase of services, infrastructure planning, economic promotion, and other activities as appropriate.

In order to contain urban sprawl and provide for efficient use of infrastructure, an urban zone should be identified within the GTA within which all development will be concentrated for the next 25 years. Areas beyond the urban zone would not be extended services or have large development proposals approved, but would be represented on the Services Board.

2.   *The Panel recommends that the Province mandate the following implementation strategy:*

- *Immediately appoint an implementation commissioner who could act as interim chair of the Greater Toronto Services Board. The implementation commissioner's mandate would be:*

  - *To establish the GTSB as a first priority.*

  - *To develop proposals for municipal consolidations, with a report by April 1997; and to implement the consolidations effective January 1, 1998.*

  - *Determine GTSB membership based on the population of the newly consolidated cities by April 1997.*[22]

---

22. Who Does What Panel, Chair David Crombie letter of honourable Al Leach, December 23, 1996

The four GTA Mayors, the Burnham Review panel, the six Metro Mayors and the Crombie "Who Does What" Panel all recommended the establishment of a Board to deal with cross regional border services such as water/sewer supply and treatment, waste disposal, economic development, tourism and transit. That Board they all agreed would have no direct taxing power. Member municipalities and their residents would pay on the basis of user charges, assessment or population. For different functions, different revenue sources would be utilized and an important function of the Board would be to act as a forum for discussion, co-ordination and innovation. This all harkens back to the old county councils established by the Baldwin Act of 1841, designed to meet the needs of a stable rural society. Fred Gardiner a former Warden (chair) of York County Council and later the first Metro Chairman described the county council as a County Debating Society, which bandied about controversial topics, session after session mired in disagreements over who would pay for what if at all.[23] To be effective such a Board as envisaged in these reports would have to have direct taxing power and a binding decision making mechanism just like Metropolitan Toronto Council and just like the Greater Toronto Area Council proposed in the Golden Report, which they had all vehemently rejected.

Towards the end of November 1996, the Harris government retained KPMG a large auditing and consulting firm to do a last minute job of finding the savings to justify amalgamation. The terms of reference read:

1. Could the replacement of the present seven governments by a single, fully-integrated entity produce savings?

2. Are there ways in which the transition from seven entities to one could be managed so as to minimize costs and maximize future savings?

3. In what ways could the new government be established and operated, so as to maximize the savings from consolidation, while also achieving substantially greater operational efficiencies?

---

23. Timothy J. Colton, Big Daddy: Frederick G. Gardiner the building of Metropolitan Toronto
(University of Toronto Press)

4. What is the range for potential net savings flowing from the creation of a new entity that removes duplication and follows basic principles of sound public sector management?

About 30 days after it had been retained on December 16, 1996 KPMG issued its report to the government entitled "Fresh Start: An Estimate of Potential Savings and Costs from the Creation of a Single Tier Local Government for Toronto", which concluded: Estimates of Savings.

> *Although the limitations of time and access did not permit a detailed examination or verification of the components of spending in the seven municipalities, on the basis of the material reviewed we can conclude that:*
>
> 1. *Moving from seven governments to one can, if properly managed, significantly lower operating expenditures through savings associated with a consolidated governance structure. The gross "consolidation savings" could be in the range of $82 to $112 million each year from 1998 onward.*
>
> 2. *An integrated entity offers considerably more scope for reducing operating costs within most of the service delivery sectors, through application of modern public management techniques and emulation of best practices from other jurisdictions. The annual gross "efficiency savings" could be in the order of $148 to $252 million by the year 2000*
>
> 3. *The total reduced operating costs of $230 to $363 million per year in 2000 could entail a reduction in the workforce in the range of 2,500 to 4,500 relative to the 1995 full-time continuing employment level of 42,400.*
>
> 4. *The total gross savings available during the period 1998– 2000 are estimated to range from $535 to $865 million, depending on the pace of implementation.*

5. The one-time transition costs associated with creating the new entity would be in the range of $150 to $220 million, which is less than the estimated annual savings associated with implementation of the consolidation and efficiency measures.

Our analysis concentrated on operating expenditures. We did not try to estimate new capital requirements or the returns available from the disposal of assets made redundant by amalgamation. [24]

Back in 1992, the equally large auditing and consulting firm of Price Waterhouse in conducting a similar study of the Municipality of Ottawa-Carleton reach a different conclusion:

"The fundamental conclusion of our analysis is that bigger is certainly not more efficient, from a financial perspective. One-tier government would be an expensive proposition. In addition, the tax effects cannot be calculated with certainty because of the unknown future infrastructure rehabilitation costs." [25]

On December 17, 1996, the day following the release of the KPMG report, in a speech to the Board of Trade the Minister of Municipal Affairs Al Leach announced the government's intention to amalgamate the six area municipalities of Toronto, North York, Scarborough, Etobicoke, York and East York and to eliminate Metro to create a "Mega City or Super City" structure.[26] Later that same day he introduced Bill 103 in the legislature, being: "an Act to replace seven existing municipal governments of Metropolitan Toronto by incorporating a new municipality to be known as the city of Toronto".[27]

---

24. KPMG Fresh Start: An Estimate of Potential Savings and Costs from the Creation of Single Tier Local Government for Toronto, December 16, 1996
25. Price Waterhouse, The Municipality of Ottawa-Carleton, Study of Financial Impact of One Tier Government in Ottawa-Carleton, Fiscal Report, August 27, 1992
26. Ministry of Municipal Affairs & Housing, Press Release, December 17, 1996
27. Bill 103 (Chapter 2, Statutes of Ontario 1997) 1st reading December 17, 1996z

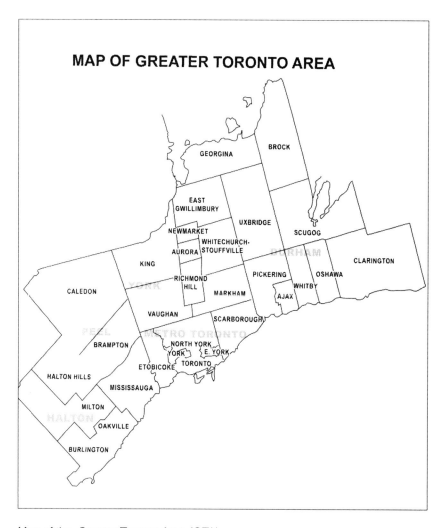

Map of the Greater Toronto Area (GTA) *(Source: Valentine De Landro 2014)*

Anne Golden
(Source: "Toronto Star/ GetStock.com")

"Changing of the Guard" incoming Ontario Premier Mike Harris (on the left) with provincial Liberal leader Lyn McLeod (in the centre) and outgoing Ontario Premier Bob Rae (on the right) *(Source: "Ken Faught/ GetStock.com")*

Old Toronto Mayor Barbara Hall
(Source: "Boris Spermo/ GetStock.com")

North York later megacity Toronto
Mayor Mel Lastman
(Source: "Tannis Toohey/ GetStock.com")

Mississauga Mayor Hazel McCallion
(Source: "The Toronto Star/ GetStock.com")

Representation on Intermunicipal Services Board

Urban Municipalities			Rural Municipalities		
City	Population*	Votes	City	Population*	Votes
Pickering	68,631	1	County #1		9
Ajax	57,350	1	Clarington	49,479	
Whitby	61,281	1	Scugog	17,810	
Oshawa	129,344	1	Uxbridge	14,092	
Vaughan	111,359	1	Brock	11,057	
Markham	153,811	2	Witchurch		
Richmond Hill	80,142	1	-Stouffville	29,454	
Newmarket	45,474	1	East Gwillimbury	18,387	
Aurora	29,746	1	Georgina	29,746	
Scarborough	524,598	5			
Toronto	635,395	6	County #2		1
East York	102,696	1	King	18,121	
North York	562,564	6	Caledon	34,965	
York	140,525	1	Milton	32,075	
Etobicoke	309,993	3	Halton Hills	36,816	
Mississauga	463,388	5			
Brampton	234,445	2			
Oakville	114,670	1			
Burlington	129,575	1			
Total Urban Members		**19**	**Total Rural Members**		**2**

* Based on 1991 Census data

The Four Mayors proposed Inter-municipal Services Board
(Source: "Tannis Toohey/ GetStock.com")

Former old Toronto Mayor and former federal cabinet
Minister, Chair of the "Who Does What Panel" David
Crombie *(Source: Fred Lum/ The Globe and Mail, December 6, 1996)*

Five of the six Metro Mayors in 1996,(from left to right) Etobicoke Mayor Doug
Holyday, York Mayor Frances Nunziata, old Toronto Mayor Barbara Hall, North
York Mayor Mel Lastman and East York Mayor Michael Prue
(Source: "Peter Power/ GetStock.com")

Scarborough Mayor Frank Faubert *(Source: 1994 election brochure Toronto Reference Library collection)*

Do you know a good thing
when you see it?

CHAPTER 7

"The name Toronto is virtually synonymous in North America with effective metropolitan administration. The 1953 creation of a federated municipality of metropolitan Toronto composed of the city of Toronto and twelve suburbs (reduced to five in a 1966 reorganization), the rapidity with which metropolitan institutions overcame serious public service deficiencies and the persistent economic and social wall – being of the city of Toronto's inner core made Toronto model an object of administration and respect for students of metropolitan affairs throughout North America."

Frances Frisken, York University[1]

"Metro Toronto is 'a jewel in the crown among metro authorities around the world'."

L.J Sharpe at the Conference on
Urban Regions in a Global Context 1995

"Fourth of 118 cities in quality of life."

Geneva Corporate Resources Group 1994

---

1. Frances Frisken, Metropolitan Governance Revisited, (Institute of Government Studios, University of California, Berkley 1998 p. 161)

"Eighth best city in the world in which to do business."

Fortune Magazine 1995

"New York run by the Swiss, the city that works"

Peter Ustinov [2]

Why did we want to spoil a good thing?

In 1994, just prior to the provincial election which resulted in him becoming the premier of Ontario, Mike Harris told an audience in Fergus, Ontario:

> *"There is no cost to a municipality to maintain its name and identity. Why destroy our roots and pride? I disagree with restructuring because it believes bigger is better. Services always cost more in larger communities. The issue is to find out how to distribute services fairly and equally without duplicating services."* [3]

According to Professor Andrew Sancton of the University of Western Ontario in his book entitled Merger Mania: The Assault on Local Government:

> *"On 5 January, 1995, the leader of the then third party in the Ontario legislature appointed the 'Mike Harris Task Force Bringing Common Sense to Metro'. The chair was Joyce Trimmer, who had retired a few months previous as mayor of Scarborough. She was actively recruited by Mr. Harris to be a Conservative candidate in the approaching election but she adhered to her decision to leave politics. There were three 'co-chairs', Al Leach, Derwyn Shea, and Morley Kells, each of whom did turn out to be a successful Conservative candidate in June 1995. The task force conducted six public hearings in Metro in February and March 1995, but the members themselves never met alone to discuss their recommendations. According to handwritten notes kept by*

---

2. Report of the GTA Task Force, January 1996
3. Fergus-Elora News Express, September 28, 1994

Ms. Trimmer, none of the approximately 30 presentations recommended a complete merger, although some suggested that there should be four municipalities within Metro rather than six. There were frequent references to the desirability of eliminating Metro, or at least to weakening its authority and reducing its budget.

"In retrospect, it appears that the existence of the task force might have had more to do with preparing for the election than with preparing for government. Recruiting Ms. Trimmer would have given the Harris campaign considerable credibility within Metro; she was certainly better known than any of her three co-chairs. Staff support for the task force came from Mr. Harris's office, notably David Lindsay and Tony Clement. At one point David Lindsay sent to Ms. Trimmer 'a first cut at an interim Report from you to Mike'. He wrote that he was sending 'a copy to Mike in North Bay for his comments and suggestions and I would welcome your thoughts and input'. Since. Ms. Trimmer was the chair, this last remark seems to speak eloquently as to how people in the leader's office viewed the independence of the task force. The 'first cut' that Mr. Lindsay referred to included drafts of a two-page covering letter dated March 30, 1995 and a six-page report. The letter listed eight 'findings'. None specifically referred to the desirability of eliminating the Metro level of government. However, in a separate paragraph in the letter, the following statement appeared:

"These observations are leading us to conclude that the Metro level of government should be eliminated. Responsibility for the delivery of some services should be moved to the local level; others, such as transportation, should be structured on an expanded regional basis beyond the current Metro boundaries. Some services may have to be assumed by the Province.

"The 'interim report' was never officially released. Indeed, the four task force members never met to discuss it. There is no evidence that any of them ever signed it. However, on April 3 during a pre-election debate on GTA issues sponsored by The Toronto Star, Mike Harris stated that, 'Last Thursday, the chair, Joyce Trimmer,

presented an update of their work.' Last Thursday was March 30, the date of the draft covering letter. During the debate Mr. Harris made a number of specific references to the work of the Trimmer task force.

He pointed out that the task force concluded that 'there are too many arbitrary political boundaries' and that the task force is leading to the conclusion 'That Metro regional government in its current form must go. Eliminating Metro government would result in the elimination of regional taxation. Under this option, local councils would negotiate a direct payment for their share of the costs of regional services. This may very well lead to the complete elimination of an entire level of government.'

"Although it was far from clear in this debate exactly what structural arrangements Mr. Harris did favour, three points were readily apparent: he supported the findings of the Trimmer task force (which, in any event, were drafted in his own office); there was no hint of a megacity, and the Metro level of government was being targeted for elimination."[4]

Why then did he change his mind?

That question has baffled a great many including those who share Mr. Harris's right of centre conservative philosophy. It is particularly difficult to understand when one considers that in 1986 British Prime Minister Margaret Thatcher, a fellow right of centre conservative, rather than amalgamating the 33 local London municipalities abolished the Greater London Council (a rough equivalent of Metro Toronto council) transferring most of its responsibilities to the local London municipalities.[5] A similar approach was advocated by the four GTA Mayors and later just prior to the introduction of Bill 103 in the Ontario Legislature by the six Metro Mayors as well. Bearing in mind what Mrs. Thatcher had done, one can understand why the Mayors would also be

---

4.   Andrew Sancton, Merger Mania: The Assault on Local Government (McGill-Queen's University Press, 2000)
5.   Ben Pimlott and Nirmala Rao, Governing London (Oxford University Press, 2002)

baffled by Mr. Harris's decision. Ronald Reagan as the Governor of California before becoming President of the United States also rejected the idea of municipal amalgamations in California because as a right of centre conservative he was opposed to big government.[6]

Some say the bureaucrats in the Ministry of Municipal Affairs got out their wish list of items that had been on the shelf for at least five years and used them to convince the new Minister of Municipal Affairs Al Leach. That was the view Professor Emeritus of York University Harvey Swartz who writing in the February 2010 issue of Policy Options said: "Mergers are based on the view that senior levels of government and its civil servants know what is best for residents.

"No," says Al Leach, most emphatically. "There were no plans on the shelf when I took office."[7] His Deputy Minister Dan Burns confirms those words.[8]

Mike Harris told me that, "If there were such plans, I didn't know about them."[9]

Others say it was inevitable that the Harris government would reject positions taken by the NDP-appointed Golden Task Force. Again, Al Leach says, "No, I like Anne Golden having worked with her a lot in the past." [10] The Golden report was not rejected because it was a NDP report, Mike Harris told me, but rather because it was a "huge bite" and Hazel McCallion didn't want Toronto to dominate a Greater Toronto Area Council as recommended by Golden.[11] William Walker writing in the Toronto Star on December 21, 1996, said that an unnamed person in the Ministry of Municipal Affairs told him that Golden's plan for the GTA was rejected because, "We were concerned about creating what would be a small country, let alone a small province." [12]

---

6.   Interview with Professor Andrew Sancton, University of Western Ontario, August 22, 2012
7.   Interview with Al Leach, November 26, 2012
8.   Interview with Dan Burns, December 19, 2012
9.   Interview with Mike Harris, November 21, 2012
10. Interview with Al Leach, November 26, 2012
11. Interview with Mike Harris, November 21, 2012
12. Toronto Star, William Walker, December 21, 1996

Still others feel it must have been the premier's frustrations with city of Toronto Mayor Barbara Hall and her council after they gave their employees a paid day off work to join the labour movement's protest against his government. "That's stupid," says Mike Harris.[13] Dan Burns who met with Premier Harris, his cabinet and his "kitchen cabinet" many times says he never heard the premier talk about lefties on city council, or remark about the day of protest.[14]

According to Sean Gadon, then an assistant to Toronto Mayor Barbara Hall, the six Metro Mayors met with Premier Harris shortly after his election victory in 1995. At that meeting Harris told them that if he could he would abolish the province of Ontario itself, if that would fix the provincial fiscal problem. He then pointed out to them that the province was transferring 75 per cent of its entire annual revenues to the municipalities and others. After that meeting, Gadon told me, everyone felt there was something in the wind and "Save Our Cities" buttons began to appear at City Hall.[15]

When the Harris government came to power in 1995, the point man in charge of the Metro and the GTA files was the new Minister of Municipal Affairs and Housing Al Leach. Al Leach was 60 years of age when he agreed to run for the Ontario Legislature. "I told Mike," he said, "I would only do it for one term so if he had any dirty jobs I would take them on."[16] Leach asked for it. He got it and he knows it.

Clearly, the municipal politicians in and around Metro wanted their system of government changed. Metro council had asked the province for it in 1994. Toronto city council had asked for it by holding a plebiscite on the question: "Are you in favour of eliminating the Metro level of government?" The Golden Task Force had recommended changes. The four GTA Mayors had recommended changes. The Burnham Review Panel had recommended changes. Etobicoke Mayor Doug Holyday,

---

13. Interview with Mike Harris, November 21, 2012
14. Interview with Dan Burns, December 19, 2012
15. Interview with Sean Gadon, December 19, 2012
16. Interview with Al Leach, November 26, 2012

addressing the legislative committee studying the amalgamation Bill said: "We all know the status quo isn't acceptable."[17] In the light of this built up momentum the status quo must have appeared to the government to definitively be unacceptable. Changes had to be made, but what?

In 1991, Dan Burns who had been the city of Toronto Commissioner of Housing was recruited by NDP Premier Bob Rae to join the provincial government as the Deputy Minister of Municipal Affairs and Housing. Despite the fact that the housing policies of the Mike Harris government were drastically different than those of the Rae government, Burns was retained by Harris as Deputy Minister of Municipal Affairs and Housing. It was Dan Burns' job to advise his Minister Al Leach on the changes to be made in Metro and GTA government.

Burns told me that Mike Harris "had come to office on a platform of shrinking government and fewer municipal politicians". While there is no doubt the Common Sense Revolution talks about fewer provincial politicians there is no mention of fewer municipal politicians. That came later. In Harris' first year in office, according to Dan Burns, he approached government in a very methodical and organized way. Initially he looked at tax and fiscal reform. Then he looked at structural change to government. As for Metro and the GTA Burns says that the provincial civil servants and cabinet Ministers in ten different Ministries looked at every possible alternative way of restructuring municipal government.[18]

But of course it was up to the Minister Al Leach to decide what he thought was best. If for instance, he abolished Metro as recommended by the four GTA Mayors and the Burnham panel, the then current Metro services such as the police, ambulance, sewers and water would have to be unwound and returned to the six local municipalities. That would mean turning back the clock to the situation that existed before 1953. Instead of one police department, for example, there would be six. Leach says, "That did not make sense to me, nor did it make sense to me to continue

17. Douglas Holyday, Legislative Asssembly of Ontario, Standing Committee on General Government – February 13, 1997
18. Interview with Dan Burns, December 19, 2012

to have one unified set of Metro services while eliminating Metro itself." What then was the way to go if you didn't unwind existing Metro services but you were expected to make changes? Leach concluded there was only one possible way to go – Amalgamation.

As for Golden's Greater Toronto Area Council, the inter-municipal cross border board recommended by both the Four GTA Mayors and the Burnham panel seemed to Leach like a safer bet, bearing in mind the fears of creating another province and Hazel McCallion's concerns about Toronto dominating Mississauga. [19]

The premier, of course, had the absolute final decision. Al Leach and Dan Burns met privately with Premier Mike Harris to discuss all of the possible options for Metro. Leach told me that he presented all the negative arguments against each option with the exception of amalgamation. On that one, he emphasized the efficiencies as well as, the equality of services and property taxes that would follow from the creation of one big city. He also pointed out to the premier the benefit to Metro builders and developers who would then have to deal with only one set of by-laws rather than seven different ones. According to Leach the idea of getting rid of the Metro cities appealed to the premier who then asked, "Can you do that?" and later told Leach "to explore it". Both Burns and Leach were surprised at how quickly Harris appeared to have made the decision.[20]

Before the final decision was actually made, however, the premier ran it by his political advisors. They didn't like the idea. Harris told me, that Tom Long his election campaign chairman said to him: "Show me where in the 'Common Sense Revolution' it says we are going to amalgamate Toronto."

Mike Harris replied, "It says we're going to cut costs and operate more efficiently." [21]

Al Leach had several more meetings with Mike Harris on the subject. But the absolute final decision was made at a meeting arranged

---

19. Interview with Al Leach, November 26, 2012
20. Interview with Al Leach, November 26, 2012
21. Interview with Mike Harris, November 21, 2012

by the premier's office, which was held at the Albany Club on October 10, 1996. Present were the Premier Mike Harris, the Minister of Municipal Affairs Al Leach, the Minister of Health and former East York Mayor Dave Johnson, the premier's chief of staff, David Lindsay, his election campaign chairman, Tom Long, Paul Godfrey and David Crombie. According to Paul Godfrey, the premier chaired the meeting and opened it by asking: "What should we do about Toronto; leave it or reduce it to four?"

David Crombie recalls it somewhat differently. He says Mike Harris only asked about amalgamation. However, both Godfrey and Crombie agree that the premier first turned to Godfrey and said: "Paul, you always have a lot to say." According to Al Leach, Godfrey then spoke out strongly in favour of total amalgamation and dominated the discussion. Paul Godfrey told me that in arriving at his decision, the catalyst was the direct election of Metro Councillors. David Crombie then followed saying, "Paul as a former Metro Chairman I never thought I would ever hear you say that but I agree with you." The catalyst for Crombie was also the direct election of Metro Councillors. They both said it made no sense to have local municipalities with directly elected Metro Councillors. The 1988 "no brainer" may have been more democratic but by severing the connection between local councils and Metro, carefully crafted by Leslie Frost and Lorne Cumming in 1953, it had destroyed the form of municipal government admired around the world. Leach, Godfrey and Crombie all agree that there was no dissent from anyone in the room. Paul Godfrey warned the premier he would face major disagreements and to expect to hear every possible reason for not doing it because everyone likes the status quo. Neither Harris nor Leach voiced an opinion but said they wanted to digest what had been discussed. Later at lunch, David Crombie recalls Tom Long saying: "If we are going to do it, we have got to do it fast and bomb the shit out of them before they know what's happened to them." [22]

22. Interviews with Al Leach, November 26, 2012, Paul Godfrey, December 19, 2012 and January 13, 2013, David Crombie, January 9, 2013

William Walker writing in the Toronto Star on December 21, 1996, said that according to the unnamed official: "Crombie was the key. When we heard the king of neighbourhoods, the guy who grew up in Swansea, say there won't be damage to neighbourhoods then we felt pretty good about it intellectually. It just put everybody at ease." [23] For some at least, David Crombie, Paul Godfrey and Dave Johnson's support for amalgamation was not a surprise. In his 1974 book The Tiny Perfect Mayor, Jon Caufield pointed out that both Crombie and Godfrey appeared to favour uniting Metro's boroughs in the long run, into a single political unit governed by a single council.[24] After Al Leach introduced Bill 103 in the Legislature, Globe and Mail columnist Colin Vaughan reminded his readers that in 1989 then East York Mayor Dave Johnson predicted in the Globe and Mail's Toronto magazine that Metro would be amalgamated by the turn of the century and was quoted at the time as saying: "It will happen pretty quickly when it comes."[25]

Al Leach sold the idea of amalgamation to his cabinet colleagues, he told me, by emphasising how it would create efficiencies, reduce bureaucracy and equalize services in Metro. Later in October, after the decision to amalgamate was carved in stone, he met with the six Metro Mayors. Despite knowing that it would change nothing, Leach gave them the 30 days that they asked for to prepare and present him with their own recommendations. After he read their recommendations, Al Leach felt it was in his words "the dumbest report". He had a further conversation with Metro Chairman Alan Tonks, who then, in Leach's words "came on side". Later, just prior to his speech to the Metropolitan Toronto Board of Trade on December 17, 1996, Leach presented his Progressive Conservative caucus colleagues with the decision, as a fete a complete. So, they had no chance to object prior to the first reading of Bill 103 that very same day.[26]

---

23. Toronto Star, William Walker, December 21, 1996
24. Jon Caufield, The Tiny Perfect Mayor (James Lorimer & Company, Publishers, Toronto 1974)
25. The Globe & Mail, February 10, 1997, Colin Vaughan
26. Interview with Al Leach, November 26, 2012

Thus the die was cast. The provincial legislative draftsmen and women were already at work during the summer of 1996 preparing Bills to amalgamate Ottawa, Hamilton and Sudbury, so it was a short leap to add Toronto. Dan Burns pointed out to me that unlike the federal lawyers who need a cabinet minute before they will start drafting legislation their provincial counterparts start to work in anticipation of events. As a result the Toronto amalgamation Bill 103, which likely would have taken a year or more to draft in Ottawa, was ready for the Minister to present to the Legislature for first reading on December 17, 1996.[27]

We now know why Al Leach opted for amalgamation but what made Premier Mike Harris do it?

Obviously the recommendation of Al Leach and the input of Paul Godfrey and David Crombie played a huge part in Mike Harris' final decision. But when I met with him fifteen years after amalgamation, his own explanation closely followed the background information bulletin for Bill 103 (The City of Toronto Act 1997), issued by the Ministry of Municipal Affairs at the time describing the new city as a tool for the economic development of the province. Mike Harris told me that he had learned when he had made trade missions abroad that everyone knew about Canada and Toronto. He had also read what Queen's University Professor Thomas Courchene had written about city states. As a result he had concluded that: "If Toronto was to make an even greater impact on the global stage it must get bigger, but not because I believe bigger is better. We were trying to resolve problems across the province," he said. The Mike Harris "Common Sense Revolution" had promised jobs for the province. Although he didn't say it, I drew from the order of his thoughts that day the feeling that he believed that Toronto had to grow bigger and create more jobs if the province of Ontario was going to grow and create the jobs he had promised in the "Common Sense Revolution".

At this point in our meeting Harris pointed out that, "Mayor Hazel McCallion wanted her Mississauga to equal the size of Toronto. She did

27. Interview with Dan Burns, December 19, 2012

not want Toronto to dominate Mississauga." This begged the question for me at least, how do you make Toronto bigger without allowing it to dominate Mississauga. Although he never said it and may not even admit it to himself the fact that his comment came in the context of our discussion concerning amalgamation left me with the impression, rightly or wrongly that the "Hazel Factor" had played a part in his thinking not only about Golden's recommendations for a Greater Toronto Area Council but also about the Toronto amalgamation. We may never know the answer to that.

The Municipal Affairs backgrounder to Bill 103 also said that amalgamation will reduce duplication and overlap; local government will be streamlined and more efficient. Fifteen years later Mike Harris repeated that same message: "We felt there would be substantial savings provided everyone did not average up. We knew there would be resistance to change and concern for lost jobs but we felt it was the right thing to do."[28]

Mike Harris may have known there would be some resistance but apparently Al Leach never expected the amount of resistance that his amalgamation announcement actually generated. "We had the endorsement of all three dailies," he noted. "All the polling we had done indicated that a majority, in the high 60s and over 70 per cent in some cases, supported the principle."[29] Obviously, his polling did not include the November 12 Environics poll which concluded that 52 per cent of Metro residents were opposed to amalgamation while only 42 per cent were in favour.[30]

Al Leach was correct, however, that all three daily Toronto newspapers the Star, the Globe and Mail and the Sun enthusiastically cheered the announcement of amalgamation or the "megacity" as they called it. It was the newspapers dream come true. Toronto newspapers had been pushing successive provincial governments to amalgamate

28. Interview with Mike Harris, November 21, 2012
29. John Ibbitson, *Promised Land: Inside the Mike Harris Revolution* (Prentice Hall Canada Inc, 1997)
30. Globe & Mail, Michael Valpy, December 19, 1996

Toronto since the end of World War II. The government was thrilled to have their support. Patting itself on the back, the government said to itself, this is certainly the right thing to do if the newspapers are all supporting it. But now having finally gotten their way the papers were free to start attacking the government for its method of implementation, for the lack of the promised cost savings and for the provincial down loadings that followed. It was a very short honeymoon.

Former Ontario Premier Mike
Harris *(Source: Mike Harris 2014)*

Former Scarborough Mayor Joyce
Trimmer *(Source: "Al Dunlop/ GetStock.com")*

Former Ontario Minister of
Municipal Affairs and Housing
Al Leach *(Source: Allan Leach 2014)*

Paul Godfrey, former Chairman of
Metro Toronto *(Source: "Toronto Star/
GetStock.com")*

Former old Toronto Mayor David
Crombie *(Source: "Eglinton/ GetStock.com")*

GREATER TORONTO

Who'll be megacity czar?

Leader of proposed GTA needs political, managerial skills

BY ELAINE CAREY
STAFF REPORTER

Several people say David Crombie is ideal for job

"Who'll be megacity czar?" *(Source: Toronto Star December 8, 1996)*

161

The Citizen Revolt

CHAPTER 8

"For Every Action there is a Reaction."

Sir Isaac Newton   III Law of Motion

"Three hostile newspapers are more feared than 1000 bayonets"

Napoleon Bonaparte

Notwithstanding that three hostile newspapers were arrayed against them reaction was not long in coming even from some members of the Ontario Progressive Conservative party itself. When Joyce Trimmer former Mayor of Scarborough, whom Mike Harris had chosen to study reforms to the GTA, heard of Bill 103, she was quoted as saying: "Appalling and dishonest, the government is playing games that threaten to leave Metro neighbourhoods whipped to death. I have always been a Conservative supporter, but I am questioning it right now."[1] Appearing before the legislative committee reviewing Bill 103, Arthur Lofsky, a card-carrying Ontario PC member, expressed his regret for voting for the government.[2] Addressing the same committee long-time PC member and former Toronto Controller Bill Archer said, "Bill 103 ignores the principles of effective representation, access and informed discussion at the area and local levels."[3]

---

1.   Toronto Star, December 20, 1996
2.   Arthur Lofsky, Legislative Assembly of Ontario Standing Committee on General Government, February 3, 1997
3.   Bill Archer, Legislative Assembly of Ontario Standing Committee on General Government, February 3, 1997

Other opponents of amalgamation soon appeared as well. The six Metro Mayors all spoke out against it, five of them very strongly. The one exception was Etobicoke Mayor Doug Holyday who was later to become the Deputy Mayor of the megacity and still later a PC MPP. According to then East York Mayor Michael Prue, Holiday was against amalgamation but didn't want to upset his friends in the provincial government.[4] "Holyday was quite ambivalent about amalgamation," says then Toronto Mayor Barbara Hall. "He went along with the other mayors but his heart wasn't in it."[5] Following a special public meeting on November 12, 1996, attended by about 200 residents, Etobicoke council voted to oppose amalgamation. But at the same meeting, council on a motion by Councillor (later megacity Councillor) Gloria Lindsay Luby, also voted to eliminate York and East York.[6]

Many observers felt that the city of York, having lost such major industries as Kodak from its property tax base, was really in a quite precarious financial position. In spite of that, however, Mayor Frances Nunziata strongly opposed the amalgamation of any of the six Metro municipalities, especially, of course, her own city of York. But, her council had other ideas. Megacity Councillor, Joe Mihevic, formerly a York Councillor, told me that he did not support either amalgamation or the status quo. While he thought that the four-city model was best he "did not want to declare war on East York".[7] With that in mind, York council voted five to four to support Mihevc's motion to oppose the megacity and support a Metro or GTA level of government while at the same time authorizing York to engage in merge discussions with what was then the old city of Toronto. The Mayor, later the speaker of the megacity council, voted against any such merger discussions.[8]

Initially, North York Mayor Mel Lastman, who later became the first Mayor of the megacity, appeared to be strongly opposed to amalgamation and to the elimination of any of the six Metro municipalities but former

---

4.   Interview with Michael Prue, December 4, 2012
5.   Interview with Barbara Hall, January 21, 2013
6.   Etobicoke Council minutes – November 12, 1996
7.   Interview with Joe Mihevc, November 20, 2012
8.   Interview with Frances Nunziata, November 7, 2012

Toronto Mayor Barbara Hall, who later opposed Lastman for Mayor of the megacity, describes his attitude this way: "At times Mel was strongly supportive in his opposition to amalgamation and other times he was less engaged."[9] However, Mel Lastman, and Councillors John Filion and George Mammoliti were the only members of North York Council to vote against a council resolution supporting the concept of four rather than six Metro municipalities. At the same meeting a majority of North York Councillors voted to discuss a merger with East York.[10] John Filion, a North York Councillor at the time who later also became a megacity Councillor, told me that he felt the provincial government might have agreed to retain four Metro municipalities, and while personally he might have agreed to a Toronto and York merger, he "couldn't do that to East York".[11]

According to Brad Duguid, then a Scarborough Councillor later a provincial Liberal cabinet Minister, the battle against amalgamation was Scarborough Mayor Frank Faubert's "fight of his life". "Frank lived for Scarborough," Duguid told me. "Amalgamation broke his heart." Duguid feels that the stress and disappointment of the battle contributed to Faubert's early death from cancer. Frank Faubert was "a personal casualty of amalgamation", says Brad Duguid.[12] Led by their Mayor, Scarborough Council voted to oppose amalgamation but supported four rather than six Metro municipalities with York and East York as the odd men out. At the same meeting, Scarborough council also voted to discuss a merger with East York.[13]

There was a general impression round about, that East York was in the same questionable financial situation as that of the city of York. "Not so," says former East York Mayor Michael Prue later a megacity Councillor and still later a provincial New Democratic Party MPP. "At the time of amalgamation, he told me, East York was financially sound."

9. Interview with Barbara Hall, January 21, 2013
10. North York Council minutes, November 12, 1996
11. Interview with John Filion, November 16, 2012
12. Interview with Brad Duguid, November 2, 2012
13. Scarborough Council minutes, December 10, 1996

Its once empty factories rewired with fibre optics had attracted high tech businesses. The municipal administration had been re-engineered. Garbage collection had been put out to tender with private contractors and municipal union staff competing for the job. There were new aerial fire trucks: "The best in Metro," Prue says. And on top of all that East York was virtually debt free with its own reserve funds. No wonder, the residents, the council and the Mayor of East York were vehemently opposed to amalgamation as well as to a merger with North York, Scarborough, Toronto or anyone else. Michael Prue still wears an East York pin in his lapel every day. [14]

For years and years Toronto City Council had been urging amalgamation but now in 1996, it was strongly opposed to the idea. Council had arrived at its new position via an interesting route. In 1992 it had voted to seek provincial legislation to permit the city of Toronto to secede from the Municipality of Metropolitan Toronto.[15] Then prior to the 1994 municipal election, Toronto council had voted to put a question on the ballot: "Are you in favour of eliminating the Metro level of government?" A majority voted yes.[16] By 1995, Toronto City Council wanted either to secede from Metro or to dissolve Metro altogether.[17] But on November 4, 1996, they voted against amalgamation and for stronger local government within Metro.[18]

The same day Bill 103 received its first reading in the legislature the government enacted an Order-in-Council appointing the Board of Trustees, which was called for in the Bill. The next day the Deputy Minister of Municipal Affairs Dan Burns met with the Chief Administrative Officers of the Metro municipalities to brief them on the role to be played by the Trustees leading up to amalgamation. According to Burns the Trustees were not expected to intervene in the affairs of the

14. Interview with Michael Prue, December 4, 2012
15. Toronto City Council minutes, October 27, 1992
16. Toronto City Council minutes, December 6, 1994
17. Toronto City Council minutes, March 31,1995
18. Toronto City Council minutes, November 4,1996

municipalities except to insure financial prudence. However, the Trustees would require each municipality to submit monthly financial reports to them for their approval even though they had been already approved by a council itself. In addition, no collective agreements were to be signed and no purchases or sales over $50,000.00 were to be made without the prior approval of the Trustees.[19] The Metro municipalities interpreted this to mean that the Board of Trustees was intended to replace the elected councils even prior to amalgamation taking effect. Perhaps with tongue in cheek, North York council reacted to this by passing a resolution requesting the provincial government to appoint a similar Board of Trustees to approve all provincial election campaign promises.[20] In hindsight based on what has happened in subsequent provincial election campaigns that would have been a very good idea. Scarborough council, however, was enraged and took the province to Court, whereupon the Honourable Mr. Justice Lloyd Brennan struck down the Trustee appointments because they had been made under the authority of a Bill not as yet enacted into law.[21]

Former Toronto Mayor John Sewell led the Toronto city residents' attack against amalgamation. Under his guidance a seventeen member volunteer steering committee calling itself the Citizens for Local Democracy (C4LD) organized and co-ordinated regular Monday night meetings every week from December 1996 to February 1997 under the slogan of "Restore Local Democracy to Toronto". Initially these meetings were attended by about 300 people, but by January and February they were drawing crowds of nearly 2,000. The key C4LD organizer was Kathleen Wynne, then a school board Trustee, later a provincial Liberal cabinet Minister and still later the Liberal premier of Ontario. She chaired most of the meetings that were held to share information, distribute the 26 newsletters published by C4LD, hand out lawn signs and listen to fiery speeches from well- known opponents of amalgamation such as Jane

19. Scarborough Council minutes, December 23, 1996
20. North York Council minutes, January 22, 1997
21. Globe & Mail, February 26, 1997

Jacobs, Margaret Attwood, John Ralston Saul, Michael Ondaatje, Liberal MPP Mike Colle and John Sewell himself. Those in attendance were urged to write letters asking for the opportunity to address the legislative committee, which would be studying and hopefully proposing amendments to Bill 103 before it was sent back to the Legislative Assembly for enactment into law. About 1,200 of these letters were delivered to the committee.[22] Toronto City Council hired consultants to prepare reports opposing amalgamation and provided some funding to help the Citizens for Local Democracy with their out of pocket expenses.[23] In addition to this money given it by the City council, C4LD received private donations in support of its efforts totalling $58,083.31.[24]

Besides the weekly C4LD meetings a great many other community organizations held meetings on their own. Sometimes as many as nine in one evening, to hear Mayor Barbara Hall and a host of other city councillors denouncing amalgamation.[25]

In mid-February, while the legislative committee was holding its hearings the C4LD sponsored a march down Yonge Street to re-enact the famous march during the Upper Canada Rebellion of 1837 led by William Lyon MacKenzie. Almost 9,000 took part in the 1997 version of that famous march to protest amalgamation.[26]

There were anti-amalgamation meetings held in the five other Metro municipalities as well. In early January 1997 the borough of East York Communications Director invited some 30 residents to a meeting in the cafeteria of the East York Civic Centre. Team East York was born that evening. Colin MacLeod was chosen as Chair to lead the team and the fight. Later I was appointed Honorary Chairman and former Mayor Willis Blair was appointed Honorary Treasurer of Team East York. Colin MacLeod together with a large dedicated group of East York volunteers rented an office staffed full time by at least five or six volunteers; held

22. Interview with John Sewell, January 14, 2013
23. Tony O'Donohue, Front Row Centre (Abbeyfield Publishers, Toronto 2001)
24. City of Toronto Archives, John Sewell Boxes 223380-3
25 City of Toronto Archives, John Sewell Boxes 223380-3
26. Interview with Kathleen Wynne, August 10, 2012

public planning meetings at the S. Walter Stewart Library every Monday night; organized a door to door canvas of residents; supervised the erection of lawn signs reading "Vote No to the Megacity" and initiated a yellow ribbon campaign which was later adopted by the C4LD and soon spread right across Metro.[27] They also organized a number of mass meetings including one at East York Collegiate where Jack Christie the long-time Chairman of East York Hydro publically ripped up his Ontario Progressive Conservative membership card.[28] East York Council offered start-up funds to anyone who wanted to organize either in support or in opposition to amalgamation. No one who supported amalgamation ever took up the offer even though Mayor Prue spoke to a number of them personally about it.[29] Team East York borrowed $4,000.00 but soon paid it back in full from public donations which included the entire reserve fund of the East York Federation of Taxpayers.[30]

The Save Our Scarborough (SOS) campaign was led by Mayor Frank Faubert himself. He was both the face and the voice of Scarborough in its fight against amalgamation. The local, very tenacious, opposition was led by Scarborough Progressive Conservative MPP Steve Gilchrist, the Parliamentary Assistant to Al Leach, the Minister of Municipal Affairs. The Mayor had a number of public debates with Gilchrist and with Scarborough Metro Councillor Norm Kelly, later a megacity Councillor and still later the Deputy Mayor of the megacity, who was another amalgamation supporter. The SOS committee, organized by Scarborough council, arranged meetings and distributed lawn signs.[31] Alan Carter the President of the Curran Hall Community Association at the time told me that although he had a "No to the Megacity" sign on his lawn, his Association didn't get involved as a group but left it up to individuals to participate in the council led anti-amalgamation campaign.[32]

---

27. Interview with Colin MacLeod, January 7, 2013
28. Interview with Michael Prue, December 4, 2012
29. Interview with Michael Prue, December 4, 2012
30. Interview with Colin MacLeod, January 7, 2013
31. Interview with Brad Duguid, November 2, 2012
32. Interview with Alan Carter, November 6, 2012

During the fall of 1996, but before Al Leach made his amalgamation announcement, North York Mayor Mel Lastman called Paul Godfrey to inquire if there was any truth to the rumours going around about amalgamation. "Mel you have a chance to become the Mayor of Toronto," Godfrey replied.[33] That might explain why former North York Councillor Denzil Minnan-Wong, later a megacity Councillor, said, "Mel played both sides of the street."[34] When I asked Minnan-Wong, who had led the North York grass roots attack against amalgamation, he referred me to former North York Councillor John Filion, a Megacity Councillor.[35] According to Filion, Mel Lastman went to Florida in the middle of the campaign so he, John Filion, with the help of 25 volunteers formed the nucleus of North York's citizen movement against Bill 103. To this day John Filion's office wall at Toronto City Hall is decorated with a vast display of anti-megacity buttons.[36] George Teighman, a former North York planner, organized another anti-amalgamation group called the "North York Taxpayers against the Megacity". It sponsored an anti-amalgamation meeting in the Council chambers attended by over 400 North York residents.[37] When the Mayor returned from Florida, rumours were flying that he had changed sides or in the words of John Filion, that "he had gone over to the dark side". But, notwithstanding the rumours, Filion persuaded the Mayor to attend a huge rally in Mel Lastman Square. When he saw the size of the crowd and read its mood Lastman became fired up.[38] "We're being carved up like a turkey and it's not even Thanksgiving," he told the cheering crowd. "You've got to vote no." [39]

Although the city of York council had voted against amalgamation, it had also agreed to begin merger talks with the "old city of Toronto" as Councillor Joe Mihevc refers to it. Mihevc, now a Megacity Councillor,

33. Interview with Paul Godfrey, December 19, 2012
34. Interview with Denzil Minnan-Wong, November 6, 2012
35. Interview with John Filion, November 16, 2012
36. George Teighman, Legislative Assembly of Ontario, Standing Committee on General Government, February 5, 1997
37. Interview with John Filion, November 16, 2012
38. Interview with John Filion, November 16, 2012
39. New York Times International, March 4, 1997

describes the attitude of York residents towards amalgamation as split east and west of Keele Street. West of Keele and in the former town of Weston there was a firmer commitment to "old York". Councillor Mike McDonald organized meetings there and co-ordinated with John Sewell's C4LD.[40] In the east end, Joe Mihevc said, there was not the same sense of pride but rather "a feeling that it was time to call it a day". Long-time east end resident and former President of the Cedarvale Community Association, Barbara Buckspan told me it was hard to drum up interest in anything there except for traffic and stop sign.[41] Irene Pagbel, a long-time resident of Cafon Court in Etobicoke was quoted in the Etobicoke Guardian as saying, "Almost all (residents of Cafon Court) are against it (Bill 103). Why change?"[42] While that appeared to be the commonly held point of view in Etobicoke, there was little leadership on the issue pro or con from Etobicoke council. So Etobicoke residents such as Janice Etter and Rhona Swarbuck went to the city of Toronto to help John Sewell's C4LD deliver their newsletters.[43] On two separate occasions Etobicoke Councillor Irene Jones invited East York Mayor Michael Prue to address meetings in her ward. Prue says, he "sensed frustration" on the part of the Etobicoke residents to whom he spoke. "They felt alone," he said, "lacking in leadership." [44]

Why were there not more members of councils publically involved for or against amalgamation? Perhaps as Jo Waterhouse, then an Executive Assistant to Scarborough Councillor Fred Johnson told me, "We were too busy preparing for the next election, which would come later that year whether or not there was an amalgamation."[45] Perhaps as Martin Horak of the University of Toronto has written: "One informant, who was an organizer with a suburban anti-amalgamation group, even pointed out that 'when I talk to people around here, the first thing I had

---

40. Interview with Joe Mihevc, November 20, 2012
41. Interview with Barbara Buckspan, December 19, 2012
42. Etobicoke Guardian, April 9, 1997
43. Interview with John Sewell, January 14, 2013
44. Interview with Michael Prue, December 4, 2012
45. Interview with Jo Waterhouse, November 10, 2012

to mention was that our group had nothing to do with John Sewell and Citizens for Local Democracy. They're seen as downtown lefties by most people in this area.'"[46] Perhaps like Mayor Doug Holyday they didn't want to offend friends at Queen's Park. Perhaps unlike Metro Councillor Norm Kelly they did not speak out in favour of amalgamation because they were intimidated by the strong anti- sentiments of their constituents. Or perhaps it was the fear of being accused of just trying to protect their own jobs, an accusation frequently made by the provincial government.[47]

All six metro area municipal councils agreed to hold local referendums on March 3, 1997, asking the question: "Are you in favour of eliminating your local municipality and the other existing municipalities in Metro Toronto and amalgamating them into a Megacity?" Getting approval for the referendum in Etobicoke was a close call, however. Only after Bob Gullins President of the Etobicoke Federation of Ratepayers and Residents Associations came out in support of a referendum did council vote seven to six in favour with Mayor Doug Holyday voting against it.[48] The municipalities called this vote a binding referendum. The Ontario government called it a non-binding plebiscite. Whatever it was called, huge numbers of Metro residents voted against amalgamation. Toronto, East York and York mailed out the ballots asking that they be sent back.[49] In Etobicoke residents were asked to come to the polls [50] while North York conducted a phone-in vote, the first of its kind in Ontario.[51] The average vote against amalgamation was 75.6 per cent. In East York its 81 per cent vote against was the highest within Metropolitan Toronto while Etobicoke's 70 per cent was the lowest. In

46. Martin Horak, The Power of Local Identity: C4LD and the Anti-Amalgamation Mobilisation in Toronto Research Paper 195, Centre for Unborn & Community Studies, University of Toronto, 1998
47. George Teighman, Legislative Assembly of Ontario, Standing Committee on General Government, February 5, 1997
48. Etobicoke Council minutes, January 7, 1997
49. John Ibbitson, Promised Land: Inside the Mike Harris Revolution (Prentice Hall Canada Inc, 1997)
50. Etobicoke Council minutes
51. Interview with North York Municipal Clerk Dennis Kelly, November 13, 2012

Scarborough, which distributed its ballots in a newspaper, there was only a 17 per cent response [52] but for Metro as a whole the response was 36 per cent better than the turnout at a typical municipal election. Over 3,500 people jammed Massey Hall on March 6 to learn the results of the vote which were:

	Yes	**%**	**No**	**%**
Toronto	43,759	26.5	121,475	73.5
York	12,892	34.7	24,213	65.3
East York	5,879	18.5	25,930	81.5
North York	31,433	20.6	121,475	79.4
Etobicoke	13,243	30.3	30,472	69.7
Scarborough	16,242	21.9	58,092	78.1
Total	123,448	24.4	381,657	75.6 [53]

Appearing at the legislative committee hearings just prior to the referendum/plebiscite "The Toronto Raging Grannies" surely must have upset government MPPs when they sang:

> *"Mr. Harris! Give us a break!*
>
> *Won't you admit now you've made a mistake?*
>
> *Megacity, oh, what a mess*
>
> *You will create here and so much distress.*
>
> *Destroying the province along with the city,*
>
> *No use in future to say what a pity!*
>
> *Mr. Harris! Give us a break!*
>
> *Won't you admit now you've made a mistake?"* [54]

52. John Ibbitson, Promised Land: Inside the Mike Harris Revolution (Prentice Hall Canada Inc., 1997)
53. Globe & Mail, March 7, 1997
54. The Toronto Raging Grannies, Legislative Assembly of Ontario, Standing Committee on General Government, February 6, 1997

But neither the Metro residents' votes nor the 550 out of 590 disputants who spoke against Bill 103 at the legislative committee [55] nor the rumoured opposition of the PC Metro MPPs swayed the Ontario government.[56] Why was that? According to John Ibbitson "… the mass mobilization may have hardened the government's resolve rather than give in to what it perceived as the predominantly 'leftist' opposition."[57] Besides, the Toronto newspapers and Minister Leach all said that most people supported amalgamation notwithstanding the vote and the disputants. Thus, Bill 103 and with it total amalgamation of metropolitan Toronto became law on April 21, 1997.[58]

The next day, as a last desperate measure, three legal challenges were launched against The City of Toronto Act 1997 (formerly Bill 103) on the basis that amalgamation was contrary to the Canadian Charter of Rights and Freedoms. The first was brought by 125 individuals incorporated as the Citizens' Legal Challenge Inc. (CLC). The second was initiated by the city of Scarborough together with Scarborough resident Alan Carter who told me he was joined as a party by the city's lawyers as a precaution to insure their Application had status before the court. Before he agreed to become a party to the proceeding Mr. Carter insisted on a written indemnification agreement with Scarborough in the event that court costs were awarded against him personally. [59] The third Application was brought by East York, York, Toronto and Etobicoke. Once again Etobicoke's participation was a close call with Mayor Holyday voting against it. [60] North York Council refused to get involved with the Application but instead, petitioned the Governor General of Canada asking him to disallow the legislation under the provisions of section 56 of the British North America Act of 1867 (now known as the

55. Legislative Assembly of Ontario, Standing Committee on General Government hearings of Bill 103, 1997
56. Toronto Sun, April 16, 1997
57. John Ibbitson, Promised Land: Inside the Mike Harris Revolution (Prentice Hall Canada Inc, 1997)
58. City of Toronto Act, Statutes of Ontario 1997
59. Interview with Alan Carter, November 6, 2012
60. Etobicoke Council minutes – April 28, 1997

Constitution Act 1982).[61] The court case was argued before the Honourable Mr. Justice Stephen Borins in the Ontario Divisional Court, who criticized the government for failing to conduct the type of public consultation, which should have preceded the introduction of the legislation and for displaying "mega chutzpah" in proceeding as it did, and in believing that the inhabitants of Metro Toronto would submit to the imposition of the Megacity without being given an opportunity to have a real say in how they were to live and be governed, but he concluded, "The charter does not guarantee an individual right to live his or her life free from government chutzpah or imperiousness." An appeal of that decision was dismissed by the Ontario Court of Appeal and The Supreme Court of Canada refused to hear a further appeal.

The Council of Europe is on record as opposing forced amalgamations. The European Charter of Local Self Government states that boundary changes are not to be made without prior consultation, possibly by way of a referendum.[62] The Canadian Federation of Municipalities has also made it clear that it "supports the rights of citizens to decide on the form and structure of their own municipal government" [63]

Eight years later as reported in the Toronto Star, Guy Giorno, a former Chief of Staff to Premier Mike Harris and subsequently the Chief of Staff to Prime Minister Stephen Harper speaking at Ryerson University in Toronto, described the Toronto amalgamation as both bad public policy and bad politics:

"It is bad public policy because, far from producing more efficient administration, it actually drives up costs. And it is bad politics at least for a Tory government because it alienates small – conservative voters."

61. North York Council minutes – May 28, 1997
62. Council of Europe, European Charter of Local Self-Government European treaty series No. 122, Strasbourg, Le Conseil, Section des publications, 1985
63. Henry Aubin, A European model to emulate, Montreal Gazette, July 4, 2001

While the Toronto amalgamation was being debated inside the government Giorno argued against it: "Mine was, however, a minority view," he said. He outlined several factors that drove the Toronto amalgamation agenda inside the government including:

- "It was an elite priority," Giorno cited the following voices in support of amalgamation: John Honderich, then publisher of this newspaper and now an adviser to Mayor David Miller, Paul Godfrey, then head of Sun Media and now president of the Toronto Blue Jays, (which he was at that time) former mayor David Crombie and the Toronto Board of Trade.
- While amalgamation was not part of the platform the Conservatives ran on in 1995, the arguments for it – "efficiency and savings" – meshed neatly with the government's publicly stated values. It also seemed to resonate with the government's downloading agenda – "a way to help local governments do better with less".
- There was an internal political champion for amalgamation: Al Leach, minister of municipal affairs. "He believed strongly in the merits of amalgamation. He was tenacious and he was fearless." His bureaucrats were also in favour of the move.
- The proponents of amalgamation managed to convince everyone that the status quo was not an option. "It was a masterful strategy because it took doing nothing off the table. But in fact, doing nothing … was a perfectly viable alternative." [64]

Were the Toronto newspapers and Al Leach correct that the majority of those within metropolitan Toronto supported amalgamation? Referring to a poll conducted for the Toronto Star/CTV prior to the 1999 provincial election following amalgamation, Frank Graves, the President of Ekos polling said: "Amalgamation is a non-issue in this campaign." [65] While it may very well have been a non-issue, Toronto MPPs Al Leach, the

64. Toronto Star, Ian Urquhart, April 11, 2005
65. Toronto Star, May 9, 1999

Minister of Municipal Affairs, Charles Harnick, the Attorney General, and Bill Saunderson, the Minister of Economic Development, chose not to run for re-election in 1999.[66] When the Harris government took office after the 1995 election, there were 30 provincial ridings in what was then the Municipality of Metropolitan Toronto. As a cost cutting measure prior to the next election in 1999, the Mike Harris government reduced the number of provincial ridings in the Megacity from 30 to 22.[67] Toronto cabinet Ministers Dave Johnson and Isabel Bassett were defeated in the 1999 election as were twelve other PCs in Toronto ridings.[68] In 1995 the Harris PCs elected a majority of sixteen MPPs in the 30 Toronto ridings. [69] In 1999 they elected only eight in the 22 Toronto ridings. [70] In the subsequent elections of 2003, 2007 and 2011, the PCs were wiped out and unable to elect any members in any Megacity riding.[71] It was not until a 2013 by-election that the Ontario PCs successfully elected a MPP in a Megacity riding.

At the farewell dinner for Metro Chairman Alan Tonks and for that matter a farewell for the Municipality of Metropolitan Toronto itself, Paul Godfrey, who had personally strongly recommended the total amalgamation of Toronto to Premier Mike Harris, called Metro a major experiment saying: "Most people who view government will conclude it was a huge success."[72] Amen!

Why did it happen? Although we blame Mike Harris, the truth is that many of us either actively or passively share the responsibility for amalgamation. Leslie Frost and Lorne Cumming created a unique form of government that was admired around the world. But we weren't satisfied with a good thing in its original form. We wanted change. At first we merged the thirteen municipalities into six. Then we broke the

---

66. Ontario Legislative Assembly Parliamentary History www.ontla.on.ca/web/members
67. Ontario Legislative Assembly Parliamentary History www.ontla.on.ca/web/members
68. Ontario Legislative Assembly Parliamentary History www.ontla.on.ca/web/members
69. Ontario Legislative Assembly Parliamentary History www.ontla.on.ca/web/members
70. Ontario Legislative Assembly Parliamentary History www.ontla.on.ca/web/members
71. Ontario Legislative Assembly Parliamentary History www.ontla.on.ca/web/members
72. Toronto Sun, December 10, 1997

strong local connection with the direct election of Metro Councillors. Next we advocated doing away with the Metro level of government altogether and replacing it with something a kin to a 1840s Ontario County Council. Finally we rejected a locally controlled GTA regional government. Only at the last minute faced with total amalgamation, something the old city of Toronto had advocated for years did we vote against the Megacity. But what did we really want in place of the Megacity? The fact is we were all over the map. So Premier Mike Harris made a decision just as Premier Leslie Frost did when the thirteen municipalities couldn't agree on what they wanted to do in 1953. A wise man once said: "In the end we get the government we deserve."

Former Etobicoke Mayor later
Toronto Megacity Deputy-Mayor
later provincial Progressive
Conservative MPP Doug Holiday
*(Source: 1994 election brochure from the Toronto
Reference Library)*

Former Etobicoke Mayor later Toronto Megacity Deputy- Mayor later
provincial Progressive Conservative MPP Doug Holyday (on the left)
with provincial Progressive Conservative leader Tim Hudak (on the right)
(Source: "Colin McConnell/ GetStock.com")

York Mayor later Toronto Megacity Deputy-Mayor
Frances Nunziata *(Source: "Toronto Star/ GetStock.com")*

Old Toronto Mayor Barbara Hall (on the left) with old Toronto
Councillor Kay Gardiner (on the right) *(Source: "Toronto Star/ GetStock.com")*

East York Mayor later Toronto Megacity Councillor and later provincial New Democratic Party MPP Michael Prue *(Source: "Toronto Star/ GetStock.com")*

Former old Toronto Mayor John Sewell *(Source: "Toronto Star/ GetStock.com")*

Kathleen Wynne former Metro Toronto
school Trustee later Ontario Liberal Party
Premier of Ontario *(Source: 2000 election brochure
in the Toronto Reference Library)*

Disentanglement AKA Off Loading

But known to us as Downloading

CHAPTER 9

"Bill 103 (City of Toronto Act 1997) will lead to efficiencies that will offer the City's 2.3 million residents lower property tax rates."

Hon. Dave Johnson MPP Don Mills
Government House Leader January 1997[1]

Toronto's credit rating reduced from AAA to AA because of pressures that provincial downloading of services has put on the municipal tax base.

Dominion Bond Rating Agency
December 1998 [2]

"Amalgamation has been a disaster."

Toronto Mayor Mel Lastman
January 2001 [3]

Hard on the heels of amalgamation came down loading. What was it that drove the provincial government to download?

One of the key reasons dates back to the federal governments' spending in the 1970s, 1980s and early 1990s. When the governments of

---

1. Globe & Mail, Martin Mittelstaedt, January 30, 1997
2. National Post, Don Wanagas, December 29, 1998
3. Toronto Star, Jim Coyle, January 11, 2001

Prime Ministers Pierre Elliott Trudeau and John Turner left office in 1984 the federal government faced a $38.5 billion annual budget deficit with a national debt of almost $200 billion.[4] When the governments of Prime Ministers Brian Mulroney and Kim Campbell left office over nine years later in 1993 the annual deficit was $38 billion while the national debt had reached $557 billion. Interest payments alone on the national debt totalled $39 billion in the 1993, $1 billion more than the entire annual federal deficit.[5] By the end of 1994 Prime Minister Jean Chretien's first year in office the national debt had risen to $596 billion. [6]

In December 1994 the Mexican peso collapsed as the result of massive government debt. [7] On January 12, 1995, the Wall Street Journal headline read: Bankrupt Canada?

> *"Turn around and check out Canada, which has now become an honorary member of the Third World in the unmanageability of its debt problem. If dramatic action isn't taken in next month's federal budget, it's not inconceivable that Canada could hit the debt wall … it has lost its triple-A credit rating and can't assume that lenders will be willing to refinance its growing debt."* [8]

Our federal government reacted to this with the now famous 1995 Paul Martin budget. The Minister of Finance Paul Martin referred to this in his budget speech as restructuring when he announced: "The debt and deficit are not inventions of ideology. They are facts of arithmetic. The quicksand of compound interest is real. The last thing Canadians need is another lecture on the dangers of the deficit. The only thing Canadians want is clear action." [9]

---

4.   Janice McKinnon, Minding the Public Purse (McGill-Queen's University Press, 2003)
5.   Brian Lee Crowley, Jason Clemens, Niels Veldhuis, The Canadian Century moving out of America's shadow (The Macdonald-Laurier Institute, 2010)
6.   Brian Lee Crowley, Jason Clemens, Niels Veldhuis, The Canadian Century moving out of America's shadow (The Macdonald-Laurier Institute, 2010)
7.   Wall Street Journal editorial January 12, 1995
8.   Wall Street Journal editorial January 12, 1995
9.   House of Commons Debates – Budget Speech 1995

That Martin budget, which now receives universal credit for Canada escaping the worst of the 2008 recession, not only slashed federal government departmental expenditures but unilaterally without consultation froze social housing subsidies and reduced federal transfer payments to the provinces for healthcare, post-secondary education and welfare assistance by $7 billion.[10] At the time Ontario Premier Bob Rae said: "It marks the end of Canada as we know it."[11] Although these changes were announced in the 1995 federal budget they did not take effect until 1996–1997. [12]

When Bob Rae's government was defeated in 1995, Ontario had an $11 billion annual deficit and a provincial debt of $49 billion.[13] Mike Harris when he succeeded Rae as premier was aware of those facts. He was also aware that federal government's down loading was about to take affect when during his successful election campaign, he promised to balance the provincial budget, cut taxes to stimulate employment and redistribute provincial and municipal government responsibilities and funding.[14]

In response to long standing complaints from the people of Ontario that the province rather than municipalities should pay the costs of education and welfare, the Rae government had begun but not finished a process of redistributing provincial and municipal responsibilities on the basis of revenue neutrality. No doubt this prompted Mike Harris' own promise to redistribute provincial and municipal responsibilities and subsequently to appoint David Crombie's "Who Does What" Panel.

10. Janice McKinnon, Minding the Public Purse (McGill-Queen's University Press, 2003)

11. Janice McKinnon, Minding the Public Purse (McGill-Queen's University Press, 2003)

12. Brian Lee Crowley, Jason Clemens, Niels Veldhuis, The Canadian Century moving out of America's shadow (The Macdonald-Laurier Institute, 2010)

13. Janice McKinnon, Minding the Public Purse (McGill-Queen's University Press, 2003); Brian Lee Crowley, Jason Clemens, Niels Veldhuis, The Canadian Century moving out of America's shadow (The Macdonald-Laurier Institute, 2010)

14. The Common Sense Revolution, the Ontario Progressive Conservative Party 1995 election platform

In his final "Who Does What" reporting letter to the Minister of Municipal Affairs, David Crombie wrote:

The review was undertaken using the same four principles which guided our work throughout:

1. Municipal government, in keeping with its historic function, should have a strong role in "hard services", such as services to property and community infrastructure ... the province should have a strong role in the provision of "soft services", such as health, welfare and education.

2. Government programs primarily aimed at income redistribution should be funded by the province.overnment programs primarily aimed at income redistribution should be funded by the Province.

3. Where possible, only one level of government should be responsible for spending decisions, and the level of government making the spending decisions should have the responsibility for funding that service.

4. There should be an appropriate balance between the allocations of responsibilities and financial resources available to support those responsibilities. [15]

Shortly after the Bill to create the Megacity of Toronto was introduced in the legislature, the Mike Harris government unveiled its program of redistribution of responsibilities and funding which it called "Local Services Realignment".[16] This was part of what some have called "mega week". It began on January 13, 1997, when the government introduced Bill 104 the Fewer School Boards Act aimed at restructuring the provincial public school system. In Toronto the six area municipal school boards were amalgamated into one city board. Although the provincial government was now said to be responsible for funding education part of the necessary funds were still to come from the municipal real estate property taxes. Unfortunately therefore, Bill 104 failed to achieve the long standing plea of municipal taxpayers for the

---

15. Who Does What Panel final reporting letter, December 1996
16. Toronto Star – Paul Moloney, June 22, 2000

province to fund 100 per cent of education costs.[17] The Crombie "Who Does What" Panel had made the following recommendation to Minister Al Leach on the subject: Education.

> *"On September 10, 1996, you and the Minister of Education and Training asked us to provide advice on how education should be funded, and who should be responsible for curriculum and standards, staffing and human resources, school transportation and capital maintenance. Our major recommendation, contained in our letter to you and Minister Snobelen of November 13, was that the province should assume increased responsibility for funding education and that the reliance of education on the residential property tax should be substantially reduced. The Panel would like to confirm its view that the province should assume increased responsibility for funding education.*

> *"It has become clear to us, however, that the only way that the province could carry out its funding responsibilities as recommended by the Panel would be to undo much of the work accomplished by the disentangling proposals such as health and welfare back down to the property tax. The Panel strongly opposes such a move. We are unanimous in the view that if there is a choice between placing education or health and welfare on the property tax, it is clearly preferable to continue to rely on property tax for the funding of education."* [18]

Although the Crombie Panel had strongly recommended that the province not fund health and welfare from the municipal property tax, the government did just that when on January 14, it announced that the municipalities would now pay 50 per cent of all welfare costs, child care costs and hostel bed costs rather than the 20 per cent they had been paying

---

17. John Sewell, The Shape of the Suburbs: Understanding Toronto Sprawl (University of Toronto Press, 2009

18. Who Does What Panel final reporting letter, December 1996

previously. The federal government had downloaded these costs to the provinces now the Province of Ontario was downloading them to the municipalities.[19] In the field of healthcare, the province had been paying 25 per cent or ½ the cost of seniors' long-term care facilities and the entire cost of women's shelters. Both were now to be paid 100 per cent from the municipal real estate property tax.[20] Crombie's Panel had recommended that "the Province should have a strong role in the provision of soft services' such as health, welfare and education" and especially that "government programs primarily aimed at income redistribution should be funded by the province". [21]

The 1995 Paul Martin budget had reduced federal social program transfer payments to the provinces by 40 per cent and had frozen all social housing subsidies.[22] Shortly after the Mike Harris government took office it announced a moratorium on the planning and building of new social housing projects. In 1997 the province began to bill Toronto for the entire annual costs of the administration and maintenance for the 63,500 seniors and families assisted housing households located in the megacity.[23] In 2001 and 2002 the Province transferred outright ownership of these homes to the city.[24]

Since the failure of the Meech Lake Accord in 1990 and the Charlottetown Accord referendum in 1992, every federal government regardless of their political affiliation has given up all further attempts to amend the Canadian Constitution Act 1982 (formerly the British North America Act of 1867). Now, federal governments relying on section 93(13) of the Constitution which gives exclusive jurisdiction over "Property and Civil Rights", to the provinces, has taken the position that funding for social housing is the absolute exclusive responsibility of the

---

19. John Sewell, The Shape of the Suburbs: Understanding Toronto Sprawl (University of Toronto Press, 2009
20. John Sewell, The Shape of the Suburbs: Understanding Toronto Sprawl (University of Toronto Press, 2009
21. Who Does What Panel final reporting letter, December 1996
22. House of Commons Debates – Budget Speech 1995
23. City of Toronto, Social Housing – Shelter, Support and Housing Administration
24. City of Toronto, Social Housing – Shelter, Support and Housing Administration

provinces. While each of Canada's provinces and territories was the recipient of the federal government's social housing downloading only the province of Ontario has seen fit to download its social housing responsibilities to its municipal property taxpayers.[25]

The Mike Harris government asked the Crombie "Who Does What" Panel for advice on the redistribution of provincial municipal responsibilities and funding. With respect to soft services, the Panel responded: "Government programs aimed at income redistribution should be funded by the Province." [26] The government did not follow that advice.

With respect to hard services, the "Who Does What" Panel advised: "Municipal government in keeping with its historic function should play a strong role in hard services."[27] On January 15, the day after downloading soft services on the municipal property taxpayers, the provincial government apparently believing it was following the Panel's advice transferred all the costs of 8,000 kilometres of road repairs to the municipal property taxpayers, since as the province said these largely serve only local needs. In that same announcement the government ended all provincial subsidies to the municipalities for public transit, GO Transit, municipal libraries and municipal policing.[28] Although the Crombie Panel had recommended that "the province consult with the municipal sector on the development of an appropriate needs –based formula for future distribution of the Municipal Support Programs", the government proceeded with this without consulting the municipalities.[29]

The next day January 16, the province also downloaded the costs of administering the property tax assessment to the municipal property tax payers.[30] To top it all off, on January 17, the government actually

25. City of Toronto, Social Housing – Shelter, Support and Housing Administration
26. Who Does What Panel final reporting letter, December 1996
27. Who Does What Panel final reporting letter, December 1996
28. John Sewell, The Shape of the Suburbs: Understanding Toronto Sprawl (University of Toronto Press, 2009
29. John Sewell, The Shape of the Suburbs: Understanding Toronto Sprawl (University of Toronto Press, 2009
30. John Sewell, The Shape of the Suburbs: Understanding Toronto Sprawl (University of Toronto Press, 2009

reduced municipal revenues with an announcement that it would stop paying provincial grants to the municipalities and that telephone companies fees paid to municipalities in lieu of property taxes would now be paid to the province.[31]

It was quite a week! Paul Martin's 1995 federal budget had downloaded $7 billion on Canada's ten provinces and three territories. [32] According to the city of Toronto staff calculations the Ontario government had now downloaded $540 million of the province's share of the federal downloading on to the municipalities.[33]

As the Crombie Panel had pointed out, municipalities should pay for hard services such as roads, sewers, water and garbage collection, police, fire, parks and recreation from property taxes, while the federal and provincial governments should pay for soft services or social services such as welfare and assisted housing from income and sales taxes. Toronto Community and Social Services Commissioner Shirley Hoy echoed the Crombie Panel when she said: "Traditionally, senior (government) levels were involved in income redistribution programs and local levels delivered hard services. Basically, now the municipalities are involved in a significant way not just in providing hard services but also human services."[34]

Social services involve a redistribution of income from all taxpayers to low income families and individuals. Property taxes are not the appropriate taxes with which to redistribute income. To require social services to be paid for from the property tax is blatantly unfair to moderate and low income homeowners. According to statistics Canada, at the time of municipal downloading, 27.6 per cent of all of the households in the former Metropolitan Toronto were defined as low income households, 10

31. John Sewell, The Shape of the Suburbs: Understanding Toronto Sprawl (University of Toronto Press, 2009
32. Janice McKinnon, Minding the Public Purse (McGill-Queen's University Press, 2003)
33. John Sewell, The Shape of the Suburbs: Understanding Toronto Sprawl (University of Toronto Press, 2009
34. Toronto Star – Paul Moloney, June 22, 2000

per cent higher than the whole of Ontario and 8 per cent higher than the whole of Canada.[35]

All levels of government like to take credit for providing services to the people they represent. No level of government wants to be blamed for increasing taxes to their electors. When the cost of government services exceeds the capacity of the tax revenues something has to give. Governments should only institute new spending when they have the tax revenues to pay for them. In 1995 the federal government tried to balance their books by downloading responsibilities on the provinces. In 1997 the province of Ontario tried to balance its books by downloading responsibilities on the municipalities. Unfortunately, there is only one taxpayer. He or she pays all of the federal, provincial and municipal taxes whatever they may be. The Crombie Panel said: "There should be an appropriate balance between the allocation of responsibilities and financial resources."[36] That has not happened. In the words of Mississauga Mayor Hazel McCallion, "The property tax was never intended to look after humans."[37]

According to the Harris government this disentanglement was revenue neutral. But, "Combining amalgamation and downloading has produced an untenable financial situation for the new city (Toronto). The city is not financially self-sufficient." – Professor Emeritus Harvey Schwartz – York University.[38]

The State of Minnesota gives the city of Minneapolis a portion of the State's sales tax.[39] Ontario has recently given Toronto the power to tax alcohol, tobacco and entertainment; to levy a land transfer tax on purchasers of used residential properties within the city and to impose a

35. Kevin K. Lee, Urban Poverty in Canada, A Statistical Profile (Canadian Council on Social Development, Ottawa, 2000), Statistics Canada, Law Income cut off
36. Who Does What Panel final reporting letter, December 1996
37. National Post – January 26, 2012
38. Harvey Schwartz, Policy Options; Trouble in the Megacity, facing a financial crisis in 2010, February 2010
39. The Stronger City of Toronto for a Stronger Ontario Act, December 14, 2005

charge on city residents renewing their motor vehicle licenses.[40] In 2008, Liberal Premier Dalton McGuinty agreed to remove a total of $1.5 billion in social services costs related to welfare and court security costs from municipal property taxpayers across the province by "uploading" them to the provincial government over a ten-year period ending in 2018. There are no present plans to "upload" any part of social housing costs.

---

40. Toronto Star – August 25, 2011

Former Ontario Premier Mike Harris *(Source: "Steve Russell/GetStock.com")*

"Megacity" means Megatax savings?

CHAPTER 10

"I disagree with restructuring because it believes that bigger is better. Services always cost more in larger communities."

Mike Harris
Progressive Conservative third party leader 1994 [1]

The KPMG Report was used by the Ontario government, publicly at least, to justify the creation of its "Megacity". The report based its calculations on the responsibilities of Metro and its area municipalities prior to the downloading or as the government referred to it, disentanglement. According to the government disentanglement did not affect the accuracy of the KPMG Report because disentanglement was a wash. It was revenue neutral or so the government said.

If disentanglement was revenue neutral, the elimination of duplication and overlap resulting from the amalgamation of the six metro area municipalities would the government said, translate into vast cost savings and tax reductions for municipal taxpayers. After all as the Minister of Municipal Affairs Al Leach said it should be less expensive to run one fire department than to pay six fire chiefs and their support staff. But when asked where the other savings would come from the government always fell back on the KPMG Report.

The government's terms of reference for the report were:

1. Could the replacement of the present seven governments by a single, fully integrated entity produce savings?

1.   Fergus – Elora News Express – September 28, 1994

2. Are there ways in which the transition from seven entities to one could be managed so as to minimize costs and maximize future savings?
3. In what ways could the new government be established and operated, so as to maximize the savings from consolidation, while also achieving substantially greater operational efficiencies?
4. What is the range for potential net savings flowing from the creation of a new entity that removes duplication and follows basic principles of sound public sector management?

According to the author of the KPMG Report:

"We were explicitly directed not to assume a general reduction in services received by the public as a principal means by which savings are to be attained. Our instructions were to look for possible savings in government structure, service management and delivery, but to assume continuation of the present overall availability and quality of public services.

"Although it makes up about 31 per cent of the total current expenditures, we assumed no reduction in the area of family and social services.

"We believe the methodologies employed provide a reasonable estimate of the expenditure reductions and new costs that can be anticipated, keeping always in mind, that we are making estimates, the realization of which are contingent upon sound management.

"The study has a four-year time horizon: January 1, 1997 to December 31, 2000. Our assumption was that the consolidated structure would be put in place in January 1998. We estimated the cumulative savings possible by the end of the year 2000 and the new costs to be generated during this same period."[2]

Prior to amalgamation, the old city of Toronto had retained Professor Andrew Sancton of the University of Western Ontario to analyze the KPMG Report. He found:

---

2. KPMG Report, "Fresh Start: An Estimate of Potential Savings and costs from the creation of a Single-Tier Local Government for Toronto dated December 16, 1996

- Because of the disclaimers made by KPMG itself, no one can claim that the report proves or demonstrates that there are any savings resulting from amalgamation.
- Amalgamation and "the new public management" are incompatible objectives anyway. In considering the merits of amalgamation, projected potential savings from "efficiency enhancements" must be ignored.
- A new structure of municipal government is only a structure: the structure itself cannot be assumed to produce any particular set of decisions. It is the councillors who make the decisions. This is what democratic local government means.
- The numbers produced by KPMG actually demonstrate that amalgamation is not a necessary policy to reduce municipal expenditures within Metropolitan Toronto.
- Either service-levels will be reduced for some tax payers; or service levels – and costs – will be increased; or there will be area rates.
- Apparently "costs" are to be saved by abolishing the existing municipalities. Then there are to be "investments" in local service centres. Why not simply keep the relatively decentralized system that already exists (and save the transition costs)?
- Vagueness is typical of all the financial calculations relating to savings that are supposed to result directly from amalgamation.
- There is good reason for caution. The evidence does not support the case that KPMG tries unsuccessfully to advance."[3]

The borough of East York retained another large consulting and auditing firm, Deloitte Touch, to analyze the KPMG Report. Deloitte's concluded:

---

3.   Andrew Sancton, "Toronto Response to the KPMG Report, "Fresh Start: An Estimate of Potential Savings and Costs from the creation of a Single-Tier Local Government for Toronto prepared for the Board of Management of the City of Toronto 1997

"As a firm of Chartered Accountants and Consultants we have substantial experience in dealing with local governments in many capacities. We believe we have a sound understanding of political climate and the administrative issues that make up any proposed restructuring of Metro Toronto. It is clear to us at this stage that there has not been put forth any concrete evidence that would support that there are savings of up to $865 million over the first three years and $300 million annually thereafter. These amounts are taken directly from the December 17, 1996 News Release Communique from the Ministry of Municipal Affairs and Housing. We believe the media has taken these figures, somewhat out of context from the way they were originally set out in the KPMG Report, and published them in various ways. As a result, the majority of the general public is of the opinion the substantial net cost savings from amalgamation of the six geographic municipalities will be realized.

"Based on information that we have reviewed we are of the opinion that great savings have resulted and will continue to result from efficiency enhancements, no matter what reasonable format of government structure is selected. We do not believe, however, that there will be any significant savings as a direct result of the proposed amalgamation over the next five-year period."[4]

These findings are consistent with a study of the Municipality of Ottawa-Carleton done by Price Waterhouse, yet another large auditing and consulting firm, in 1992:

"The fundamental conclusion of our analysis is that bigger is not certainly more efficient, from a financial perspective. One-tier government would be an expensive proposition. In addition, the tax effects cannot be calculated with certainty because of the unknown future infrastructure rehabilitation costs."[5]

---

4. Deloitte and Touche, Letter to Glenn Kippen, Treasurer, Borough of East York, February 2, 1997
5. Price Waterhouse, "The Municipalities of Ottawa – Carleton Study of the Financial Impact of One-Tier Government in Ottawa – Carleton Final Report", August 27, 1992

What were the savings that the KPMG Report identified? They could be classified as follows:

> *"1. Moving from seven governments to one can, if properly managed, significantly lower operating expenditures through savings associated with a consolidated governance structure. The gross "consolidation savings" could be in the range of $82 to $112 million each year from 1998 onward.*[6]

In 2000, two and a half years after amalgamation, the megacity of Toronto issued a report entitled "Building the New City of Toronto". This report pointed out that the great majority of expenditures in the new city, 73 per cent in fact related to previously amalgamated services under Metropolitan Toronto including social services, police services and the Toronto Transit Commission while only 27 per cent of the expenditures related to services that were amalgamated by the government. The city report compared the actual and estimated yearly savings to those referred to in the KMPG report as follows:

Year	Megacity	KPMG
1998	$48 million	$82-$112 million
1999	$72.5 million	$82-$112 million
2000	$29.3 million	$82-$112 million

6. KPMG Report, "Fresh Start: An Estimate of Potential Savings and costs from the creation of a Single-Tier Local Government for Toronto dated December 16, 1996

The city report broke down their yearly cost savings as follows:

Year	Salary & Benefits	Non Salary	Total
1998	$43.4 million	$4.8 million	$48 million
1999	$41.3 million	$31.2 million	$72.5 million
2000	$19.3 million	$10.0 million	$29.3 million [7]

Next KPMG reported:

"2. An integrated entity offers considerably more scope for reducing operating costs within most of the service delivery sectors, through application of modern public management techniques and emulation of best practices from other jurisdictions. The annual gross "efficiency savings" could be in the order of $148 to $252 million by the year 2000.[8]

According to the City of Toronto Report, however, amalgamation produced no efficiency savings because:

"Given that the city has a high proportion of unionized staff, these types of internal cost drivers are closely tied to labour agreements. Significant shifts in internal cost drivers are therefore unlikely to occur in the near future

Council has yet to address the issue of contracting out and outsourcing with respect to a number of municipal services and council's direction with respect to this issue still has to be determined. It is, therefore, difficult to predict savings arising from this area in the short-run.

In addition to the above, it should be noted that the provincial [KPMG] study did not recognize that the seven former municipalities had realized sizeable efficiencies and made reductions in their budgets

---

7.   City of Toronto, "Building the New City of Toronto, Status Report on amalgamation, January 1998 - June 1999, Toronto 1999

8.   KPMG Report, "Fresh Start: An Estimate of Potential Savings and costs from the creation of a Single-Tier Local Government for Toronto dated December 16, 1996

in the years preceding amalgamation ...this had the effect of limiting
the potential for further efficiency savings after consolidation.

It is unlikely that the magnitude of efficiency savings estimated
in the Provincial study can be readily achieved in the short-run.[9]

Immediately following amalgamation, the Megacity changed all of the previous garbage collection routes. Was this done to achieve greater efficiency? Or was it done as Councillor Denzil Minnan-Wong believes, to ensure that it would be impossible for anyone to possibly compare unfavourably the performance of the megacity with the local garbage collections before amalgamation?[10]

Robert and his brother Mark Champion were home renovators.They know all about municipal government efficiencies. Prior to amalgamation while renovating a home in East York if they needed the water turned off at the street for a short time, they would call the East York water department. A water works employee would arrive almost immediately in a modest car, turn of the street valve, and then leave until called to return to turn the water back on again. Shortly after their East York experience, while renovating a home in the old city of Toronto, they called the city water department for the same service. Following a long wait, four city workmen arrived in a truck pulling a trailer. The men searched in vain for the shut off valve, finally they admitted to the brothers that they couldn't find it. As the brothers were showing them where the shut off valve was located, a city supervisor arrived. When the four workmen saw their supervisor coming, they quickly covered up the valve and explained to their supervisor that they couldn't find the shut off valve. After the supervisor left, they uncovered the valve and turned off the water. The brothers told the city workers that they would call when they wanted the water turned on again. But instead of driving away, the four city workmen all climbed into their enclosed tailor and stayed there until it was time to turn the water on again. However, it was a cold day so the city workers asked the brothers for some wood to heat the stove in the trailer so they could keep warm while they waited to turn the water on again.[11] Has the Megacity of Toronto now achieved the same level of efficiency demonstrated by the former Borough of East York?

The owner of a small discount gas station knows about the present Megacity efficiency. He watched, while a contractor put down several blocks of new concrete sidewalk during the course of which all of the water shut off valves were covered over with concrete. When this was pointed out to the contractor, he replied: "Don't worry, the city employees will remove the new concrete, uncover each valve and fill the hole with asphalt. Does this happen all the time?" Fortunately in this case, the gas station owner alerted his Councillor who saw to it that it was the contractor not the city tax payers who paid to uncover the valves. But where was the city inspector?[12]

KPMG's third category of savings:

"*3. The total reduced operating costs of $230 to $363 million per year in 2000 could entail a reduction in the workforce in the range of 2,500 to 4,500 relative to the 1995 full-time continuing employment level of 42,400.*[13]

The city report showed the actual staff reductions as:

Year	Staff Reduction Target	KPMG
1998	1295	
1999	486	
2000	*182*	
Total	1963	2500–4500[14]

11. Interview with Robert and Mark Champion – May 1, 2011
12. Interview with small business owner – July 11, 2012
13. KPMG Report, "Fresh Start: An Estimate of Potential Savings and costs from the creation of a Single-Tier Local Government for Toronto dated December 16, 1996
14. City of Toronto, "Building the new City of Toronto, Status Report on amalgamation, January 1998 – June 1999, Toronto 1999

KPMG's Report stated:

4. The total gross savings available during the period 1998–2000 are estimated to range from $535 to $865 million, depending on the pace of implementation.[15]

The city reported the gross savings during the period 1998–2000 as:

Year	Cumulative Amalgamation Savings	KPMG
1998	$48.2 million	
1999	107.7 million	
2000	*150.0 million*	
Total	$318.9 million	$535-$865 million[16]

KPMG said:

5. The one-time transition costs associated with creating the new entity would be in the range of $150 to $220 million, which is less than the estimated annual savings associated with implementation of the consolidation and efficiency measures.[17]

15. KPMG Report, "Fresh Start: An Estimate of Potential Savings and costs from the creation of a Single-Tier Local Government for Toronto dated December 16, 1996
16. City of Toronto, "Building the New City of Toronto, Status Report on amalgamation, January 1998 - June 1999, Toronto 1999
17. KPMG Report, "Fresh Start: An Estimate of Potential Savings and costs from the creation of a Single-Tier Local Government for Toronto dated December 16, 1996

The actual transition costs totalled $275 million.

According to the provincial government the realignment of responsibilities was to be revenue neutral. According to the city report in 1999 it was revenue neutral only because the city applied its cost savings of $120 million from amalgamation as follows:

Provincial Downloading of Programs	$ 61 million
Provincial Downloading of T.T.C. Capital Costs	$ 46 million
Other Pressures (e.g. police wage increase)	$ 13 million
Total:	$120 million[18]

To help balance the Megacity budget in 1998, the provincial government made the city of $200 million interest free repayable loan and a one-time $50 million grant.[19]

The city also reduced the level of services from those existing before amalgamation. As former East York Mayor Michael Prue pointed out: "Grass used to be cut in our parks eight to ten times each summer; now it's four to five times." Tree pruning was reduced and city attractions such as the Marine Museum were closed while its valuable artifacts were locked away in a city storage warehouse.[20] All were needed in order to help balance the budget.

In 1997 the year before amalgamation, the combined operating costs budget of Metro, old Toronto, North York, Scarborough, Etobicoke, York and East York totalled $4,595 million. After amalgamation the Megacity operating cost budget was:

---

18. City of Toronto, "Building the New City of Toronto, Status Report on amalgamation, January 1998 - June 1999, Toronto 1999
19. Julie-Anne Boudreau, Roger Keil and Douglas Young, Changing Toronto: Governing Urban Neoliberalism, (University of Toronto Press, 2009)
20. Henry Aubin, Montreal Gazette – July 6, 2001, Henry Aubin, Who's Afraid of Demergers (Vehicule Press 2004)

1998	$5,600 million
1999	$5,500 million
2000	$5,900 million [21]

Why was it that the city was unable to achieve the savings that KMPG Report had estimated? According to Premier Mike Harris in his letter to Megacity's first Mayor Mel Lastman at the time, it was, "The fact that your council chose to forgo many of those savings and to increase spending – rather than taking advantage of opportunity to reduce costs – was not a provincial decision"[22] In spite of Minister of Municipal Affairs Al Leach's assertion that it would be less expensive to run one fire department rather than six, after amalgamation the one big fire department cost thirteen per cent more than the six put together. [23] It was impossible to reduce the number of firefighters in fact the numbers were increased. An arbitrator harmonized wages at the highest rate paid to the six former municipalities and all firefighters were given wage parity with a first-class Toronto police constable.[24] The wage adjustment to the highest level did not just apply to the fire department, of course, but bearing in mind that there were 56 separate collective agreements to be negotiated or arbitrated it became the norm for the entire municipal work force.[25]

Fifteen years after amalgamation and the downloading Mike Harris told me that he "knew there were challenges in social spending" but he felt "there would be substantial savings provided everybody didn't average up".[26]

"It didn't work out as well as we hoped," Al Leach said. "We wanted to plan the first budget with the city but Scarborough took us to court."[27]

21. Metropolitan Toronto and the City of Toronto Operating Cost Budgets 1997 and 1998
22. Toronto Star – June 22, 2000
23. Chief Administrator's Office, City of Toronto, "Building the New City of Toronto, Final Three year Status Report on Amalgamation - January 1999, John Sewell, the Shape of the Suburbs: Understanding Toronto's Sprawl (University of Toronto Press, 2009)
24. Globe and Mail – March 14, 2001
25. City of Toronto Staff Report Summary of Amalgamation Savings and Costs 1999
26. Interview with Mike Harris – November 21, 2012
27. Interview with Al Leach - November 26, 2012

The former Deputy Minister of Municipal Affairs Dan Burns told me, "We accepted most of Crombie except for education. To achieve what we hoped for – revenue neutrality – we had to download social services on the municipalities. We said that we would take them back over time. Harris uploaded ambulance services. McGuinty uploaded welfare."[28]

In his 1953 OMB decision the wise Chairman Lorne Cumming had this to say: "Amalgamation would result in increased taxes due to bringing all suburban wages and salary scales and working conditions up to city levels. Costs would increase with the size of the municipality because of the larger number of employees per unit of population and per capita costs in general tend to increase with the size of a municipality. A large city is able to pay more than a small one and to afford an almost endless list of desirable but unnecessary expenditures."[29]

In 1998 the city had 45,860 employees; by 2008 that had increased to 50,601.[30]

28. Interview with Dan Burns – December 19, 2012
29. OMB 1953 decision – "Cumming Report"
30. Harvey Schwartz, Policy Options, February 2010

Logistic Manager
Marketing Manager
Human Resources Manager
Security Manager
IT Manager
Communication Manager
Project Manager
Internal Supervisor
PR Manager
Product Development Manager
Jose

"If it is to achieve the KPMG Report staffing reduction target the Megacity may have to lay off Jose" *(Source: Alan Redway)*

Father and Mother Know
Best or do they?

CHAPTER 11

"For Jane Jacobs, the city-region is defined by how far its 'economic energy' extends. The city-region emanating from Toronto would correspond to the area we think of as the Golden Horseshoe – the urban area from Niagara to Oshawa with Toronto as its centre."
A footnote in the 1996 Anne Golden Report.

Long before the Toronto Megacity was created, even before the Municipality of Toronto was established, questions were being raised about boundaries as well as about the people, goods and services crossing those boundaries.

As you will recall in his 1953 Ontario Municipal Board decision recommending the creation of Metropolitan government for the then thirteen separate municipalities Lorne Cumming wrote:

"The board does not consider it necessary or desirable at this time to determine the proper limits of the future metropolitan area, provided that the boundary recommended in the initial period is deemed a temporary boundary only and that there be no repetition of the errors of the past in neglecting to provide for growth."

Then in his 1965 Royal Commission report Carl Goldenberg stated:

"The Toronto brief submits that: 'A unique requirement of government at the local level is to accomplish periodic adjustments of the units of government in response to the growth of urban areas.' I have said, in Chapter XIII of this report, that increasing

urbanization in the fringe areas points to an eventual extension of Metro's boundaries. The city admits that 'the extent of urban development which needs to be enclosed may be a factor in deciding which is more practical, amalgamation or federation'. If federation should be continued, the most likely way of adding territory would be to take in some further municipalities and to give them the status which now applies or is then assigned to local municipalities within the present boundary line. If we amalgamate, the outer boundary could be extended by adding whole or part municipalities, which would thereby be brought into the enlarged city."

Toronto City Controller Bill Archer in his personal brief to the Goldenberg Commission identified the future boundaries as stretching from Oshawa to Niagara Falls when he said:

"The brief from the city of Toronto has raised the question of the location of outer boundaries. It is my submission that in those cases where it becomes necessary to alter the outer boundaries of Metropolitan Toronto, it can be done more easily through a district system than through a totally amalgamated system. The essential point of our system of government in this area is that we must retain a high degree of flexibility for the future. The rigidity of total amalgamation would place restrictions on the future growth and development of our area and make it difficult, if not impossible, to develop regional government for the urbanized area that exists between Oshawa and Niagara Falls."

In 1969 former Metro Chairman Fred Gardiner wrote in the Toronto Daily Star:

"If Ontario's Municipal Affairs Minister Darcy McKeough persists in his plan to freeze the boundaries of Metropolitan Toronto, he will be making a tragic mistake."[1]

---

1. Toronto Star – October 11, 1969

And editorially the Star said: "Torontoland won't be fit to live in unless we get the go-ahead to expand."[2]

But despite the calls for the expansion of the metropolitan area boundaries, Premiers Robarts and Davis took the same approach as that of Prime Minister Pierre Elliott Trudeau when he introduced wage and price controls with the famous words: "Zap your frozen." The rationale for the freeze began when the Robarts' government appointed a Select Committee of the legislature to "Investigate the Municipal Act and Related Acts". Hollis Beckett the MPP for York East, the same man who played an important role in saving York and East York from extinction in 1967, chaired that committee. It recommended the creation of Metro like regional governments throughout Ontario.[3] Next the government established the Ontario Committee for Taxation (OCT) with Lancelot Smith a chartered accountant as Chairman to recommend changes in the provincial-municipal financial relationship. Smith recommended the creation of nine Metro like and seventeen other regional governments.[4] Those findings were quickly endorsed by another Select Committee of the legislature chaired by John White MPP, a future Provincial Treasurer.[5] The provincial bureaucrats were also delighted with the idea since regional government would strengthen municipal borrowing power allowing municipalities rather than the provincial treasury to pay for local infrastructure improvements.[6] In 1965 egged on no doubt by Bill Davis MPP for Brampton the province agreed to build the Central Peel pipeline to provide water and sewage for Brampton, Bramalea and present day Mississauga. In so doing it crushed Metro's hopes for any westward expansion.[7] The Beckett Committee had supported the idea of creating

---

2.   Toronto Star – February 7, 1970
3.   Frances Frisken, The Public Metropolis: The Political Dynamics of Urban Expansion in Toronto Region (Canadian Scholars' Press Inc. Toronto, 2007)
4.   Frances Frisken, The Public Metropolis: The Political Dynamics of Urban Expansion in Toronto Region (Canadian Scholars' Press Inc. Toronto, 2007)
5.   Darcy McKeough unpublished autobiography
6.   Michael Fenn interview October 30, 2012
7.   John Sewell, The Shape of the Suburbs: Understanding Toronto's Sprawl (University of Toronto Press, 2009)

regional governments based on the existing counties.[8]   Regional government soon followed for the Counties of Halton, Peel, York and Durham completing the Metro boundary freeze.

However, as time passed it became more and more obvious to the provincial government and to the residents of what was now being called the Greater Toronto Area (the GTA) that the relationship of Metro Toronto and the Regions of Halton, Peel, York and Durham transcended local municipal boundaries in terms of commuting, transportation, development and planning. Economic social and physical ties united the residents regardless of the legal boundaries. If the Metro boundaries had not been frozen this problem might never have developed.

Provincial involvement in planning for the GTA and beyond actually started in 1962 with the Metropolitan Toronto and Region Transportation Study known as MTARTS, a joint effort on the part of the province and Metro Toronto covering territory as far east as Bowmanville, as far north as Barrie and as far west as Hamilton. The province was and still is concerned with promoting growth.[9] According to Michael Fenn a former Deputy Minister of Municipal Affairs, the MTARTS planners considered two competing theories of urban growth. The long standing American view that transportation determines growth and a more recent British theory that growth follows economic development.[10]

The American theory of urban growth must have appealed to premier Robarts because in 1967 his government took the first step towards the province becoming a two-headed monster, when it created the GO transit to provide train and bus service to Metropolitan Toronto from the rest of the GTA.[11] Not only was it to continue to be the government of the province of Ontario but at the same time it was becoming the regional government for the Greater Toronto Area or as it

---

8.   Frances Frisken, The Public Metropolis: The Political Dynamics of Urban Expansion in Toronto Region (Canadian Scholars' Press Inc. Toronto, 2007)

9.   Michael Fenn interview October 30, 2012

10.   Michael Fenn interview October 30, 2012

11.   A.K. McDougall, Robarts: His Life and Government (U of Toronto Press, 1986)

would later be renamed shades of Bill Archer's brief to the Goldenberg Commission, the Greater Golden Horseshoe Area.[12]

In 1970 while the door was still open for Metro boundary expansion, the Ontario government opened a can of worms when based on MTARTS it published "Design for Development: Toronto Centred Region", which if implemented would have expanded Metropolitan Toronto's planning area from 240 to 8600 square miles.[13] But the province made a hasty retreat opting instead to make the Metro boundary freeze permanent by surrounding it with new regional governments.

Then in the mid-1970s the province took another step to becoming the "GTA Regional Government" when it built the York-Durham trunk sewer to take water from the Toronto intake and filtration plant to York Region and carry its sewage to the Duffin Creek Sewage Treatment Plant in the town of Pickering in Durham Region.[14] Now it was following the British theory, that growth is determined by economic development

The provincial Liberal government of premier David Peterson edged even closer to becoming the Regional Government of the GTA when in 1988 it established a provincial in house bureaucracy for the "Regional Municipality of the GTA", known as the Office of the Greater Toronto Area (OGTA) with a staff headed by an Assistant Deputy Minister who reported to the Deputy Minister of Municipal Affairs and Housing.[15]

The role of the OGTA was to assist Metro, its four surrounding regional municipalities of Halton, Peel, York and Durham and their 30 local municipalities to act as an interdependent economic unit. It identified three new decision making models for the GTA: 1) a "Joint Review Committee" composed of both municipal and provincial representatives, 2) a "Special Purpose Body" appointed by the Ontario

12. Andrew Sancton, the Limits of Boundaries: Why City-regions Cannot be Self-governing (McGill-Queen's University Press, 2008)
13. Michael Fenn interview October 30, 2012
14. John Sewell, The Shape of the Suburbs: Understanding Toronto's Sprawl (University of Toronto Press, 2009)
15. Michael Fenn interview October 30, 2012

cabinet and 3) a "Supra Body" comprising only elected municipal officials. But at the same time the provincial government made it clear that it was "premature to discuss the restructuring of governance arrangements since it would only provide a great and inconclusive debate within the GTA".[16]

In 1995 NDP Premier Bob Rae appointed the Anne Golden Task Force to define a system and style of government for the GTA. In her report Golden recommended abolishing the five regional governments and replacing them with a small Greater Toronto regional government similar to that of the existing Metropolitan Toronto Council but at the same time retaining all of the local municipalities. The municipal governments liked the idea of retaining the local municipalities but opposed the Greater Toronto regional government, proposing instead a board to co-ordinate a limited number of cross-border services which they variously named an "Inter-municipal Services Board", a "Co-ordinating Committee", and a "Local Municipal Coordinating Board".

Before the newly amalgamated megacity opened for business on January 1, 1998, the Harris government commissioned another study, appointing a former provincial civic servant Milt Farrow to report on the subject of a Greater Toronto Services Board (GTSB). The name had been recommended by the Crombie "Who Does What" Panel. The subject of the Report appeared to be based not only to the recommendations of the Crombie Panel but also those of the Libby Burnham Report, the four GTA Mayors' Report "Moving Forward Together", and the six Metro Mayors' Report "Change For The Better" as well.

The Milt Farrow Report, which he called "Getting – Together" recommended that the GTSB should be composed of three committees:

    1. An Executive Committee – to manage the day-to-day operations of the GTSB and to make final decisions for that which the GTSB is responsible. It was to be responsible for the co-ordination of sewers and water, inter-regional transit including GO Transit, inter-regional roads, waste management and economic

---

16. Andrew Sancton Governing Canada's city-regions (Institute for Research on Public Policy, Monrreal, 1994)

development. It was to be made up of the Mayor of Toronto, four regional Chairs of Halton, Peel, York and Durham, nine additional Mayors and fourteen Councillors. In addition the region of Hamilton-Wentworth was to have three representatives when GO Transit issues were on the agenda. Initially the Chair of the Executive Committee was to be appointed by the province.

2. An Urban Issues Advisory Committee – to advise the Executive on urban issues and to liaise with primarily urban municipalities on these issues.

3. A rural Issues Advisory Committee – to advise the Executive on rural issues and to liaise with primarily rural municipalities on these issues.

Milt Farrow recommended the GTSB have a small staff with one senior manager responsible for day-to-day operations relying on the professional expertise of the various GTA municipal officials. As for who was to pay for what the report recommended that the GTSB have no taxing power but failing a consensus on who was to pay the Executive was to "implement a decision and then apportion the costs".[17] All this brings to mind once again Fred Gardiner's remarks about the old York County Council, which he described as the County Debating Society which bandied about controversial topics session after session mired in disagreements over who would pay for what if at all. Without taxing powers the GTSB could not possibly be effective.

Acting on the Milt Farrow recommendations the Mike Harris government established the Greater Toronto Services Board (GTSB) in 1999. It was made up of representatives from the new city of Toronto, as well as Halton, Peel, York and Durham Regions. Alan Tonks, the last Chairman of Metropolitan Toronto council was appointed by the province to chair this new creation. Simultaneously the province established something called the Greater Toronto Transit Authority Chaired by former Metro Councillor Gordon Chong to finance and to operate the GO system.

---

17. Getting-Together report by Milt Farrow, 1999

The GTSB, like Fred Gardiner's York County Council soon proved fragmented, antagonistic and unable to make decisions. According to Mike Harris, "There was not much consensus and no credibility."[18] The government dissolved both the GTSB and the Greater Toronto Transit Authority in 2001. According to Michael Fenn the news that the Transit Authority was being shut down, came as a great shock to Gordon Chong. But now the GO system was on its own once again.[19]

Now with no GTSB, no Inter-municipal Services Board, no Co-ordinating Committee, and no Local Municipal Co-ordinating Board or any other such GTA regional authority in place, Mike Harris recognizing the problem, established a provincial in house organization called the "Smart Growth Secretariat" to fill the void. Michael Fenn told me, the idea originated with the Canadian Urban Institute. It was sold to the premier says Fenn, not only as a way of managing growth, but by appealing to his interest in hunting, fishing and the outdoors.[20] Hannah Evans the Director of Partnerships and Consultation with the Ontario Growth Secretariat says, Premier Harris was influenced by the work being done at that time in the United States under the direction of President Bill Clinton and Vice President Al Gore, and in the States of Maryland and Oregon, which they called "Smart Growth". This led the Harris government to purse its own "Smart Growth" initiative.[21] "There is no such thing as a new idea," Mike Harris told me, "we unabashedly steal successful ideas."[22] The Smart Growth Secretariat was mandated to focus on the problems of gridlock, smog, urban sprawl, green space, the Oak Ridges Moraine, and population growth for an area referred to as the Central Ontario Smart Growth Zone, which included the GTA plus the cities of Brantford, Hamilton, Guelph, Barrie, Orillia, Peterborough and Kawartha Lakes, the Counties of Brant, Northumberland, Peterborough, Haldimand, Wellington, Dufferin and Simcoe and the regions of Niagara, Waterloo and Haliburton.[23]

---

18. Mike Harris interview – November 21, 2012
19. Michael Fenn interview October 30, 2012
20. Michael Fenn interview October 30, 2012
21. Hannah Evans interview August 26, 2012
22. Mike Harris interview – November 21, 2012
23. Hannah Evans interview August 26, 2012

This was 2001. Back in 1995 the Anne Golden Task Force was asked to report on Metro Toronto, Halton, Peel, York and Durham (the GTA), which she called "not just a geographic area but a powerful single economy, an independent planning unit and an emergent political jurisdiction". In her report, however, Golden wrote that a revision of the external boundaries of the Greater Toronto region should be consistent with the criteria of commuter shed, cohesiveness and anticipated development. For Jane Jacobs to whom Golden referred in her report, the Toronto region corresponded to the area we generally think of as the Golden Horseshoe – the urban area from Niagara to Oshawa with Toronto as its centre.

Five short years later, the provincial Smart Growth Secretariat had revised these regional boundaries far beyond either the original Anne Golden study area or the area envisaged by Jane Jacobs. The Central Ontario Smart Growth Zone boundaries, harken back to those of the 1970 Ontario government document "Design for Development: Toronto Centre Region" put forward and then quickly withdrawn by then Minister of Municipal Affairs Darcy McKeough. Did the Secretariat merely dust off their old plans from 1970 trotting them out this time under the name of the Central Ontario Smart Growth Zone? If so, no one will admit it.

When the Liberal government of premier Dalton McGuinty took office in 2003, the Smart Growth Secretariat originally a Division of the Ministry of Municipal Affairs was renamed the Ontario Growth Secretariat and now is a division of the Ministry of Infrastructure. It presently has a staff of 40 reporting to the Minister of Infrastructure. In 2005 the McGuinty government passed "The Places to Grow Act". According to that Act, the Ontario government assumed the planning role for what they now call the Greater Golden Horseshoe area, which the Act defines as the cities of Toronto, Hamilton, Brantford, Guelph, Barrie, Orillia, Peterborough, Kawartha Lakes, the Counties of Brant, Northumberland, Peterborough, Haldimand, Wellington, Dufferin, Simcoe and the regions of Niagara, Waterloo, Halton, Peel, York, Durham, but this time Haliburton was not included.[24] The Places to Grow

---

24. Hannah Evans interview August 26, 2012

Act gives the Minister of Infrastructure the authority to establish "growth plans" for designated areas referred to in the legislation. The Growth Plan for the Greater Golden Horseshoe area, which includes the Toronto megacity, was issued by the government in 2006. It aims to curb urban sprawl, revitalize downtowns, create complete communities, and increase housing and transportation choices. It requires municipalities in the Greater Golden Horseshoe area to adopt an Official Plan amendment to conform to the policies of the Growth Plan. One of those policies encourages increased housing density.[25] That policy may be welcomed in some Toronto neighbourhoods but it certainly has generated sparks in many others. The city of Toronto has adopted an Official Plan approved by the OMB in 2006 that provides for the same Growth Plan densification policy. The city specifically pushes for mid-rise (five to eleven storey developments) condominiums on main streets as key areas for intensification.[26] Ontario Premier Kathleen Wynne says, "The government is seeking to balance agricultural land, commercial and housing interests. In doing so it must balance local needs and provincial needs. The public can be helped to understand provincial policies through consultation and education."[27] But the former Mayor of Burlington got it right when he was quoted as saying, "The only thing more unpopular than urban sprawl is urban densification."[28]

In 2006 the McGuinty government established the Greater Toronto Transportation Authority not to be confused with the Harris governments' Greater Toronto Transit Authority, which ceased to exist in 2001. The Greater Toronto Transportation Authority merged with the GO system in 2009 and is now called Metrolinx. It has developed a transportation plan for the GTA, which includes the Air Rail Link from Toronto to Pearson International Airport in Mississauga, the Eglinton-Scarborough Crosstown

---

25. Growth Plan for the Greater Golden Horseshoe 2006, Ontario Ministry of Infrastructure
26. National Post – July 7, 2012
27. Kathleen Wynne interview August 10, 2012
28. Michael Fenn interview October 30, 2012

light rail transit from Black Creek Drive to the Scarborough Town Centre, the York Viva bus line and the Mississauga Bus Rapid Transit lanes, but its plan is at the mercy of provincial government funding.[29] Currently GO is planning to expand rail service to Kitchener-Waterloo, Niagara and Guelph.[30] Any and all of Metrolinx's plans as well as any highway plans of the Ministry of Transportation within the Greater Golden Horseshoe area must conform to the Growth Plan.

This applies to hard services as well. They too, must conform, although the province leaves the financing of hard services including: water, sewers and waste disposal exclusively to the cities, counties and regions within the Greater Golden Horseshoe area. The province will only provide funding where health and safety are considerations. Recently provincial priority funding has focused on hospitals, court houses and Ontario provincial police facilities.[31]

Officially the province does not get involved in either creating or being a regional government for the Greater Golden Horseshoe area; however, in reality the province is the de facto regional government, because every provincial ministry and every municipality involved in cross boundary issues in the Greater Golden Horseshoe area must conform to The Places to Grow Act.

What kind of a job has the Ontario government been doing in its role as a regional government? Not a very good one according to long-time supporter of both amalgamation and the provincial Liberal government, John Honderich of the Toronto Star. Writing in his paper on March 30, 2012 Honderich said: "When is the Greater Toronto region going to get its economic act together. If we wait for the tumbleweed of GTA governments to start acting and planning as one economic region we could wait forever."[32] An organization endorsed by the Toronto Star, called the Greater Toronto Civil Action Alliance,

29. Michael Fenn interview October 30, 2012
30. National Post – July 7, 2012
31. Hanah Evans interview August 26, 2012
32. Toronto Star – March 30, 2012

has identified a number of possible agencies, councils and working groups to forge co-operation on inter-boundary issues across the GTA,[33] but the Ontario government seems intent on pursuing the dual role as the government of Ontario and at the same time as the government of the GTA now expanded to be known as the Greater Golden Horseshoe area.

Anne Golden in her 1996 Task Force Report had something to say about that:

> *"The Task Force believes that, regardless of how the government of Ontario is structured, it is inherently unable to meet Greater Toronto's co-ordination needs effectively. The region must develop its own identity and focus as a city-region if it is to compete with other city-regions internationally. The provincial government, by definition, cannot achieve this focus because it defines its constituency Ontario-wide. It also lacks the capacity to advocate freely and effectively on behalf of the city-region, a function that is essential to the GTA's ability to influence federal and provincial policies affecting the region.*
>
> *"A regional co-ordination function would be both more accountable and less expensive than a provincial one."*[34]

While delivering a speech to the Annual Meeting of the Sierra Club, in 1976, Darcy McKeough said, "The government of Ontario also has planning objectives, and these will not always be compatible with municipal wishes. I am not saying that local planning policies are sometimes wrong; only that they sometimes differ from our broader provincial requirements. This is understandable."[35]

In other words, in pursuing a dual role as the government of the province of Ontario and as the government of the Greater Golden Horseshoe area, the Ontario government has a major conflict of interest.

---

33. Toronto Star – March 30, 2012
34. Report of the GTA Task Force, January 1996
35. Darcy McKeough unpublished autobiography

However, the residents of the Greater Golden Horseshoe area either don't care or more likely are completely unaware that the province is now acting as their regional government.[36] So, apparently to date, at least Father and Mother do know best.

---

36. Andrew Sancton, the Limits of Boundaries: Why City-regions Cannot be Self-governing (McGill-Queen's University Press, 2008)

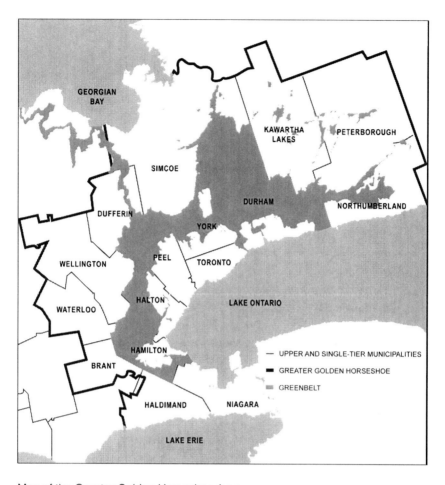

Map of the Greater Golden Horseshoe Area *(Source: Valentine De Landro 2014)*

Throwing the Baby Out
with the bath water

CHAPTER 12

"Access to elected representatives diminishes as the population within a jurisdiction increases . . . . The smaller municipality increases the importance of each constituent opinion. Hence, districts with fewer constituents represent more effective government from the perspective of representation."

Igor Vojnovic – Texas A&M University

Journal of Urban Affairs Volume 22, Number 4, pages 385–417

Local government has two major roles: the delivery of services and as access points for residents to voice their opinions and concerns on issues affecting their homes, neighbourhoods and communities.

Addressing the 1950 OMB hearings on amalgamation Leaside's Mayor Howard Burrell maintained that small scale governments were more accessible to the taxpayers and more familiar with their local problems. In his 1953 decision on the subject OMB Chairman Lorne Cumming wrote:

"It is unrealistic to expect a single council to give sufficient consideration to the many difficult problems in an area of more than 240 square miles and over one million people.

"An amalgamated city might be strong and efficient and well organized but it would not be local government. Local government in a democracy, however, at least to the majority of Ontario people, means a government which is very close to the local residents ..."

Is the Toronto Megacity government really a local government as Cumming described it? Is it accessible to the local taxpayers as was the government of the Municipality of Metropolitan Toronto? Is it realistic to expect the present number of Toronto council members to devote the same personal attention to the individual problems of the over two million people in the city as council members did under the former metropolitan system?

At the time of amalgamation there were 107 elected local representatives serving Metropolitan Toronto. When the Megacity was created by the Mike Harris government, the number of elected municipal representatives was reduced to 57. Prior to amalgamation each elected municipal councillor represented between 10,270 residents and 25,416 residents. After amalgamation from 1998 to 2000 each elected municipal councillor represented 39,926 residents as shown in the following table:

TABLE: Prepared by Beth Moore Milroy [1]

Jurisdiction	Elected regional Reps	Elected municipal Reps	Total elected Reps	Population	Ratio
(Chair)	1	1	-	-	
East York	1	9	10	102,696	1:10,270
Etobicoke	4	13	17	309,993	1:18,235
North York	7	15	22	562,564	1:25,571
Scarborough	6	15	21	524,598	1:24,981
Toronto	8	17	25	635,395	1:25416
York	2	9	11	140,525	1:12,775
Total Metro	29	78	107	2,275,771	-
Amalgamated	-	57	57	2,275,771	1:39,926

1.   Beth Moore Milroy, Toronto's Legal Challenge to Amalgamation, McGill-Queens University Press

Shortly after amalgamation the Mike Harris government passed the Fewer Municipal Politicians Act, which reduced the number of the Megacity Councillors from 57 to 44, meaning that each councillor now represented 50,573 residents.

Some such as former Megacity Deputy Mayor Doug Holyday believe that "a small council would be more accountable to the electorate for its actions and this would contribute to better government". According to Holyday, "Council could operate far more effectively with only one Councillor per ward and a Mayor supported by two deputy Mayors, one elected in the eastern half of the city, the other in the west."[2]

In that case, based on the same population as at the time of amalgamation, each elected municipal official would represent 91,031 residents. Is that local government? Of course, the Deputy Mayor was concerned with the efficiency of the city council meetings, rather than the accessibility of the city residents to their representatives.

Others including retired Toronto Star urban affairs columnist, David Lewis Stein, have written that cutting "city council from 44 to 22 would be a huge mistake". "You can't take phone calls from 2.5 million people who live in Toronto. You couldn't even expect city councillors to be responsible to wards of 100,000. They would be overwhelmed trying to sort out conflicting demands." Stein went on to argue: "One promise of amalgamation was that people who had been isolated in the old suburban councils would be heard in the new, amalgamated city council. Instead, the new council foolishly cut its numbers from 59 to 44. Then, because Mayors could not lead even that diminished council, they pushed to concentrate power in the Mayor's office. Instead of cutting city council, in half," according to Stein, "double its size. Go from 44 to 88 members or more. That would be a truly radical change. But it would restore the tradition of independent city councillors."[3]

In a 2002 article entitled "Urban Governance Reform in Toronto: A Preliminary Assessment of Changes Made in the Late 1990s", Anne

2. Toronto Star, October 7, 1998
3. Toronto Star, October 14, 1998

Golden and Enid Slack wrote: "Some observers have suggested that the reduction in the number of city councillors in Toronto has already fundamentally altered decision-making dynamics at the city council. For example, developers may now have more influence at city council because councillors are reportedly taking a "hands-off" to zoning decisions outside their own wards. In other words, if a ward councillor supports a local development proposal, there is little likelihood that an application to rezone will be challenged by other members of council."

"Before amalgamation, citizens' deputations to city council were the most visible measure of citizen participation. City officials and councillors alike suggest that there is frustration with the inefficiencies associated with this traditional form of public consultation. Deputations use up staff energy and resources that could, for example, be more effectively spent delivering programs and services. Some argue that the volume of deputations is irrelevant to council's final decision. At the same time lobbyists are becoming more powerful and central to council's deliberations than ever before."

"The curtailing of evening hours for council and standing committee meetings has certainly made a difference. Before amalgamation, full meetings of council would often continue into the evening. Now a procedural by-law prevents (in most circumstances) council meetings from continuing past 7:30 p.m., severely limiting the ability of citizens who work during the day to attend or make deputations before council or standing committees. Lobbyists have moved in to fill the vacuum, and councillors have come to rely increasingly on informal conversations with them rather than on direct citizen participation."[4]

Writing in the Toronto Star shortly after amalgamation the former Mayor of the city of York now the Speaker of Toronto city council, Frances Nunziata agreed:

---

4. Anne Golden & Enid Slack, Urban Governance Reform in Toronto: A Preliminary Assessment of Changes Made in the Late 1990s, part II Canadian Metropolitan Cases, Metropolitan Governing: Canadian Cases, Comparative Lessons, Edited by Eron Razin and Patrick Smith, The Hebrew University MAGNES Press, Jerusalem 2006

"There is also little doubt from my perspective that constituents in York are also finding the new city less accessible than the former city of York. One of the advantages of our smaller municipality was the close interaction between residents and their nine elective representatives. In a Megacity with 58 representatives facing a myriad of issues – and a mountain of paper – accessibility became one of the first casualties of amalgamation."[5]

When I met with Megacity Councillor Joe Mihevc in his City Hall office, I saw for myself one of those mountains of paper otherwise known as a council meeting agenda. I thought at the time if I stood on top of it and jumped off I would likely break my leg. No wonder citizen accessibility suffers.

The Harris government tried to provide for citizen accessibility in their amalgamation legislation with something they called "Neighbourhood Committees". Bill 103 authorized city council was to establish at least one such committee per ward to be composed of volunteers to help preserve neighbourhood identity and to provide feedback and advice about the needs of the local community. Although the right to establish them is still provided for in the City of Toronto Act, neighbourhood committees have never seen the light of day.

The City of Toronto Act also provides for the concept of local community councils. Tony O'Donohue in his book The Tale of a City, has written: "And Dave Johnson the former Mayor of East York who was the provincial minister of education ripped the guts out of the original legislation. He insisted that the old municipal identities in some form should be retained with the introduction of the local community councils."[6] Community councils were added to Bill 103 at the last minute before it became law. When I asked Al Leach directly if that was so he said, he couldn't remember.[7] Dave Johnson declined to comment.[8]

---

5. Toronto Star, October 14, 1998
6. Tony O'Donoue, The Tale of a City, The Dundurn Press, 2005
7. Al Leach email, March 19, 2013
8. Dave Johnson email, October 16, 2012

According to the provincial legislation Toronto Council may delegate responsibilities to its committees. Therefore, the community councils are not local councils but rather merely committees of the Toronto City Council. Originally there were six community councils, one for each of the six local metropolitan municipalities. But in 1999 shortly after the creation of the Megacity, when the provincial legislature passed the Fewer Municipal Politicians Act, it removed Toronto's ability to determine the size of its own council as well as its own ward boundaries. That Act divided each of the 22 federal ridings as they existed at the time in one half, to establish the present 44 city wards. The 1953 Municipality of Metropolitan Toronto Act enshrined the principle of maintaining the integrity of existing local municipal boundaries. The Megacity ward boundaries do not correspond to those of the former local Metro municipalities. The principle of maintaining historic local municipal boundaries, initiated in 1953 by Premier Leslie Frost had been consistently followed by the governments of premiers Robarts, Davis, Miller, Peterson and Rae. By violating those historic municipal boundaries the Fewer Municipal Politicians Act further undermined the concept of local government and of the residents' sense of their own community.

By reducing the number of city councillors from 57 to 44 the Fewer Municipal Politicians Act also meant that the city had to revise the boundaries of each community council. In order to avoid a conflict of interest or a political gerrymander the City Hall staff rather than council members were authorized to hold hearings in each of the former local municipalities to determine new boundaries for each community council. No doubt discouraged by the lack of consultation prior to amalgamation and having been left with the feeling that government would do what it wanted regardless of what the public wanted it to do, only 114 residents attended the six hearings. As a result six new community councils were established respectively called: Scarborough, Toronto, East York, Midtown, Humber York and Etobicoke.[9]

---

9. City of Toronto

This structure lasted only four years. Because of concerns of unequal resident representation and the unequal workloads among councillors, city council reduced the number of community councils from six to four.

So, as of 2006 the makeup and representation of the community councils was the following:

Name	Number of Councillors	2006 Population Represented	Ratio of Representatives to Population
Etobicoke	11	595,320	54,120
North York	11	635,220	57,747
Toronto East York	12	642,895	53,575
Scarborough	10	602,575	60,258 [10]

Initially the Toronto East York community council was just called the Toronto community council; however, after a great many passionate representations by "a very, very proud East Yorker" Donna-Lynn McCallum, the name was changed to the Toronto East York community council. [11]

What does a community council's actually do?
City council has delegated to each community council the following:
- The power and authority to hold public meetings required under the Planning Act regarding proposed Official Plans, Official Plan Amendments, Zoning By-laws and Zoning By-law Amendments that relate to lane that lies totally within the community council area.

10. City of Toronto
11. Donna-Lynn McCallum, interview December 26, 2012

- The responsibility, within the part of the urban area it represents, to hear public deputations and make recommendations to Council on other neighbourhood matters requiring a municipal by-law or commitment of unbudgeted City funds, including:
  - Exemptions to fence, sign, ravine and tree by-laws;
  - Business Improvement Area streetscape improvement plans and traffic;
  and
  - Parking regulations.
- The responsibility, within the part of the urban area it represents, to hear deputations on staff decisions regarding:
  - Construction-related permits;
  - Billings related to snow removal, cleaning and clearing of debris an cutting of weeds and long grass;
  - Encroachments on municipal property; and
  - Requests to remove trees and damage caused by trees on municipal property
- The responsibility, within the part of the urban area it represents, to involve citizens in neighbourhoods issues to:
  - Identify recreational needs and safety concerns;
  - Monitor the well-being of local neighbourhoods; and
  - Report to Council on how well community needs are being met.
- The responsibility, within the part of the urban area it represents, to nominate citizens as numbers of:
  - The community panels of the Committee of Adjustment;
  - The community panels of the Property Standards Committee; and
  - Local recreational facility boards of management.

What can a community council not do?
They have:
- No authority to pass by-laws;
- No authority to issue debentures;
- No power to expropriate land;
- No power to enter into agreements, or to sue or be sued;

- No ability to hold title to property;
- No power to appoint municipal officers or to hire fire staff;
- No authority to make grants.

But remember they are only committees of city council. They must report their recommendations to city council, which can then either approve, reject or table those recommendations.[12]

In reality the recommendations of community councils are virtually universally rubber stamped by city council itself. Why? Because as OMB Chairman Lorne Cumming wrote in 1953, "It is unrealistic to expect a single council to give sufficient consideration to the many difficult problems in an area of more than 240 square miles."

Megacity councillor Joe Mihevc underlined that statement when he told me, "What do I know about speed bumps in Scarborough." He pointed out: "Downtown issues differ dramatically from those in the suburbs. Downtown issues are soft services and the homeless. In the suburbs the concerns are garbage and getting to work."[13]

A Canadian national census is held every ten years. After every census, a Federal Electoral Boundaries Commission in each province reshapes the federal riding boundaries by increasing or decreasing the number of constituencies to reflect population changes. According to John Meraglia, the Manager of Elections and Registry Services for the city of Toronto, the 2006 City of Toronto Act no longer requires the city to match federal or provincial riding boundaries but allows city council to change its ward boundaries as it wishes.[14] It appears that ward boundaries will not be changed as a result of changes in federal riding boundaries. However, as the total population of Toronto increases and new condominium high rise developments increase the population density in some parts of the city at least, city council will inevitably come under

---

12. The City of Toronto Act 1997
13. Councillor Joe Mihevc, interview November 20, 2012
14. John Meraglia, Manager of Elections and Registry Services City of Toronto, emails August 8, 9 and 10, 2012

pressure to make changes to the ward boundaries, which is more than likely to mean changes in the composition of the present community councils. Hopefully any such changes will reflect the historic local Metro municipal boundaries. If not those changes will only reinforce the destruction of long established communities and neighbourhoods.

As the population represented by an elected representative increases public access to that elected representative decreases and the public is left to deal with councillors' assistants or with Megacity bureaucrats. The truth is that the smaller the municipality the greater the importance of each resident's opinion. A member of the public with a beef or problem usually prefers more personal interaction with the person he or she elected as their representative. Denzil Minnan-Wong and John Filion both told me that the "political culture" in the city of North York before amalgamation was "to keep the customer satisfied."[15]

Alf Edwards a resident of the former city of York, addressing his council's final meeting prior to amalgamation told the councillors: "I am a member of the community, I work with sports, I work with helping assist neighbours, and church work. I am concerned because what we were thinking is bigger is not necessarily better. We need good government and good government can only come starting at the local level. The bigger complaints can be addressed, they get the media, they get the attention, but the small complaints will become a real chore. Just think if you had to go down to City Hall with a complaint of your own and three years later you would probably still be looking to address it. These are realities. Working together is the sensible solution. You have taken six Mayors and got together jointly to oppose, which will probably if it comes to be a nightmare, but working together with your communities as one gentleman said Metro has achieved successes, but all successes isn't all Metro's. There is a great success within our own community with our identity. I don't think we want to lose that; as a matter of fact, we want to keep it and I challenge this council to

15. Councillor Denzil Minnan-Wong – interview November 6, 2012

work diligently to challenge us to challenge Metro and the bureaucratic government that we will fight to keep our identity and we will fight."[16]

Has the reduced size of council really saved money as was intended? The cost of elected council representatives in the Metro system totalled less than ½ of 1 per cent of local government expenditures.[17] Proportionate cost savings cannot be achieved just by decreasing the number of elected council members because fewer representatives per capita always results in higher remuneration for the councillors as well as a greater number of assistants for each of them. Mayors and councillors in smaller municipalities receive much less remuneration and most certainly do not need the same numbers of assistants because with fewer residents to represent they have the time to do the work themselves. The larger the municipality the greater the councillors' need for a larger the number of assistants to do the work for them and with the increased responsibility of managing a large staff they can justify a greater remuneration since fewer councillors result in a greater work load for each councillor. This means the costs of elected officials under the Megacity and those under the Metro system are identical even though the Metro system provided many times more representation and citizen access for the same number of residents. In addition to that, the cost of running for office under the Metro system was much less expensive than under the Megacity thereby making it possible for an individual citizen to stand for election as a municipal candidate without having to receive campaign contributions from special interest groups and lobbyists.

City council has authority to delegate responsibilities not only to community councils but also to its bureaucracy. It's inevitable with large government that a great many responsibilities are delegated to the bureaucrats. One has only to observe the federal and provincial governments to understand how this works. Former Megacity Councillor and former Mayor of the Megacity David Miller in his 1998 "Discussion

---

16. City of York Council minutes November 13, 1996
17. Robert L. Bish, Canadian Journal of regional Service XXIII:1 (Spring 2000) 77-78

Paper on the Roles and Responsibilities of community councils in Toronto" wrote: "Delegating as much as possible to staff to free up community council and city council agendas," is one solution to reducing their workloads.[18] Of course that means that residents who formerly accessed local government through their elected representatives whom they often knew on a first name basis now must access local government over the telephone or by mail or email with a faceless bureaucrat whose responses will always reflect policies, procedures and rules laid down in writing with no flexibility or wiggle room to reflect special circumstances.

The late professor of Economics at the University of Chicago, Milton Friedman, noting the shift in power in the United States from politicians to bureaucrats once remarked: "The government has become a self-generating monstrosity. We don't have government of the people by the people for the people. We have government of the people by the bureaucracy for the bureaucracy."[19]

Addressing the Town of Leaside Council in 1965, on the need to retain truly local government as had been defined by OMB Chairman Lorne Cumming in his 1953 report, Mayor Beth Neilson said, "In today's complex and changing society there is emerging an increasing emphasis on bureaucratic methods and procedures . . . the need for that kind of local government in our society is even more important today." [20]

Speaking to the city of York council, just before it ceased to exist, York resident, Helen Pressey had this to say on the coming amalgamation: "I don't have anything big to say, I have a bit of kitchen or domestic observations. I worked for a bureaucracy for ten years and the waste that I saw really, really upset me. Filling out forms that was not the focus of my job, my job was to help people, but in the process of helping them I had to fill out forms, duplication, replication, triplication, and quadruplication. In order to transfer a file when completed to another file, I had to fill out at least seven forms. I am talking about one page or two

18. Discussion Paper on the Roles and Responsibilities of Community Councils in Toronto, March 1998

19. National Post, No Cannes do by Peter Foster – November 2, 2011

20. Mayor Beth Nealson, Town of Leaside Council minutes

pagers. This is what this monster city represents to me. How many people are going to be filling out forms and wasting our money?"[21]

Toronto has been called racoon city. Some say there are more racoons than people in Toronto. In response to complaints concerning destructive racoons, the Megacity's Animal Services bureaucrats say: "It's up to residents to racoon proof their homes."[22] City Councillor Josh Matlow has been quoted as saying: "While it's true the city needs to address the racoon issue, it's not a problem that is going to be solved overnight."[23]Before amalgamation the borough of East York's Works department provided residents with humane cages to catch racoons that were damaging homes and property after which a municipal employee removed the humanely caged animals and released them in a conservation area.

It's interesting to note that some people believe that former local municipalities are better off and have better services now than before amalgamation.[24] There are many others, however, such as Alan Carter, perhaps nostalgic for days gone by, who point to the differences between what services and councillors use to be under Metro and what they are now under the Megacity. Carter told me that whenever someone running for municipal office knocks on his door he asks them: "Can you bring back the city of Scarborough?"[25] Even those in Toronto's neighbouring municipalities see a difference. Jack Heath the Deputy Mayor of Markham told me: "Amalgamation doesn't save any money and you can't call your councillor."[26] Markham of course is part of the Regional Municipality of York with a government structure similar to that of our former Metro Toronto system. It's interesting to reflect on why the

21. City of York Council minutes – November 13, 1996
22. Toronto Sun – June 5, 2011
23. Toronto Sun – June 5, 2011
24. Anne Golden & Enid Slack, Urban Governance Reform in Toronto: A Preliminary Assessment of Changes Made in the Late 1990s, part II Canadian Metropolitan Cases, Metropolitan Governing: Canadian Cases, Comparative Lessons, Edited by Eron Razin and Patrick Smith, The Hebrew University MAGNES Press, Jerusalem 2006
25. Alan Carter, interview November 6, 2012
26. Deputy Markham Mayor Jack Heath discussion, October 27, 2012

provincial government didn't amalgamate the Regions of York, Halton, Peel and Durham when it created the Megacity of Toronto.

On the other hand, according to the Toronto Star, the residents in the four houses at the north end of Gough Avenue are happy with the megacity.[27] Those four homes were in East York before amalgamation, just outside the boundary of the old city of Toronto. When the old city annexed property north of the Danforth it included every house that was built at that time. Inevitably many houses now north of that line, were built in East York after that. Today the garbage collection, snow ploughing etc., on Gough Avenue is handled by one rather than two works departments. The Robarts' Royal Commission Report recommended that all of Gough Avenue north of the Danforth be included in East York but the old city of Toronto objected and as Darcy McKeough has written: "I rejected rather quickly any boundary changes."[28] A slight adjustment at that time one way or the other could have solved the problem years ago.

Scarborough resident Jo Waterhouse told me that she likes amalgamation because rather than calling her Metro Councillor or her local Councillor, she calls the city 311 telephone number to get action.[29] Of course technology continues to advance so no doubt Metro and its local municipalities if they had continued to exist would have instituted a similar system. Apparently, however, Ms. Waterhouse is one of the lucky callers because according to Toronto ombudsman Fiona Crean in her 2012 annual report: "Toronto's dealing with its citizens continues to be plagued by bad communications, in addition to being kept in the dark, people got poor service or were denied service; enforcement was unpredictable, and there were unreasonable decisions and delays."[30] In 2013 Crean reported her office received 28 per cent more citizen complaints than in the previous year. This resulted in one councillor calling for the creation of another bureaucracy to police the existing city bureaucracy.[31]

---

27. Toronto Star – January 26, 1999
28. Darcy McKeough, unpublished autobiography
29. Jo Waterhouse – interview November 10, 2012
30. Toronto Star, February 15, 2013
31. Toronto Sun, February 13and 14, 2014

Despite citizen protests prior to amalgamation, public opinion polls conducted in 1999 reported that the vast majority of residents were happy with the Megacity and that amalgamation had become a non-issue. The city's Status Report claimed:

> " "*In the spring of 1999, 70 per cent of Toronto residents stated that they were satisfied with life after amalgamation (Environics Research). Another survey revealed that 66 per cent of Torontonians who stated an opinion, felt that amalgamation was a success (Ekos Research). In June 1999, 79 per cent of Toronto residents felt that Council was on the right track in terms of where it was taking the new city of Toronto (Angus Reid Group)."* [32] *Perhaps, however, the real truth lies in the Globe and Mail headline of April 22, 1997: "Megacity legislation has broken Civic Spirit."* [33]

It has been said that before amalgamation the residents of Etobicoke, York, North York, East York, and Scarborough when asked where they lived would inevitably answer Toronto. But not all of residents considered themselves Torontonians. Physically they lived in part of Metropolitan Toronto but psychologically they were residents of Etobicoke, York, North York, East York, and Scarborough.

Former Leaside Mayor Howard Burrell addressing the Cumming OMB hearing said something else of great significance: "The town's community spirit would disappear if it were merged with Toronto."

Deliberately or otherwise the Megacity is stamping out all signs of the community identities that existed under Metro. Street signs which formerly indicated the local municipalities are being replaced with big blue and white street signs. Local municipal flags cannot fly on city flagpoles. Local Recreation volunteer programs are being replaced by similar programs run by city bureaucrats at a significant cost to taxpayers. Referring to one of those programs still in the hands of volunteers, one

32. Building the New City of Toronto January 1998 – December 2000, Chief Administrative Office, Toronto, Michael Garrett
33. Globe & Mail, April 22, 1997

city official at least has been quoted as saying: "The Leaside Tennis Club is a pain in the ass."

As the symbols of the community identity disappear and roles previously played by volunteers are assumed by paid bureaucrats our community spirit is disappearing as well. Long-time residents may still feel a local pride, but anyone born after 1997 and new residents in a former local municipality, will never know what they missed.

I suppose that's what the city council and the city staff wants. But is it what the residents really want?

De-Amalgamation

CHAPTER 13

"To Dream the Impossible Dream."

- The Man from La Mancha

"... *back in 1997 before our forced amalgamation, when the borough of east york residents were about to see property taxes decrease due to the fact we were about to make the final payment on the East York Civic Centre ... not only did we have the lowest taxes in all Metro Toronto, we had our own dedicated civil service, a fleet of brand new garbage trucks, our own municipal vehicles, eight part-time councillors and our own Mayor. On top of that we had strong reserves of funds in the bank, along with the highest rate of satisfaction with delivery of municipal services in all of Metro Toronto ...*

"... *what benefit have we really gained through this forced amalgamation, and indeed, what have all other former metro municipalities gained as well?*

"*It certainly hasn't been any real decreases in operating costs, for as we know, there are more civil servants working for the city than before amalgamation. I do not think greater efficiency has been achieved; just look at the tug of war that we've had with the rest of the city for access to funds and services with amalgamation . . . .*

"*Experts in municipal affairs on both the right and left of the political spectrum warned back in the 1990s not to amalgamate because it had been proven to not work. Former Ontario Premier*

Mike Harris finally ended up stopping further amalgamations in Ontario because they were not saving money . . . .

"The bottom line is that the former borough of East York had a working formula to keep property taxes low and deliver services high. Given how dysfunctional and polarized our current municipal structure has become, is it really wrong to re-introduce the idea of de-amalgamation?"

Joe Cooper regular weekly columnist writing in the East York, Leaside and Riverdale Mirror" – May 31, 2012

Before 1990, who among us would ever have dreamed in our wildest imagination that the Union of Soviet Socialist Republics (the USSR) would ever de-amalgamate? But it has happened. The former Soviet Union Republics of Russia, Ukraine, Estonia, Latvia, Lithuania, Belarus, Moldova, Georgia, Armenia, Azerbaijan, Turkmenistan, Tajikistan, Uzbekistan, Kyrgyzstan, and Kazakhstan are now all separate and sovereign countries. How many of us anticipated the peaceful de-amalgamation of Czechoslovakia? But that too has taken place.[1]

Montreal is the best Canadian example of what is possible. Prior to 2002, the Montreal Urban Community was made up of the city of Montreal and 27 suburban municipalities. But that year the Parti Quebecois government of Premier Lucien Bouchard amalgamated the 28 municipal governments into a new "Megacity" of Montreal. The very next year, however, Peter Trent the former Mayor of Westmount, one of the amalgamated municipalities, acting on behalf of a number of anti-merger groups retained a retired judge Lawrence Poitras to study and report on the possibility of a de-amalgamation of Montreal. The Poitras Report issued on the eve of the 2003 Quebec provincial election revealed that there had been a number of municipal demergers in the province of Quebec, in the recent past. He cited Buckingham and Gatineau as only two examples. As well the Report pointed out, how inter municipal

---

1. Dissolution: Sovereignty and the Breakup of the Soviet Union by Edward W. Walker 2003

agreements were used to provide inter municipal services for the demerged communities.

During the election campaign that followed, Jean Charest leader of the provincial Liberal Party, promised that if his party formed the government after the election they would submit Montreal and other Quebec municipal mergers to local referendums. Charest was elected. Then, in spite of furious attacks from Montreal Councillors who would of course lose their jobs if demerger occurred, Premier Charest carried through with his commitment. The Quebec National Assembly enacted Bill 9 setting out the terms upon which a municipal demerger could take place. A local referendum must be held in the former municipality with at least 35 per cent of the registered voters casting a ballot, a majority of whom must approve of demerger before it could occur.

On June 20, 2004, referendums were held in 87 former municipalities within parts of 29 amalgamated municipalities. Thirty-one former municipalities that were part of twelve different amalgamated municipalities met the required criteria and de-amalgamated. Twenty-two of those 31 former municipalities voted to demerge from Montreal and regain their former independent status. Five former municipalities opted not to hold demerger referendums. On January 1, 2006, demerger became a reality for fifteen of the municipalities voting in favour of it. In the other seven municipalities, even though the voters favoured demerger, voter turn-out did not meet the 35 per cent threshold and so they remained a part of Montreal.[2]

Today, the Island of Montreal has sixteen independent municipalities, one of them being the city of Montreal. But it is interesting to note that following the demerger the city of Montreal, itself, was divided into nineteen boroughs. Although the boroughs are not separate

---

2. The Merger Delusion by Peter Trent
    Emails and interview August 22, 2012 with Professor Andrew Sancton
    Municipal Mergers and Demergers in Ontario and Quebec prepared for the Annual Meeting
    of the Canadian Political Science Association, York University June 1, 2006 by Andrew Sancton
    Annual Meeting of Canadian Political Science Association – June 1, 2006

corporate entities, each has a minimum of five borough councillors including a Mayor. Each Mayor and, with one exception, at least one other borough councillor sits on the city of Montreal Council. A total of forty borough councillors are elected to serve locally. Montreal City Council is composed of 64 members including the Mayor of Montreal and nineteen borough Mayors. The boroughs have the same responsibilities as the demerged municipalities, namely:

- Fire prevention
- Removal of household waste and residual materials
- Funding of community
- Social and economic development agencies
- Planning and management of parks and recreational
- Cultural and sports facilities, organization of recreational sports and sociocultural activities
- Maintaining local roads
- Issuing permits
- Public consultations for amendments to city planning bylaws
- Public consultations and dissemination of information to the public
- Land use planning and borough development

These are all very similar to the responsibilities of the local Metro Toronto municipalities before amalgamation. However, while Metro Toronto, local municipalities had provincial authority to levy their own taxes to pay for the local services, the Montreal boroughs, but not the de-amalgamated municipalities, need the consent of Montreal City Council to levy their own taxes. So rather than levying their own taxes the Montreal boroughs rely on an annual grant from the Montreal City Council for their funding. The Montreal boroughs hire their own employees subject to the city's union collective agreements. A joint board for the Island of Montreal provides firefighting services for the city of Montreal and all the other fifteen demerged municipalities.[3]

---

3. Municipal Mergers and Demergers in Ontario and Quebec prepared for the Annual Meeting of the Canadian Political Science Association, York University, June 1, 2006 by Andrew Sancton

Some may feel that the Montreal demerger initiative was unique, the only one of a kind. But that's not so, community demerger efforts are happening all the time in North America. Staten Island, for example, the smallest of the five New York City boroughs was amalgamated in 1898. In 1989, almost 100 years later, the New York state legislature passed a bill signed into law by then Governor Mario Cuomo authorizing a referendum asking the question: "Should the borough of Staten Island separate from the city of New York to become the city of Staten Island." In 1995 the residents of Staten Island voted by an overwhelming 81 per cent to secede from New York City. If its residents had been successful in their efforts to de-amalgamate, Staten Island would have been the 40th largest city in the United States. However, to do so they needed the final approval of the New York state legislature. Faced with the fact that the much larger borough of Queens was contemplating similar action, the New York State Assembly narrowly defeated a Bill to charter Staten Island as a separate and independent city.[4]

The San Fernando Valley community has been part of the city of Los Angeles since 1915. But in 2002 a majority of its residents voted to secede from the city of Los Angeles. Under California law at the time the proponents of separation first had to collect the signatures of at least 20 per cent of the valley's registered voters on a "detachment petition" to ask for the vote to be held. Approximately 25 per cent of the registered voters signed the petition. Next the proponents were required to prepare a feasibility study for a state agency mandated to oversee local restructuring. The agency had the authority to approve or turn down the "departure" initiative based on whether the plan was financially sound. In this case the valley proponents received approval to hold a referendum. The state legislation, however, required a majority vote not only in the valley but also in the entire city of Los Angeles before the de-amalgamation could succeed. Fifty-one per cent of the valley voters approved of succession but 67 per cent city wide voted against the

---

4.   New York Times Archives July 26, 2012

proposal. In Quebec 35 per cent of eligible voters were required to casting their ballots in the referendum in order to succeed, but there was no similar threshold voting requirement in California.[5]

Here in Ontario, a number of communities have initiated efforts to de-amalgamate since the amalgamation of Toronto in 1998. One of the first was the Regional Municipality of Haldimand-Norfolk. It had been created by the Davis government in 1973 from what had previously been two counties and 28 local municipalities including six towns, eighteen townships and the police villages of Canfield, Fisherville, St. Williams, Selkirk and Vittora. The regional government had been established anticipating large scale industrial development at Nanicoke on the shores of Lake Erie. That development never took place. In 1998, Haldimand-Norfolk consisted of a regional government plus six local municipal governments. Both Haldimand and Norfolk are predominantly farm country although each has a different type of soil. Neither has an urban hub. Each has historical links to different areas outside the region. As a result of these differences, a grass roots organization sprang up calling itself "Residents Against Tax Hikes (RATH)" which brought pressure on their Progressive Conservative MPP Toby Barrett to advocate for a demerger of the regional municipality. In 1998 and again in 1999, Barrett introduced a Private Member's bill in the Ontario legislature entitled "An Act to Eliminate Regional Government, End Duplication and Save Taxpayers Money". The Bill called for the dissolution of the regional government of Haldimand-Norfolk. But rather than a complete demerger restoring all of the original municipalities, it provided for the elimination of the six local municipal governments while creating two new independent municipalities, one called Haldimand, the other Norfolk with boundaries mirroring those of the former counties. As with virtually all Private Members' Bills as opposed to Bills put forward by the government, Barrett's Bill never became law.

But "RATH" didn't give up. In October 1999, it commissioned a

---

5. Governance restructuring in Los Angeles and Toronto: Amalgamation or Secession by Roger Keil, International Journal of Urban and Regional Research Vol. 24.4 December 2000

poll, which revealed overwhelmingly that the Haldimand-Norfolk residents favoured splitting the regional municipality along the former county lines as set out in Toby Barrett's Private Member's Bill. "RATH" then very astutely, took the position that by reducing the existing seven municipal governments to just two the Harris government could achieve its announced objectives of fewer politicians and saving taxpayers' money.

Since no politician would deliberately vote themselves out of a job and since no bureaucrats would recommend a policy which could eliminate their jobs, the seven municipal councils of Haldimand-Norfolk could not agree. In fact they were all over the map on this issue. But after a provincially commissioned study, conducted by that same former Deputy Minister of Municipal Affairs Milt Farrow, the Harris government agreed to a demerger of Haldimand and Norfolk, while at the same time merging the seven existing local municipalities, thus creating two separate municipalities of Haldimand and Norfolk with the former county boundaries.[6]

In contrast to Toronto where the anti-amalgamation movement has never pressed for a demerger, the anti-merger movement in Flamborough, which was forcibly amalgamated with Hamilton in 1999, continued their efforts for a demerger right up to and after the provincial election of 2003. In 1999 Flamborough's Progressive Conservative MPP, Toni Skarica, resigned his seat in the legislature, after having told his constituents, while running for re-election in 1995 that as long as he was their MPP a PC government would not force an amalgamation in the Hamilton area. Of course, subsequently the Harris government did just that. During the by-election following Tony Skarica's honourable resignation, which was held before the merger had actually been implemented, the Liberal leader of the Official Opposition in the legislature, soon to be the next premier of Ontario Dalton McGuinty, told the voters of Flamborough in an open letter that: "If I were premier today, I would not proceed with this forced

---

6.   Report of Special Advisor Haldimand – Norfolk Review Matt Farrow November 1999

amalgamation proposal. My party proposed amendments to the municipal referendum legislation allowing for binding referenda on municipal amalgamation issues. Our bill would place the power where it belongs, with local residents." Dalton McGuinty's Liberal candidate won the by-election in a traditional PC riding. Not long after this the Mike Harris government announced there would be no more forced amalgamations in the province.

During the 2003 general election campaign in an email to the leader of the demerger activists in Flamborough dated 26 June 2003, Dalton McGuinty wrote:

> *"Thank you for your email regarding the issue of the future structure of Flamborough. I appreciate the deep feeling you have for your community. I believe in local democracy. Local residents should have the right to decide on the future of their municipality. Unlike Mike Harris and Ernie Eves – I will not sit in my Queen's Park office and dictate the future of our communities. As to whether we would reverse past amalgamation the Ontario Liberal position is to allow a binding referendum when there is a substantial degree of public support. As to how we would determine there was substantial support for a referendum for the de-amalgamation of a municipality, we will take into account all signals of a community's wishes – petitions, letters, and municipal council resolutions. We do not have a cast-in-stone, one-size-fits-all number or percentage or cut-off for holding a referendum. Similarly, we will not dictate a province-wide formula that insists that this minimum cut-off for a referendum applies to only one former community in an amalgamated municipality, a certain percentage of former communities, or every community in that amalgamated city.*
>
> *"Lastly, I do not believe in unilateral separation – all residents of an amalgamated municipality will have a say in what happens to their city. But that does not mean that the residents of one former community in an amalgamated city have a veto over the democratic desires of another former community.*
>
> *"It was the Harris-Eves government's dictatorial style that resulted in these sometimes unwanted amalgamations – we will not*

change these amalgamations with a similar made in Queen's Park forced resolution. Unlike Ernie Eves, we realize that each community in Ontario is unique. A set of referendum rules that may work for the community of Kawartha Lakes, Meaford or North Grenville may not work for Flamborough or Chatham-Kent. My plan for resolving the future shape of our municipalities recognizes that each community is different and require a unique system of democratically determining the future."

The 1999 Flamborough by-election winner Liberal Ted McMeekin was re-elected in the general election of 2003. That election brought Dalton McGuinty to power as the Liberal premier of Ontario. When the legislature commenced its sittings after the election MPP McMeekin presented a petition in the Assembly signed by 11,129 Flamborough voters representing over 50 per cent of those eligible to vote. In his reply to the petition the Minister of Municipal Affairs, John Gerretsen stated that he was turning the matter over to the Mayor of Hamilton. No doubt as the former Mayor of Kingston, Minister Gerretsen was not in the least surprised by the Mayor of Hamilton's response: "My mandate is to make the amalgamated city work." So there the matter ended, at least to date.[7]

On January 1, 2001, the Harris government forcibly amalgamated the sixteen municipalities of Victoria County to create the new city of Kawartha Lakes. The largest of these municipalities was Lindsay, the hometown of the man who was instrumental in creating Metro Toronto, late former Premier Leslie Frost. Once again unlike the Toronto anti-amalgamation activists, the Victoria County anti-merger opponents calling themselves the "Voices of Central Ontario (VOCO)" didn't fade away but continued their opposition. After the city of Kawartha Lakes or as some called it the city of Kawartha "Mistakes" had come into existence, "VOCO" not only collected an 11,000 signature petition requesting demerger but conducted its own referendum in which 96.5 per cent of the 6,209 who cast ballots voted to de-amalgamate.

---

7. Municipal Mergers and Demergers in Ontario and Quebec – Andrew Sancton

In October of 2001 Liberal opposition leader Dalton McGuinty had told the residents of Victoria County that: "Ontario Liberals believed that past amalgamations could be reversed by a local referendum if there was a substantial demonstration of public support for holding a referendum." He went on to say that, "The petition campaign in Victoria County has clearly met the threshold." In early 2002 in an email to a leader of VOCO, McGuinty renewed that commitment.

Victoria County's MPP at the time was a Progressive Conservative member of the Harris government, Chris Hodgson. In 2001 Mike Harris had appointed Hodgson as his Minister of Municipal Affairs. When Harris resigned as premier in 2002 his successor PC Premier Ernie Eves reappointed Hodgson to that same portfolio. Now poor Chris Hodgson was really on the hot seat with his own constituents. Under extreme pressure he finally agreed to hold a referendum asking the question: "Are you in favour of a return to the previous municipal model of government with an upper –tier municipality and sixteen lower-tiered municipalities." Rather than wait for the results Hodgson retired from politics altogether before the vote was even held. Forty-eight per cent of the eligible voters in the city of Kawartha Lakes cast ballots. 16,802 voted to de-amalgamate while 15,918 voted to retain the new city.

Understandably, the "VOCO" activists assumed that demerger would follow in due course, especially when Dalton McGuinty became the premier of Ontario. But that was not to be. The final act in this drama ended with two letters from Premier McGuinty's Minister of Municipal Affairs John Gerretsen, the first dated February 18, 2004 read:

> "As I have stated previously, there is no provincial funding available for municipal de-amalgamation. This is a direct result of the deficit left by the previous government. While your current single-tier configuration may not necessarily be the most appropriate municipal structure for your area, I remind you that it was not put in place by this government.

> "As the Minister of Municipal Affairs, my first responsibility is to help ensure that the people of Ontario are privileged to enjoy the security and benefits that come from living in financially viable

and sustainable municipalities that deliver services we expect from local governments. I would be betraying the trust placed in me if I were to establish a new municipal structure that resulted in municipalities financially unable to provide ongoing delivery of those services. I have reason to believe that a number of the previous sixteen lower-tier municipalities that would result from de-amalgamation would experience significant financial challenges, given their present day roles and responsibilities. The government will therefore not be implementing the de-amalgamation of the city of Kawartha Lakes at this time."

Later Minister Gerretsen wrote again:

"I remain willing to give consideration to proposals submitted by municipal councils that would improve local governance and service delivery systems and that meet the reasonable criteria of property tax fairness for all residents and assured fiscal sustainability of all resulting communities. In my February 18, 2004 letter to council, I also expressed concern about the creation of any new municipal structures that would be unable to meet the fiscal and service delivery challenges that face our municipalities, given their present day roles and responsibilities. I would expect any restructuring proposal from your council to address those concerns."

Gerretsen or the provincial bureaucrat who likely wrote the letter for him to sign ignored completely the fact that the rationale for the amalgamation of the sixteen Victoria county municipalities in the first place was to save money not fiscal sustainability. The letters also ignored the fact that prior to the amalgamation there was no indication that the sixteen separate municipalities were unable to meet their fiscal and service delivery challenges. According to the Kawartha Lakes' city engineer, the amalgamation caused a great deal of cross subsidization of municipal services among the former municipalities. Some of those services, at least a number of the communities did not want or demand.[8]

---

8.   Municipal Mergers and Demergers in Ontario and Quebec – Andrew Sancton

In 2002 Mayor Hazel McCallion launched a campaign to allow the city of Mississauga to secede from the regional municipality of Peel. The Mayor said Mississauga taxpayers were subsidizing Brampton and Caledon taxpayers for the programs delivered by the regional municipality of Peel. The issue of cross subsidization was the same issue raised, in the efforts to de-amalgamate the city of Kawartha Lakes. A citizens' task force appointed by the Mississauga council to study the matter, recommended that the Peel regional government be phased out within five years and that the city of Mississauga become a separate municipality with expanded authority to deliver local services. After receiving this report Mississauga Council passed a resolution: "That the province of Ontario be requested to permit the transition of the city of Mississauga to a separate city."

Next the Mayor sent out a questionnaire on the subject to every household in the city. Ninety-nine per cent of the 20,000 questionnaires returned favoured the separation of Mississauga from the region of Peel. This ammunition was augmented by a financial report from the city auditors estimating that Mississauga was overpaying for the services it received from the region. A further city staff report identified a $32 million annual saving if the city seceded from the region. When Mayor Hazel presented all this to Premier McGuinty, he told her the province would take no action unless the councils of Peel region and those of Brampton and Caledon agreed. It must have been obvious to the premier that this was most unlikely since they were the beneficiaries of the cross subsidization. But Hazel didn't give up. She pressed for and was given a further interview, this time with the premier and his Finance Minister Greg Sobara. But now, however, the response was even clearer. The province would not allow Mississauga to demerge. That message was later reinforced by a letter from Mr. Sobara to Mississauga Council in which he stated: ". . . major reorganization is not part of our agenda at this time."[9]

---

9.   Her Worship: Hazel McCallion and the Development of Mississauga by Tom Urbaniak

The province's rejection of the efforts of Flamborough, Kawartha Lakes and Mississauga to de-amalgamate has not stopped others from trying. The town of Essex is the product of the Harris government's forced amalgamation of the former town of Essex, the town of Harrow, and the townships of Colchester North and Colchester South. In February 2008 the Essex town council was presented with a petition from the "South Colchester-Harrow Action Committee" signed by 5,000 people representing almost 90 per cent of the electorate in the southern half of the town calling for the municipality to be divided into two new towns. The Essex town council in the absence of the Mayor supported the thrust of the petition sending it to the province and to Essex county council for comment. The county took no action. But in March 2008 the then Minister of Municipal Affairs Jim Watson, formerly the Mayor of the amalgamated city of Ottawa, responded by repeating the criteria previously set out by his predecessor John Gerretsen in the case of Kawartha Lakes. The town must demonstrate fiscal sustainability for all resulting municipalities and property tax fairness to all taxpayers. Invariably in an amalgamation there is cross subsidization that did not exist before, so if there is a de-amalgamation, someone is going to lose the tax advantage they received, fairly or not from the amalgamation.

Quite understandably of the Chief Administrative Officer of the town of Essex who would likely lose his job if a demerger occurred, threw cold water on the idea. When he reported to council concerning Minister Watson's letter, he cited the province's response to Kawartha Lakes. He also drew council's attention to the Harris government's regulation 216/96. That regulation specifically forbids "a restructuring that results in an increase in the number of local municipalities". Unfazed by this regulation and the overt opposition of the town CAO, the "South Colchester-Harrow Action Committee" retained the services of Peter Tomlinson of the Department of Economics of the University of Toronto together with his associates Professor Andrew Sancton of the Department of Social Science at the University of Western Ontario and Adam Found a University of Toronto PHD candidate in economics at the time to prepare a de-amalgamation report. That report revealed that the existing town of Essex was incompatible with the wishes of its residents in that the southern half of the town (South Colchester and Harrow) who preferred lower taxes and fewer services, while the more populous north wanted higher service levels and were prepared to pay for them.

Unfortunately, for the residents of South Colchester and Harrow, the town of Essex bureaucrats, who might have lost their jobs in a de-amalgamation, refused the consultants access to the town's financial information and accordingly they were unable to meet the provincial requirement for a proper fiscal impact study. Although the consultants' report was endorsed in the absence of the Mayor when the Mayor, who could also have lost his job in a demerger, returned for the next meeting, council reversed its endorsement. Needless to say Minister Watson was delighted with council's change of heart and wrote congratulating the town on deciding to remain amalgamated.[10]

The consultants' findings that the residents in one part of Essex preferred lower taxes and fewer services, while the residents in another part wanted a higher level of services and were prepared to pay for them, can also be applied to the present Megacity of Toronto where differing priorities also account in part at least for what some have called the dysfunctional nature of the city. The residents in some parts of the Megacity have entirely different priorities from those in other parts. That should be abundantly clear, when one remembers that all parts of the Megacity do not elect their provincial MPPs from the same political party. In the words of Megacity Councillor Mike Del Grande: "We have two cities in Toronto . . . the old city of Toronto it's a socialistic mindset . . . the rest of Toronto it's the have nots."[11]

In 2009, following the receipt of a report entitled "Governing Ottawa", a public forum was held in Ottawa on the subject of de-amalgamation. The present Mayor of Ottawa is once again Jim Watson who as Ontario Minister of Municipal Affairs congratulated the town of Essex on its decision to remain amalgamated,[12] so you

10. Interview and emails with Peter Tomlinson July 23, 2012
11. Toronto Sun February 16, 2014
12. Interview and emails with Adam Found, July 23, 2012 and August 15, 2012 (Agenda for Public Forum March 30, 2009) Department of Economics, University of Toronto

know why the idea of de-amalgamation has gone nowhere in Ottawa to date.

No Mayor of an amalgamated city will ever support or recommend de-amalgamation and the provincial government knows that. As the Mayor of Hamilton said, he was elected to make the amalgamation work.

During the summer of 2013 de-amalgamation gathered steam in the former township of Sydenham, not far from Owen Sound, where a committee initially headed by Peggy Richardson and originally calling itself the "Sydenham Separatists", was collecting the signatures of over 50 per cent of the households on a petition calling for a demerger from the municipality of Meaford. The rolling hills and vast agricultural fields of Sydenham were forcibly amalgamated with the town of Meaford and the township of St. Vincent in 2001 to create the municipality of Meaford. In a letter to the editor of the Meaford Independent on August 9, 2013, one Sydenham Township resident wrote: "For 150 years, simple bucolic Sydenham Township was able to run its affairs just fine. It had no CEO, no HR Department, no purchasing agent and no engineer in charge of roads. It ran with eight staff. It didn't get involved with the entertainment business. It did not charge extra for weekly garbage pick-up. It had no costly legal wrangles to conduct." The previous week the editor of the that newspaper had written, "As much as I am fond of the entire municipality of Meaford, if I lived in Sydenham, I would want to separate, too."

During the autumn of 2013, separation was also being actively pursued by some of the residents of the former township of Goderich in south western Ontario. However, Kingston Councillor Jeff Scott who represents the former township of Countryside and his colleague Councillor Brian Reitzel, who represents the former Pittsburg Township in eastern Ontario, were both seeking a separation referendum.[13]

So in spite of all the provincial government's efforts to throttle it the issue of de-amalgamation is still alive and thriving in Ontario. But de-amalgamation will only actually happen if the provincial government listens to the peoples' concerns and makes it happen.

---

13. Kingston Whig Standard November 25, 2013

Former Ontario Premier Dalton McGuinty   (Source: "David Cooper/ GetStock.com")

QUO VADIS TORONTO?

Where does the City go from here?

CHAPTER 14

"Amalgamation leaves a legacy of dysfunction"

Toronto Star – August 17, 2012

Six years after amalgamation, a long time Scarborough resident called the Toronto City Hall columnist of the National Post newspaper, Don Wangas, to say: "We used to be a proud city that lived within its financial means and still managed to provide residents with decent services. It's embarrassing what has happened here since amalgamation. There's got to be some way to return things to what they were before."

National Post – July 8, 2003

Fourteen years after amalgamation Christopher Hume of the Toronto Star wrote: "Toronto is a city at war with itself. This wouldn't have been an issue in the old days. But then amalgamation happened. Fourteen years later it has yet to justify the upheaval it caused. Turns out the arguments about bureaucratic efficiency and economic scale were simply wrong. Neither occurred.

"As cumbersome as pre-amalgamation arrangement might have been, each of the jurisdictions at least had its own council.

"Tellingly, even efforts to harmonize planning rules have faltered. Perhaps one size does not fit all. What's appropriate in, say Scarborough doesn't necessarily work downtown and vice-versa.

"'There was an outcry when harmonized by-laws were adopted,' recalls Sheena Sharp, chair of the Ontario Association of Architects. 'The city practically stopped issuing building permits. Council repealed the new by-laws but still hasn't dealt with the issues. It's very, very frustrating.'

"Not only did amalgamation not streamline the approval process, getting approvals is slower and more bureaucratic than ever," Sharp says.

"Some argue all Torontonians now, urban or suburban, should get over our differences.

"The legacy of amalgamation, however, is a dysfunctional administration and a clash of civic cultures and lifestyles that has left the city divided and seething with self-hatred.

"Many issues are local. Ignoring them has led to cynicism and feelings of disconnection and resentment.

"Toronto's former chief planner, Paul Bedford, declared in 2010 that amalgamation 'exists only on paper'.

"The underlying point is that we've yet to broach the subject of governance despite its obvious failings."

Christopher Hume Toronto Star August 17, 2012

And Joe Cooper of the East York, Leaside and Riverdale Mirror wrote: "Why has the city of Toronto become such a dysfunctional municipal organization, given that it was once one of the best run municipalities in the world?

"It began with the creation of Metro Toronto in 1953, which at the time was a revolutionary idea. What the Metro system provided, which a big city government can't, was a 'wholesale' source of reasonably priced services to its various municipalities.

"Each municipality would be able to determine what their needs were based upon their unique policies and demographics....

"By the late 1960s the success of Metro Toronto was apparent. Cities of similar size to Toronto in the United States were seeing urban crime rates soar, rioting over social inequality, visible environmental decline and unchecked development.

"One of the best examples of how citizens could influence municipal policy was demonstrated with the Spadina Expressway proposal. Working at a grassroots level and with limited funds, ordinary citizens banded together to stop the expansion of the Spadina Expressway, which they did in 1969.

"It also created a political climate in Metro Toronto that put people and communities ahead of big development. Due to its people-first policy, Metro Toronto became the envy of the world.

"The main failing of the provincial government of Mike Harris in the 1990s was that the opportunity was there to expand the successful Metro system to the entire GTA. This would have allowed for a region-wide means of dealing with big issues such as transit, gridlock and developing a level playing field of economic development....

"We now have two choices: we can continue on the current path and watch the failed amalgamation experiment collapse, or return to a model of success with a GTA metro system and Toronto turned into four working cities. It is not too late to do so and it will cost a lot less than what we will be facing if we continue as we are."

> Joe Cooper weekly columnist writing in the East York, Leaside and Riverdale Mirror - June 14, 2012

Joe Cooper offers us a ray of hope. Ideally a Montreal like demerger would return Toronto to what many have described as the city's "golden age".[1] That being the Municipality of Metropolitan Toronto as it existed

---

1.   Interview with Professor Enid Slack – August 7, 2012

from 1967 to 1987 with a Metro regional government, as currently exists in Halton, Peel, York and Durham, and six local governments called either community councils or boroughs as they are called in the city of Montreal. Each local community would elect a Mayor and several local councillors as is done now in Montreal. The local Mayors would each sit on the Metro regional council as would an appropriate number of local community councillors in accordance with the principle of representation by population depending on the number of residents in that local community. Metro regional councillors would not be directly elected to that council but would also sit on their local councils reflecting the views of their local communities as envisaged by former Premier Leslie Frost when Metropolitan Toronto was created. As in Toronto's "golden age" the Metro councillors would choose a Chair who has demonstrated leadership ability from among their own members.

The Metro regional council and the local community or borough councils would each have clearly defined responsibilities and taxing powers. This would accommodate different levels of local services, acceptable to local residents as was the case during Toronto's "golden age". The Metro Council would have the same responsibilities and provide the same services as it did during Toronto's "golden age" with the addition of fire-fighting.

Many are likely to say that a Metro system would be disruptive. But John Sewell has pointed out: "Two-tiered arrangement will mean that the regional and local levels of government will often seem to be at odds with each other as they express different values and perspectives. This was often the case in Toronto, and some took it as a sign of failure. Instead, it was a sign of success – public debate means that the values at issue become very evident, trade-offs made at decision-time become obvious. The openness of the debate between the interests often dictates that decisions be taken carefully, often in an environment of compromise.

"That more than anything, was what gave the Toronto system
such a stellar international reputation: two tiers of government
ensured that neighbourhoods had a voice, and that the regional point

of view did not run roughshod over local interests, as happened in so many other cities. [2]

It is interesting to note that when I mentioned giving neighbourhood interests a voice during my meeting with former Premier Mike Harris, he said: "That makes sense. We hoped something like that would happen." [3]

Addressing the legislative committee studying the megacity Bill 103 in 1997, Kathleen Wynne then not yet a MPP and not yet the premier of Ontario, told the members of the committee that as Chair of the Citizens for Local Democracy (C4LD) weekly meetings, she had learned that Metro citizens were outraged, not only because of the undemocratic process being followed, but also because the Bill was removing accessible local representation. [4] Citizen Kathleen Wynne was right then. Hopefully Premier Kathleen Wynne still believes that now.

While according to the 1996 KPMG study, amalgamation would reduce costs by achieving economies of scale, American econometric studies conducted by Professor Arthur O'Sullivan show that a local municipal population of only 100,000 people, not a population of over 2,000,000 as in the case of the Megacity, is all that is required to achieve a municipal economies of scale. [5] A more recent study by Adam Found of the University of Toronto concluded that a municipal population of only 76,000 will achieve economies of scale. The same studies have found that municipalities with larger populations have lower productivity than municipalities with smaller populations. Adam Found's work reveals that in the province of Ontario, municipalities with populations over 76,000, result in increased costs rather than cost savings. [6] When the

---

2.   John Sewell, The Incredible Lightness of the Two-tiered Model of Local Government (Towards a New City of Toronto Act) Zepher Press 2005
3.   Interview with Mike Harris – November 21, 2012
4.   Kathleen Wynne – Appearance before the Ontario Standing Committee on General Government, February 12, 1997
5.   Arthur O'Sullivan, Urban Economics, seventh edition, (McGraw Hill, New York, 2009)
6.   Peter Tomlinson, Toronto's Fiscal Outlook 2011 through 2014, a paper prepared for the University of Toronto's Cities Centre, November 30, 2010 and interviews and emails with Peter Tomlinson and Adam Found July 23, 2012

province began planning regional government, Darcy McKeough placed the bar even lower: "I suggest that the minimum population for local government in a two-tiered system should be 8,000 to 10,000." [7]

To bring back a city that worked would require a demerger of the Megacity by the province of Ontario. At the present time the provincial government's Regulation 216/96 (section 3) prohibits municipal restructuring resulting in an increase in the number of local municipalities, in other words a demerger or a de-amalgamation. Presently the provincial government's response to the demerger efforts in Flamborough, the city of Kawartha Lakes and Essex, reveals that three conditions must be met before the province will consider the de-amalgamation of a municipality:

1. Demonstrate the fiscal sustainability of all the demerged municipalities.
2. Demonstrate the property tax fairness to all taxpayers.
3. Must be endorsed by the existing city council. [8]

In the province of Quebec the Montreal and other municipal demergers require only that the residents, not the present members of council, vote in favour. What are the chances of the Toronto Megacity Council voting to de-amalgamate? Can you imagine any councillor or anyone else for that matter voting to eliminate his or her own job? The creation of Metropolitan Toronto, the reduction of the local municipalities from thirteen to six and amalgamation itself clearly demonstrate that the provincial government must take the lead and accept the responsibility for its actions. When she was the Minister of Municipal Affairs Kathleen Wynne told me: "It's up to the city (read city council) to make the decision."[9] But now she is the premier of Ontario. She is no longer the team player and obedient follower of the leader. She is the leader. Either the residents should make that decision as they did in Montreal or the provincial government should appoint a Royal Commission to make

---

7.   Darcy McKeough unpublished autobiography
8.   Interview July 23, 2012 and emails with Adam Found
9.   Kathleen Wynne – interview August 10, 2012

recommendations as was done in the past in the case of the Goldenberg and Robarts' Royal Commissions. That would give the citizens of the city a chance to have their say as the premier advocated in 1997. It would also shift the responsibility for the decision and take the premier and the government off the hook. Not only that but it could make Toronto's municipal government more accessible to the public, something she also advocated in 1997 while at the same time solving the problem of the dysfunctional Megacity government. Darcy McKeough says: "Like it or not municipalities are creatures of the Province. Had they not been creatures Metro Toronto would never have happened."[10]

How many viable local communities are there in Toronto? If we use Darcy McKeough's figures all thirteen of the original municipalities that existed when Metro Toronto was created in 1954 would qualify. However, based on the research done by Arthur O'Sullivan and Adam Found the more likely number is the six that existed just before amalgamation.

After amalgamation was announced the borough of East York, which at that time was the 18th largest municipality in Ontario and the 35th largest in Canada, published the following fact sheet about that municipality:

East York is:

1. **Accessible** – Walk into the Civic Centre and speak directly with senior staff or the Mayor. Attend a Committee or council meeting and make a deputation.
2. **Accountable** – Streamlined services and decision making allow a small staff to service a large population. Public consultation plays a major role. East York residents, businesses and organizations are a part of all decision-making processes.
3. **Community** – One in seven people volunteer in East York compared with one in ten province-wide. A "small town in the big city" and yet not so small! A population of 102,000 demands and receives the services of a large city.

---

10. Darcy McKeough unpublished autobiography

4. **Fiscally Responsible** – The municipal portion of the tax bill has not increased in FOUR [4] consecutive years. East York does not run at a deficit. East York councillors are paid only part-time and share one Administrative Assistant among eight councillors.
5. **Responsive** – Responsive – Provincial revenues have decreased more than 57 per cent since 1992. East York has met these challenges without reducing services. Economic development strategies have responded to the new economic climate. Heavy industry is being replaced by major retail and new media. East York is in its fourth year of increased business permit growth. Capital projects are funded from current revenues leaving the municipality virtually debt-free in the year 2000.[11]

On the other hand the council of the former city of York on the eve of amalgamation over the objections of Mayor Frances Nunziata voted by a majority of only one to discuss the merger of York with the former city of Toronto. If the residents of the former city of York or the residents of any other local community wish to join a de-amalgamated city of Toronto, then demerger could be limited to those voting in favour of it and the number of local councils could be more or less than six.

An alternative to de-amalgamation or perhaps a preliminary step towards it could be further decentralization of the existing system. Presently, without further provincial legislation Toronto City Council can decentralize further by delegating the following responsibilities to the community councils:
1. Local area parks maintenance
2. Local recreation programing
3. Local by-law enforcement
4. Local roads and sidewalk maintenance
5. Local sewer and water maintenance
6. Local waste collection and disposal
7. Hire and maintain a staff to carry out all or any of the above[12]

11. Borough of East York Facts 1997
12. City of Toronto Act 2006
Emails with John D. Elvidge & John Meraglia, City of Toronto – August 13-21, 2012

City council cannot delegate its power to adopt or amend the city budget. However, it could allocate a budget to each of the community councils so that they could carry out these additional responsibilities.[13] Without further provincial legislation, however, city council cannot delegate the power to pass zoning by-laws or amend an official plan under the provincial Planning Act to a community council.[14] This is an essential power for a local community if it is to control its own destiny. According to OMB Chairman Lorne Cumming in his 1953 decision that is what local government means.[14]

There are those who tell us nothing has really changed with amalgamation. Our neighbourhoods remain the same just as they were before. That may be so but more and more our neighbourhoods are being subjected to major changes. We have lost the ability to control the changes to our own neighbourhoods.

During the public consultation in 1998 conducted by then Megacity councillor (later Megacity Mayor) David Miller concerning the newly legislated community councils, one resident suggested that city council should allocate funds to each community council to be used at the community council's discretion, so as to carry out the declared plan of the Megacity's first Mayor Mel Lastman when he said: "Our plan places community decisions in the lap of our citizens and community councillors, where they rightfully belong. Our plan is really very simple – the Megacity should look after the big things and the community council can do everything else."

That person went on in his submission to then Councillor Miller to write: "But I must confess that the main reason for me coming with this recommendation of funding for community councils is that I am deeply

---

13. City of Toronto Act 2006
Emails with John D. Elvidge & John Meraglia, City of Toronto Clerk's Department – August 13 – 21, 2012
14. City of Toronto Act 2006
Emails with John D. Elvidge & John Meraglia, City of Toronto Clerk's Department – August 13 – 21, 2012

concerned about losing those wonderful, area-unique community agreements that happen when a local government can extend funding to a neighbourhood project. For example, a need for a playground can involve contributions from sharing space arranged by the school board to a local business sharing costs with council for needed playground equipment. These agreements evolve around grassroots neighbourhood needs, and are initiated by the local residents. For centuries, healthy communities have always had them. They work, they share costs and, best of all, they are maintained because the people want them there and care about them. They are excellent examples of "citizen-focus being kept alive", and without encouragement, in all forms, they simply disappear and usually very quickly. When our community councils can give real support to our neighbourhood "agreements", then we are keeping alive that age-old working tradition of the community determining its needs first. Then we can all work together to make good things happen." [15]

The City of Toronto Act 2006 now allows Toronto City Council to eliminate or create more community councils and to determine their composition. The number of community councils could remain at four or could be increased to five or six or more to accommodate local preferences. This type of decentralization should meet head on provincial government concerns about sustainability and property tax fairness to all taxpayers.

The Municipality of Metropolitan Toronto government model was admired all over the western world. It was eliminated on January 1, 1998, and with it went accessibility to local government, local community spirit and local government frugality and responsiveness. There are a great many who believe that the Megacity is dysfunctional but they also believe the powers at be will never change it. As the Globe and Mail headline read on April 22, 1997: "Megacity legislation has broken Civic Spirit." But the Quebec government did change it in Montreal and other Quebec municipalities. City council can start the process of change in Toronto by decentralizing. After all the Etobicoke, York, North York, East York and

15. David Miller, The Roles and Responsibilities of Community Councils in the City of Toronto, March 1998

Scarborough Civic Centres as well as Toronto City Hall and Metro Hall are all still publicly owned and still used by city government and the public.

In 1999 Dalton McGuinty addressing the Board of Trade was quoted as saying: "To reopen that can of worms or put toothpaste back in the tube. No."[16] But that was 1999, today almost fifteen years later, the provincial government can start the process of change by initiating a long overdue review of the Megacity government.

When the Municipality of Metropolitan Toronto was established on January 1, 1954, the provincial government of then Premier Leslie Frost promised to review its experience within five years. In fact the province conducted its review of the Metro government chaired by OMB Chairman Lorne Cumming, only three years later. Five years after that, the provincial government now led by Premier John Robarts appointed Carl Goldenberg to conduct a Royal Commission on Metro Toronto resulting in the original thirteen local municipalities being reduced to six. Ten years later in 1975 the Bill Davis' provincial government appointed his predecessor John Robarts as a Royal Commissioner to once again review all aspects of Metro's government. In 1986 the David Peterson government conducted another but more limited study by its Ministers of Municipal Affairs Bernard Grandmaitre and John Ekins. Then in 1995, Premier Bob Rae established the Greater Toronto Area Task Force chaired by Anne Golden to examine not only the governance of Metro Toronto but that of the entire GTA. When the new government of Premier Mike Harris received the Golden report in 1996, it commissioned a further study by another Task Force chaired by Libby Burnham to review the findings of the Golden report. Later that same year it initiated another study called the "Who Does What" Panel led by former Toronto Mayor and federal cabinet Minister David Crombie, to report on a restructuring of municipal/provincial responsibilities and financing. Following the

16. Toronto Star – May 23, 1999

receipt of those reports the Harris government repealed the Municipality of Metropolitan Toronto Act replacing it with the City of Toronto Act, 1997. That Act has never been publically reviewed.

Leslie Frost said that metropolitan government should be reviewed each decade.[17] We are long overdue for another provincial Royal Commission to review the Megacity government.[18] After it took office in 2003 the Dalton McGuinty government always claimed that it was up to the Mayor and council of the city of Toronto to ask for changes to its government structure. Ultimately, however, major changes in local government can only come about through the government of the province of Ontario. Section 92(8) of the Canadian Constitution Act gives the province the exclusive right to make laws in relation to municipal institutions. It is a cop out to expect the Toronto Mayor and council and/or their city staff to recommend changes that might eliminate their own jobs. Premier Kathleen Wynne is fond of saying: "We're going to have those conversations."[19] Well, let's have a conversation about de-amalgamation or at least decentralization to make our city government more accessible to its citizens.

> *"First they ignore you. Then they ridicule you. Then they fight you. Then you win"*
>
> *Mahatma Ghandi*

---

17. Don Stevenson & Richard Gilbert, Restructuring Municipal Government in Greater Toronto – July 30, 1999
18. Peter Tomlinson, emails July 20, 2012
19. Toronto Star – January 26, 2013

Former Quebec Premier Jean Charest   *(Source: Jean Charest)*

Former Ontario Premier Leslie M. Frost QC , father of the city that worked

(Source: C 306-0-0-373 , May 6, 1958 International Press Limited from the files of the Archives of Ontario)

Former Ontario Premier Leslie Frost QC (on the Left)
with OMB Chairman Lorne Cumming QC *(Source: The
Globe and Mail, February 26, 1953)*

Ontario Premier Kathleen Wynne *(Source: "David Cooper/ GetStock.com")*

Bibliography

Archives of Ontario, *Leslie Frost papers,* B292272-1 RG 3-24 Boxes 35 & 36

Archives of Ontario, *John Robarts papers,* RE 7-1-0-1026 Box 40

Aubin, Henry. *Who's Afraid of Demergers?,* Vehiculé Press, 2004

Bish, Robert L. Professor Emeritus, University of Victoria, *Evolutionary Alternatives to Metropolitan Areas: The Capital Region of British Columbia,* Canadian Journal of Regional Science XX111: 1 p. 73-87, Spring, 2000

Bish, Robert L. & Vojnovic, Igor. *The Transitional of Municipal Consolidation,* Journal of Urban Affairs, 22, No. 4, 2000

Bish, Robert L. Local *Government Amalgamations, Discredited Nineteenth Century deals Alive in the Twenty-First Century,* The Urban Papers. C.D. Howe Institute Commentary, No 150, Toronto, March, 2001

Bonis, Robert R. *A. History of Scarborough,* Scarborough Public Library, 1965

Boudreau, Julie-Anne, Keil, Rogers and Young, Douglas. *Changing Toronto: Governing Urban Neoliberalism,* University of Toronto Press, 2009

Boylen, J.C. *York Township: An Historical Summary, The Municipal Corporation of the Township of York and the Board of Education of the Township of York,* 1954

Caro, Robert A. *The Power Broker,* Alfred A. Knopf, New York, 1974

Caulfield, Jon. *The Tiny Perfect Mayor,* James Lorimer & Company Publishers, Toronto, 1974

Citizens for Local Democracy, *Newsletters,* 1997, 1998

City of Mississauga, *Running the GTA Like A Business: Recommendations for GTA Reform,* August, 1995

City of Toronto Archives, John Sewell papers, Boxes 223380-3

City of Toronto, Treasury & Financial Services Division. *Provincial Downloading – Local Service Realignment,* Report Prepared for the Policy and Finance Committee by the Chief Financial Officer, December 1, 1999

City of Toronto Council Minutes, City of Toronto: *Staff Report to the Board of Control*, November 5, 1928

City of Toronto: *Works Commissioner R.C. Harris Report to the Board of Control*, October 31, 1931

City of Toronto, *Social Housing-Shelter, Support and Housing Administration*, 2012

City of Toronto, *Operating Cost Budgets*, 1997

City of Toronto, *Building the New City of Toronto, January 1998 – December, 2000*, Michael Garrett, Chief Administrative Office, Toronto, 1999

City of Toronto, *Staff Report, Summary of Amalgamation Savings and Costs* prepared by Chief Administrative Officer for the Budget Advisory Committee, 2001

Colton, Timothy J. *Big Daddy: Frederick G. Gardiner- The Building of Metropolitan Toronto*, University of Toronto Press, 1980

Council of Europe, *European Charter of Local Self-Government, European Treaty, service No. 122*, Strasbourg, le Conseil, Section des publications, 1985

Crombie, David. *Who Does What Panel*, December 23, 1996

Crowley, Brian Lee. Clemens, Jason & Veldhuis, Niels. *The Canadian Century: moving out of America's shadow*, The MacDonald-Laurier Institute, 2010

Cruickshank, F.D. & Nason J. *History of Weston*, University of Toronto Press, 1983

Currell, Harvey. *The Mimico Story*, Town of Mimico & Library Board, 1967

Darke, Eleanor. *Call Me True: a biography of True Davidson*, National Heritage/Natural History Inc. 1997

Davidson, True. *The Golden Strings*, Griffin House, Toronto, 1973

Davidson, True. *The Golden Years of East York*, Centennial College Press, Toronto, 1976

Deloitte and Touch, *Letter to Glenn Kippen, Treasurer, Borough of East York*, February 2, 1997

Etobicoke Guardian, April 9, 1997

Farrow, Milt. *Report of Special Advisor Haldimand,* Norfolk Review, November, 1999

Farrow, Milt. *Getting – Together Reports,* 1999

Fergus – Elora News Express, September 28, 1994

Flint, Anthony. *Wrestling with Moses: How Jane Jacobs Took on New York's Master Builder and Transformed the American City,* Random House Trade Paperbacks, New York, 2009

Four Mayors, McCallion, Hazel, Lastman, Mel, Hall, Barbara and Diamond, Nancy. *Moving Forward Together, A Discussion Paper,* January, 1996

French, William. *A Most Unlikely Village: an Informal History of Forest Hill, Corporation of the Village of Forest Hill,* 1964

Frisken, Frances. *The Public Metropolis: The Political Dynamics of Urban Expansion in the Toronto Region 1924-2003,* Canadian Scholars Press Inc., Toronto, 2007

Frisken, Frances. *York University – The Greater Toronto Area in Transition: The Search for New Planning & Servicing Strategies Metropolitan Governance Revisited,* Institute of Government Studies, University of California, Berkley, p. 161, 1998

Given, Robert A. *Etobicoke Remembered,* Pro Familia Publishing, Toronto, 2007

Glazebrook, G.P. De T. *The Story of Toronto,* University of Toronto Press, 1991

Globe & Mail, January 9, 1950, November 15, 1965, December 19, 1996, January 30, 1997, February 10, 1997, February 26, 1997, April 22, 1997, March 14, 2001

Golden, Anne. *Greater Toronto Area Task Force Report,* January 1996

Golden, Anne & Slack, Enid. *Urban Governance Reform in Toronto: A Preliminary Assessment of Changes Made in the Late 1990s, Part II Canadian Metropolitan Cases: Metropolitan Governing: Canadian Cases, Comparative Lessons,* Edited by Razin, Eran & Smith, Patrick J. The Hebrew University Manes Press, Jerusalem, 2006

Graham, Roger. *Old Man Ontario: Leslie M. Frost,* University of Toronto Press, 1990

Guillet, Edwin C. *Pioneer Life in the County of York: Volume One*, Hess-Trade Typesetting Company, Toronto, 1946

Harris, Mike, Manning, Preston & McMahon, Fred, *Is Toronto on Decline*, Fraser Institute, Vancouver, 2008

Hart, Patricia. *Pioneering in North York*, General Publishing Company Limited, Toronto, 1968

Hayes, Esther. *Etobicoke from Furrow to Borough*, Borough of Etobicoke, 1974

Hogen-Esch, T. *Urban Succession and the Politics of Growth: The Case of Los Angeles*, Urban Affairs Review, 6 (6), p. 783-809, 2001

Horak, Martin. *The Power of Local Identity: C4LO and the Anti-Amalgamation Mobilization in Toronto*, Research Paper 195, Toronto Centre for Urban Community Studies, University of Toronto, 1998

House of Commons, *Hansard Budget Speech*, 1995

Hoy, Claire. *Bill Davis*, Methuen Publications, Toronto, 1985

Ibbitson, John. *Promised Land: Inside the Mike Harris Revolution*, Prentice Hall Canada Inc. 1997

Jacobs, Jane. *The Death and Life of Great American Cities*, Vintage Books, New York, 1961

Jacobs, Jane. *The Economy of Cities*, Vintage Books, New York, 1970

Keenan, Edward. *Some Great Idea: Good Neighbourhoods, Crazy Politics and the Invention of Toronto*, Coach House Books, Toronto, 2013

Keil, Roger. *Governance Restructuring in Los Angeles and Toronto: Amalgamation or Succession*, International Journal of Urban and Regional Research, 24 (4), p. 758-81, 2000

KPMG, *Fresh Start: An Estimate of Potential Savings and Costs from the Creation of Single Tier Local Government for Toronto*, December 16, 1996

Lee, Kevin K. *Urban Poverty in Canada: A Statistical Profile*, Canada Council on Social Development, Ottawa, 20000

Lemon, James. *Toronto since 1918*, James Lorimer & Company Publishers & National Museum of Manitoba, national Museums of Canada, Toronto, 1985

MacDonald, Donald C. *The Government & Politics of Ontario*, Van Nostrand Reinhold Ltd., Toronto, 1980

MacKinnon, Janice. *Minding the Public Purse: The fiscal crisis, political trade-offs and Canada's future*, McGill-Queen's University Press, 2003

McDougall, A.K., *Robarts: His Life and Government*, University of Toronto Press, 1986

McKeough, W., Darcy. *Unpublished autobiography*, 2012

McMahon, Michael. *Metro's Housing Company: The First 35 years*, University of Toronto Press, 1990

Meaford Independent, August 2, 2013, August 9, 2013

Memories of Scarborough: a Bicentennial Celebration, The Scarborough Public Library Board, 1997

Metropolitan Toronto Council minutes, April 14, 1993, March 11, 1964, October 19, 1965

Metropolitan Toronto Review Committee Response, April 1987

Metropolitan Toronto, Operating Cost Budget, 1997

Miller, David. *The Roles and Responsibilities of Community Councils in Toronto, discussion paper,* March 1998

Milroy, Beth Moore. *Toronto's Legal Challenge to Amalgamation, Urban Affairs: Back on the Policy Agenda*, McGill-Queen's University Press, p. 157, 2002

Montreal Gazette. July 6, 2001, April 11, 2005

New York Times International, March 4, 1997

New York Times Archives, July 25, 2012

O'Donohue, Tony. *The Tale of a City: re-engineering the urban environment*, The Dundurn Group, Toronto, 2005

O'Donohue, Tony. *Front Row Centre*, Abbeyfield Publishers Toronto, 2001

Oliver, Peter. *Unlikely Tory: The Life & Politics of Allan Grossman*, Lester & Orpen Dennys Limited, Toronto, 1985

Ontario Legislative Assembly, *The Municipality of Metropolitan Toronto Act*, Bill 80, 1953

Ontario Legislative Assembly, *Hansard,* April 26, 1966, p. 2599

Ontario Municipal Board decision *concerning the application of the Town of Mimico for an interurban administration area for the 13 area municipalities including Toronto and the application for the City of Toronto for the amalgamation of the 12 area municipalities,* dated January 20, 1953

Ontario Progressive Conservative Party, *Common Sense Revolution,* 1995

O'Sullivan, Arthur. *Urban Economics, 7th edition,* McGraw Hill International Edition, 2009

Paine, Thomas. *Common Sense,* Free Patriot Press, Surfside Beach, South Carolina, 2010

Phillips, Nathan. *The Mayor of All the People,* McClelland and Stewart Limited, 1967

Pimlott, Ben & Rao, Nirmals. *Governing London,* Oxford University Press, 2002

Pitfield, Jane. Leaside, *National Heritage/National History Inc.,* Toronto, 1999

Plumtre, A.F.W. *Report on the government of the Metropolitan Area of Toronto to the Hon. David Croll, Minister of Municipal Affairs in the Province of Ontario,* June 20, 1935

Poitras, Hon. Lawrence *A. retired Judge Counsel to Borden Ladner Gervais LLP,* Montreal, La Défusion Municipale au Québec, 2003

Price Waterhouse. *The Municipalities of Ottawa-Carleton, Study of the Financial Impact of One-Tier Government in Ottawa-Carleton,* Final Report, August 27, 1992

Progressive Conservative Party of Ontario. *The Road Ahead,* Toronto, May, 2003

Province of British Columbia. *Primer on Regional Districts in British Columbia,* 2006

Province of Ontario. *Municpal Act, 2001 Overview,* Ministry of Municipal Affairs and Housing, 2003

Province of Ontario. *Bill 53, An Act to Revise the City of Toronto Act,* December, 2005

Province of Ontario. *The New City of Toronto Act,* 2007

Province of Ontario. *White Paper, Government Statement on the Review of Local Government in the Municipality of Metropolitan Toronto,* dated May 4, 1978

Province of Ontario. *Ministry of Municipal Affairs and Housing: Municipal Act 2001, Overview,* 2003

Province of Ontario. *Bill 26: The Savings and Restructuring Act,* November, 1995

Province of Ontario. *Bill 103, An Act to incorporate the City of Toronto,* December 17, 1996

Province of Ontario. *Ministry of Municipal Affairs and Housing,* Press Release, December 17, 1996

Province of Ontario. *Legislative Assembly of Ontario, Standing Committee on General Government,* February 3, 5, 6, 12 & 13, 1997

Province of Ontario. *Ministry of Infrastructure: Growth Plan for the Greater Golden Horseshoe,* 2006

Province of Ontario. *The City of Toronto Act,* 1997

Province of Ontario. *Ministry of Infrastructure, Growth Plan for the Greater Golden Horseshoe Office Consolidation,* January, 2012

Report of the Royal Commission on Metropolitan Toronto, June 10, 1965 by Commissioner H. Carl Goldenberg*Report of the Royal Commission on Metropolitan Toronto, June 1977* by Commissioner John P. RobartsRose, Albert. *Governing Metropolitan Toronto: a social & political analysis,* University of California Press, 1972

Sancton, Andrew. *Governing Canada's City Regions, Institute for Research and Public Policy,* Canada, 1994

Sancton, Andrew. *Merger Mania: the Assault on Local Government,* McGill-Queen's University Press, 2000

Sancton, Andrew. *The Limits of Boundaries: Why City regions cannot be Self-governing,* McGill-Queen's University Press, 2008

Sancton, Andrew. Why *Municipal Amalgamations: Halifax, Toronto, Montreal* (unpublished)

Sancton, Andrew. *Municipal Mergers and Demergers - Ontario and Quebec,* prepared for the Annual Meeting of the Canadian Political Science Association, York University, June 1, 2006

Sancton, Andrew. *Globalization Does not Require Amalgamation,* Policy Options, November 1999

Sancton, Andrew, James, Rebecca, Ramsay, Rick. *Amalgamation vs. Inter-Municipal Co-operation: Financing Local Infrastructure Services,* ICURR Press, Toronto, 2000

Saunders, Leslie Howard. *An Orangeman in Public Life: Memoirs of Leslie Howard Saunders,* Britannia Printers Limited, 1981

Sauriol, Charles. *Remembering the Don,* Consolidate Amethyst Communications Inc., Scarborough, 1981

Schwartz, Harvey, *Trouble in the Megacity, facing a financial crisis in 2010,* Policy Options, February 2010, Policy Options, February 2010

Sewell, John. *The Shape of the Suburbs: understanding Toronto's Sprawl,* University of Toronto Press, 2009

Sewell, John. *The Incredible Lightness of the Two-tiered Model of Local Government: Towards a New City of Toronto Act,* Zephyr Press, 2005

Six Mayors, Hall, Barbara, Lastman, Mel, Holyday, Doug, Faubert, Frank, Nunziata, Frances, Prue, Michael: *Change for the Better,* December 12, 1996

Statistics Canada. *Low Income Cut Offs*Stevenson, Don. *Democracy and the Urban Landscape: a talk at the Democracy Café,* June 14, 2010

Stevenson, Don. *Notes for Remarks to the ABC Residents Association,* February 10, 1977

Stevenson, Don, Gilbert, Richard. *Restructuring Municipal Government in Greater Toronto,* July 30, 1999

Stevenson, Don, Gilbert, Richard. *Municipal Government in the Greater Toronto Area: Structure, Function, Issues and Intergovernmental Relations,* Canadian Urban Institute, September, 1992

Stevenson, Don, Gilbert, Richard. *Background Paper with respect to the Question on the Ballot, City of Toronto Municipal Elections,* November, 1994, Canadian Urban Institute, August 31, 1994

Task Force on Representation and Accountability in Metropolitan Toronto: Analysis and Options for the Government of Metropolitan Toronto, Report, November, 1986

Tomlinson, Peter. *Toronto's Fiscal Outlook: 2011 Through 2014*, a paper prepared for the University of Toronto's Cities Centre, November 30, 2010

Tomlinson, Peter. *Partitioning the Amalgamated Two of Essex into Tow Municipalities*, prepared for South Colchester-Harrow Action Committee, September 12, 2008

Tonks, Alan. *Letter to the Honourable Al Leach*, November 28, 1996

Toronto Star. March 2, 1937, October 1, 1985, January 11, 1966, August 28, 1965, April 26, 1966, January 22, 1966, October 11, 1969, February 7, 1970, October 29, 1994, April 4, 1997, December 8, 1994, December 20, 1996, December 21, 1996, May 9, 1999, April 11, 2005, January 11, 2001, June 22, 2000, August 25, 2011, March 30, 2012, October 7, 1998, October 14, 1998, January 26, 1999, February 15, 2013, May 23, 1999, January 26, 2013

Toronto Sun. April 16, 1997, December 10, 1997, June 5, 2011

Toronto Telegram. January 10, 1950, September 12, 1963

Toronto Transition Team. *New City New Opportunities*, December, 1997

Town of Leaside Council minutes (City of Toronto Archives)

Town of Mimico Council minutes (City of Toronto Archives)

Town of New Toronto Council minutes (City of Toronto Archives)

Town of Weston Council minutes (City of Toronto Archives)

Township of East York Council minutes (City of Toronto Archives)

Township of Etobicoke Council minutes (City of Toronto Archives)

Township of North York Council minutes (City of Toronto Archives)

Township of Scarborough Council minutes (City of Toronto Archives)

Township of York Council minutes (City of Toronto Archives)

Trent, Peter F. *The Merger Delusion: How Swallowing Its Suburbs Made an Even Bigger Mess of Montreal*, McGill-Queen's University Press, 2012

Urbaniak, Tom. *Her Worship: Hazel McCallion and the Development of Mississauga*, University of Toronto Press, 2009

Village of Forest Hill Council minutes (City of Toronto Archives)

Village of Long Branch Council minutes (City of Toronto Archives)

Village of Swansea Council minutes (City of Toronto Archives)

Vojnovic, Igor. *Municipal consolidation in the 1990s: an analysis of five Canadian municipalities,* Plan Canada, 38:4, p. 28-48, July 1997

Vojnovic, Igor. *Transitional impacts of municipal consolidations,* Journal of Urban Affairs, 22:4, p. 385-417, 2000

Walker, Edward W. *Dissolution: Sovereignty and the Breakup of the Soviet Union,* Rowan & Littlefield Publishers Inc., Maryland, USA, 2003

Wall Street Journal, January 12, 1995

Whelan, R. Joncas, P., *Montreal Demergers: An Update,* Inroads 16, Winter-Spring, p. 94-9, 2005

White, Graham. *The Government Politics of Ontario, 5th edition,* University of Toronto Press, 1997

Interviews

1 Blair, Willis, former Mayor of East York, January 9, 2012 & February 10, 2013

2 Buckspan, Barbara, York activist (telephone), December 19, 2012

3 Burns, Dan, Retired Deputy Minister of Municipal Affairs, December 19, 2012

4 Carter, Alan, Scarborough resident & party to Court application under The Charter, November 6, 2012

5 Champion, Robert & Mark, home renovators, May 1, 2011

6 Coté, André, Manager, Programs & Research, Institute of Municipal Finance & Governance, The Munk School, University of Toronto August 7, 2012

7 Crombie, David, former Mayor of Toronto, June 8, 2011 & January 9, 2013

8 Duguid, Brad, Ontario Minister, former Scarborough & Metro Councillor. November 2, 2012

9 Evans, Hannah, Director, Partnerships & Consultation, Ontario Growth Secretariat, August 27, 2012

10 Fenn, Michael, Retired Deputy Minister of Municipal Affairs, October 30, 2012

11 Filion, John, former North York Councillor, currently City of Toronto Councillor, November 16, 2012

12 Found, Adam, University of Toronto PhD candidate in economics, July 23, 2012

13 Gadon Sean, (formerly Getz-Gadon), former Executive Assistant to Minister Hosek, Mayor Hall & Mayor Lastman, currently Director, Affordable Housing Office, City of Toronto, December 10, 2012

14 Godfrey, Paul, former Chairman of Metro Toronto, December 20, 2012 & January 3, 2013

15 Hall, Barbara, former Mayor of Toronto, currently Chair of the Ontario Human Rights Commission January 21, 2013

16 Harris, Mike, former Premier of Ontario, November 21, 2012

17 Leach, Al, former Minister of Municipal Affairs, November 26, 2012

18 MacLeod, Colin, Chair of Team East York (telephone), January 7, 2013

19 McCallum, Donna-Lynn, East York activist & member of Team East York, December 26, 2012

20 Mihevic, Joe, former York Councillor, now Toronto Councillor, November 20, 2012

21 Minnan-Wong, Denzil, former North York Councillor, currently Toronto Councillor, November 6, 2012

22 Nunziata, Frances, former Mayor of York, currently Speaker for the Toronto City Council, November 7, 2012
23 Peterson, David, former Ontario Premier (telephone), January 17, 2013
24 Prue, Michael, MPP, former Mayor of East York, currently Ontario Member of Parliament, December 4, 2012
25 Sancton, Andrew, University of Western Ontario, August 22, 2012
26 Sewell, John, former Mayor of Toronto, January 14, 2013
27 Slack, Enid, University of Toronto Professor, August 7, 2012
28 Stainton, Ketih, former Leaside Councillor, October 5, 2012
29 Stevenson, Don, retired Ontario Deputy Minister, November 20, 2012
30 Tomlinson, Peter, University of Toronto Lecturer, July 23, 2012
31 Tonks, Alan, former Chairman of Metro Toronto, December 28, 2012
32 Waterhouse, Jo, former executive Assistant to Scarborough Councillor Fred Johnson (telephone), November 20, 2012
33 Wynne, Kathleen, Ontario Minister of Municipal Affairs & Housing, currently Premier of Ontario, August 10, 2012

Correspondence & Email
1 Balkissoon, Bas, former Scarborough Councillor, currently Ontario Member of Parliament
2 Elridge, John, City of Toronto, Director, Secretariat, City Clerks Department, August 13 & 21, 2012
3 Farrow, Ron, former Deputy Minister of Municipal Affairs
4 Kanter, Ron, former Metro Councillor & MPP, August 7, 2012
5 Kelly, Dennis, former Municipal Clerk of the City of North York, November 13, 2012
6 Kelly, Norm, former Scarborough Metro Councillor, currently Toronto Councillor
7 McKeough, Darcy W. O.C. LLD., former Minister of Municipal Affairs & former Minister Treasury Economics & Inter-Governmental Affairs
8 Meraglia, John, City of Toronto, Manager, Elections & Registry Services, August 13 & 21, 2012
9 Mundle, Mary, August 1, 2013
10 Richardson, Peggy, August 10, 2013
11 Rohmer, Richard O.C. CMM, DFC, O.ONT. K STJ., CD, Of.L., QC, advisor to Premier John Robarts

Too Ill for Interview
1 Davis, William, former Premier of Ontario

Declined to be Interviewed
1   Harnick, Charles, former Ontario Attorney General
2   Holyday, Doug, former Mayor of Etobicoke, currently Toronto Deputy Mayor
3   Johnson, David, former Mayor of East York & Ontario Cabinet Minister
4   Lastman, Mel, former Mayor of North York & Toronto
5   Lindsay-Luby, Gloria, former Etobicoke Councillor, currently Toronto Councillor
6   McCallion, Hazel, Mayor of Mississauga
9   Milczyn, Peter, former Etobicoke Councillor, currently Toronto Councillor

Did Not Answer Request for Interview
1   Bernardinetti, Lorenzo, former Scarborough Councillor, currently Ontario Member of Parliament
2   Giorno, Guy, former Chief of Staff for Premier Mike Harris
3   Long, Tom, former Election Campaign Chairman for Premier Mike Harris
4   Shea, Derwyn, former Ontario MPP

Acknowledgements

Although this book is focused on the megacity of Toronto and the surrounding area, I am only too well aware that the issues of merger, amalgamation, centralization, demerger, de-amalgamation, separation and decentralization have already or sooner or later will become the concerns not only of other North American municipalities but in municipalities across the western world. Some examples of which, I have cited in the book. I believe that the analysis and the solution I have proposed for Toronto can be applied to numerous other municipalities as well.

First and foremost I wish to express my thanks to all of the residents of the former Borough of East York where I grew up and where my strong beliefs in local involvement and participation in the municipal decision making process were forged and ingrained in me.

I also owe a debt of gratitude not only to each and every member of the East York and the Metropolitan Toronto Councils with whom I had the honour of serving during my ten years in municipal office but also to the many local East York community volunteers and activists all of whom have demonstrated to me so clearly the vast superiority of the Metro system of government over what I observe in the present amalgamated megacity of Toronto.

This book would not have been possible without the enormous help and encouragement of the friendly librarians and staff at the former Urban Affairs Library, the Toronto Reference Library, the Toronto Archives and the Archives of Ontario. In particular my special thanks go to Kathleen Wyann, Cynthia Fisher and Judy Curry who assisted me at both the Urban Affairs and the Toronto Reference Library, and Christine Bourolias at the Archives of Ontario. Nor can I overlook the very many listed elsewhere in this book who shared with me their views and recollections when we met or corresponded.

There are no words to adequately describe the debt I owe to Professor Andrew Sancton of Western University (formerly the University of Western Ontario), Peter Tomlinson and Adam Found of the University of Toronto. Leading academic authorities in municipal amalgamations and demergers, in addition to enlightening me concerning other Canadian and international examples of both successful and unsuccessful of municipal demergers they each provided me most generously with the information, insights, helpful comments and encouragement .The fact that they shared my views, reinforced my own strongly held beliefs in the superiority of a federated system of local municipal government.

A very extra special thanks to Professor Andrew Sancton for reviewing an early draft of the book and providing me with many most helpful and insightful criticisms and comments.

There would be no at all book but for the typing expertise of Sarah Said and Anna Malandrino who transcribed my hand written original draft into a version which was both readable and absolutely essential for publication.

I have been guided through the hoops of publishing a book by a great number of knowledgeable people including: James Lorimer, Terry Fallis, Jane Gibson, Barry Penhale, Lorna Krawchuk, Harry Goldhar and Mary Mundle to all of whom I am most grateful.

This book would not have had a cover nor maps but for the excellent work of Valentine De Landro nor would there have been any photographs either but for the help of MaryJo Lavelle of GetStock.com at the Toronto Star, Andrea Gordon of Canadian Press and the Globe and Mail, Linda Winstone and Christine Bourolias at the Archives of Ontario, Hector Vargas and Gillian Reddyhoff of the city of Toronto Archives and Kathleen Wyann of the Toronto Reference Library, Jennifer Wing at the city of Toronto and of course my wonderful photo editor Tracy Choy.

To all those who have spoken out in favour of the Metro system of local government as devised by former OMB Chairman Lorne Cumming and by former Ontario Premier Leslie Frost in which Metro councillors are first elected to their local councils, my sincere thanks and appreciation.

Any and all errors in this book are mine alone and should be attributed to me and none other.

I am pleased to dedicate this book to my family, especially to my wife and very best friend Louise.

282

Index

Page references in *italics* indicate an illustration.

E

East York

fact sheet on, 258–259

financial stability of, 164–165

opposition to Bill 103, 164–165, 167–168

response to KPMG report, 195–196

East York township, 9–10, *17*, 26

Economies of scale, municipal size for, 256

Education, restructuring, 185–186

Edwards, Alf, 229–230

Election (direct) of Metro councillors, 103–106, 123, 126, 154

Elections, cost of running for office, 230

Electoral ridings

reduced, 176, 221, 222

ward boundaries and, 228–229

Essex, de-amalgamation, 248–249

Etobicoke, opposition to Bill 103, 163, 170

Etobicoke township, 6–7, 10, *14, 17*, 26

European Charter of Local Self-Government, 174

Evans, Hannah, 213

F

Farrow, Milt, report on GTSB, 211–212

Faubert, Frank, *145*, 164, 168

Fenn, Michael, 209, 213

Fewer Municipal Politicians Act, 222, 225

Fewer School Boards Act, 185–186

Filion, John, 164, 169, 229

Fiscal neutrality, 128, 190, 193, 202, 204

Flamborough, de-amalgamation, 242–244

Flynn, Dennis, 101, *116*

Forest Hill, 7, 11, *15*

4-city proposal

I

Income redistribution and property tax, 189–190
Infrastructure
    development, 44, 54, 88–89, 208, 210
    financing, 208, 216
    pressure on post WWII, 18–19
Intermunicipal Services Board, 124, 125–126, *143*

J

Jacobs, Jane, 45–46, *56,* 88–89, 214

K

Kanter, Ron, 103, *118*
Kawartha Lakes, de-amalgamation, 244–246
Kingston, de-amalgamation, 250
KPMG Report
    Deloitte Touche analysis of, 195–196
    estimates of savings, 137–138
    Sancton analysis of, 194–195
    sources of savings, 197–202, *205*
    terms of reference, 136–137, 193–194

L

Lamport, Allan, 30, 31, 38, *39,* 62, *77*
Lastman, Mel, *141, 144*
    on Alan Tonks, 103
    on amalgamation, 163–164, 169
    boundary changes, Metro, 96
    Changes for the Better committee, member, 129
    Metro Toronto Council Review Committee, member, 103
    Moving Forward Together committee, member, 123
Leach, Al, *160*
    amalgamation, 129, 138, 151, 152–155, 203
    Burnham Panel, 126, 127

Greater Toronto Transit Authority, 212, 213
Metrolinx, 215–216
Spadina Expressway, 88–89
Trimmer, Joyce, *159,* 162
Trimmer Task Force, 147–148, 149

V
Volunteerism, effect of Megacity on, 234–235

W
Wards, relationship to electoral boundaries, 228–229
Water and sewer, expansion, 44, 54, 208, 210
Waterhouse, Jo, 233–234
Weston, bankruptcy, 10, *17*
White Select Committee, 208
Who Does What Panel. *see* Crombie Panel
Wynne, Kathleen, *181, 267*
    advocate for citizen access, 256
    member of Citizens for Local Democracy, 166

Y
York
    6-borough proposal, 63
    merger with Toronto, 163, 169
    opposition to Bill 103, 163, 169–170
York-Durham trunk sewer, 210
York township
    annexations, 7, 8, 9
    bankruptcy, 10, *17*
    opposition to amalgamation (Metro), 26

About the Author

Alan Redway is a recently retired lawyer, born in Toronto, with a degree in Commerce and Finance from the University of Toronto and a law degree from Osgoode Hall Law School. Mr. Redway served for six years as Mayor of the Borough of East York and as a member of Metropolitan Toronto Council and Executive Committee. Later he was elected to the parliament of Canada where he served for almost ten years as a Progressive Conservative member of the House of Commons and as Minister of State (Housing). In 1997 as Honorary Chair of Team East York he actively opposed the Toronto amalgamation.

CPSIA information can be obtained at www.ICGtesting.com
Printed in the USA
LVOW12s1921130215

426960LV00002B/345/P